Critical Muslim 47

Evil

Critical Muslim is published quarterly by C. Hurst & Co. (Publishers) Ltd. on behalf of and in conjunction with Critical Muslim Ltd. and the Muslim Institute, London.

All editorial correspondence to Muslim Institute, Canopi, 7-14 Great Dover Street, London, SE1 4YR
E-mail: editorial@criticalmuslim.com

C. Hurst & Co (Publishers) Ltd., New Wing, Somerset House, Strand, London, WC2R 1LA

ISBN:9781805260486 ISSN: 2048-8475

To subscribe or place an order by credit/debit card or cheque (pounds sterling only) please contact Kathleen May at the Hurst address above or e-mail kathleen@hurstpub.co.uk

A one-year subscription, inclusive of postage (four issues), costs £60 (UK), £90 (Europe) and £100 (rest of the world), this includes full access to the *Critical Muslim* series and archive online. Digital only subscription is £3.30 per month.

A Cataloguing-in-Publication data record for this book is available from the British Library

Critical Muslim

Subscribe to Critical Muslim

Now in its twelfth year in print, *Critical Muslim* is also available online. Users can access the site for just £3.30 per month – or for those with a print subscription it is included as part of the package. In return, you'll get access to everything in the series (including our entire archive), and a clean, accessible reading experience for desktop computers and handheld devices — entirely free of advertising.

Full subscription

The print edition of *Critical Muslim* is published quarterly in January, April, July and October. As a subscriber to the print edition, you'll receive new issues directly to your door, as well as full access to our digital archive.

United Kingdom £60/year
Europe £90/year
Rest of the World £100/year

Digital Only

Immediate online access to *Critical Muslim*

Browse the full *Critical Muslim* archive

Cancel any time

£3.30 per month

www.criticalmuslim.io

CM47

SUMMER 2023

CONTENTS

EVIL

EVIL

INTRODUCTION: COMBING MEDUSA'S HAIR

Robin Yassin-Kassab

Published in France in 2006, Jonathan Littell's novel *Les Bienveillantes* sold over 700,000 copies and won the Prix Goncourt. Translated into English as *The Kindly Ones*, it made much less of an impact. This is a shame, because it's surely one of the greatest literary achievements of the century, both a historical novel involving detailed and apparently accurate recreations of Nazi atrocities, and a study in individual and systemic evil.

The novel's great set pieces include the Holocaust by shooting in Ukraine, the later Holocaust by starvation and gassing in the death camps, the siege of Stalingrad, and Germany's descent into apocalyptic chaos at the end of the war, culminating in the fall of Berlin. The action is seen through the eyes of an SS officer, Max Aue, and told in his voice many years later – for he survives the war, no doubt unjustly, and lives a bourgeois life now under an assumed name, with a family and a job in the lace industry.

'It was the systematically cultivated nature of the Holocaust that makes it unique in the annals of genocide,' writes Richard Appignanesi in his essay 'Evil in the Absence of God'; and Littell's Max Aue is a cultivated man. Even as a young man, Aue is highly cultured, a man of taste, intelligence and education. But he is also a convinced Nazi, emerging from a society of convinced Nazis. When stationed in the Caucasus he engages in fascinating scholarly discussions of the local ethnicities' tribal, linguistic and religious affiliations, and all with the purpose of determining which communities are to be exterminated.

Aue is an enthusiastic organiser of and participant in the bloodshed. Even as he remembers it later, he is largely unrepentant, though he demurs finally from justifying his crimes by reference to any political end. He starts off as an ideological Nazi but the horror he helps to unleash, its pointlessness, becomes its own end. At a late stage in the narrative Aue goes properly mad, but this only begs the question of what sanity means, given his murderous behaviour while calm, collected and supposedly healthy. The most decent thing he does in a thousand pages is suffer a breakdown, but he soon recovers, and is able to resume normal functioning in his second, staid, lace-manufacturing life. A monster, but all too human, and ultimately rather ordinary. The novel opens with this invocation: 'Oh my human brothers …'

So why is such a book of cruelties titled *The Kindly Ones?* In reference to the Eumenides, or Furies, Greek deities of vengeance who were named 'the kindly ones' euphemistically, because the reality was too awful to name – and alluding too to the standards of Greek morality, which disconnect the notions of good and evil from the idea of intention. Actual results are what count, as the Greek tragedies illustrate. Oedipus doesn't know that the man he kills is his father, nor that the woman he marries is his mother. Nevertheless, these crimes are terrible, and Oedipus must pay the price.

To an extent Islam agrees that the result of an act determines whether it is good or evil. 'You may hate a thing, but it is good for you,' says the Quran, and the story of Khidr shows that apparently evil actions can have good results. In general, though, Islam follows the logic of the hadith: 'Actions are judged according to intentions'.

In his essay 'Ordinary Folks', Julian Baggini disaggregates evil thus: 'The seriousness of a bad action is related to consequences, but its basic nature – foible, misdemeanour, wicked – is generally related to intention.'

We cannot know the end results of our actions – perhaps this is the point of the Khidr story – so it's important at least that we mean well, that we attempt to engage life in a moral sense. That's what we do when we call something or someone 'evil'. At least, it's one of the things we may be doing when we use the word.

Because that's what 'evil' is – it's a word. An intensifier of 'bad'. Like all words, its referent is debatable. Unlike most words, its referent is often debated. As it is here. In this issue of the *Critical Muslim*, evil is considered morally, psychologically, philosophically, socially, politically, and artistically.

In John Liechty's reading of the complementary stories of Nabi Yunus in the Qur'an and Jonah in the Old Testament, evil is found in a denial of responsibility, a refusal to do what you should, a rejection of your God-given purpose. Yunus/Jonah, ordered to preach to Nineveh, tries to escape from God by boarding a ship. But the ship is beset by a storm. Yunus ends up overboard, and then is swallowed by a fish. At last, he repents and accepts his mission. Freed from the fish, he preaches to Nineveh, causing the city's repentance and reform, which leads to God's forgiveness.

It's the earlier part of the story that interests Liechty most (and in the Old Testament version, the latter part too, because Jonah falls back into petulance, becoming 'angry enough to die' when God relents from destroying Nineveh). The point is that Yunus knows what he must do but runs from doing it – a very common human response. 'The reluctant messenger does not seem to be an isolated type, so much as a universal one,' Liechty writes, linking the figure to 'people aware of a calling in life who get side-tracked or lose the plot altogether, owing in part to circumstances beyond their control, but above all to their own Jonah-like propensity to fly from responsibility.'

Perhaps the ISIS fighters who destroyed Mosul's Nabi Yunus Mosque in 2014 were aware of better callings. Perhaps their lives had been sidetracked from more wholesome plots. Mosul is the successor city to Nineveh, built on the same spot. God spared the city, but ISIS – rather like the Old Testament version of Jonah – decided they knew better.

They also decided to vandalise churches, and to shoot non-Sunni truck drivers dead at checkpoints, and to rape and enslave Yazidi women and children. In the name of Sharia law, they made a mockery of law. In the name of submission to God they forced submission to their own gangster rule. According to Liechty, this is everybody's business: 'God's initial call to go to Nineveh suggests that rising to the challenge of evil is a human responsibility.' Furthermore, we can't escape responsibility by claiming ignorance, because 'at bottom we know evil when we see or feel it. Human beings are equipped with the capacity to know right from wrong, good from bad – that we are not always willing or able to use the equipment does not mean it isn't there.'

We can use the equipment in various ways according to our means. This is reminiscent of one of the hadith on jihad, which states that we should fight evil physically, with our hands, and if that isn't possible then with our tongues, by speaking out, and if that isn't possible then with our hearts, by at least feeling that the evil behaviour is evil.

Whatever our means, we must use the equipment. Remaining silent over enormous injustices and cruelties, failing to offer solidarity to the victims, is itself a form of evil. Oz Katerji's Last Word 'On Denial' focuses not just on cowardly and irresponsible silence but, worse, on the active denial of war crimes. War reporting done properly, by contrast, should be a force for good: 'If conflict journalism isn't a direct opponent of atrocity denial, then it is nothing but war tourism and propaganda.' For Katerji, open-source intelligence (OSINT) – this age's key addition to the journalistic toolkit – is a practical means to resist evil.

Sometimes evil is not a matter of ignoring a good intention or calling, or of stifling the voice of conscience, but of following a misguided intention, of causing harm from a state of ignorance. Nazism, for instance, followed the pseudo-science of social Darwinism and – in a way – the values of evolutionary humanism. If a Nazi actually believed the nonsense that certain 'races' were 'subhuman', and that their genes, if mixed with those of 'superior races', would pollute those races and cause them to degenerate – and such nonsense was taught in German schools – then the total segregation and even complete annihilation of the 'subhumans' became a necessary act, a duty to future generations. Yes, on the one hand, it was hard to burn babies and gas old men, but on the other, it would be worse for untold millions of future humans to fail to reach their superhuman potential and to be sunk in disability and disease instead.

Here the evil of the belief, the ideology, precedes the evil of the act. When the weight of social authority is added to bad ideology, we arrive at the casual, bureaucratic evil of 'office murderers' and those who 'followed orders', at what Hannah Arendt called 'the banality of evil'. Arendt's studies of twentieth century totalitarianism are, unsurprisingly, referenced in several of the essays collected here, usually approvingly, but Richard Appignanesi strikes a critical note, pointing out that the anti-totalitarian scholar fell in love with the 'shifty Nazi' Martin Heidegger, and arguing that Heidegger's perspectives clouded her work. 'The student has reconfigured the secret king's philosophy to produce an exoneration of evil,' he writes, 'to the dismay of her own sense of morality – and to the bewilderment of ours ... No one can be anything but appalled by Arendt's conclusion that evil is a matter of "banal thoughtlessness".'

Perhaps evil is not mere thoughtlessness then, but a kind of incomprehension. Gwen Adshead, whose essay 'The Seven' explores 'how the concept of the seven deadly sins might fit with contemporary psychiatric ideas about evil,' writes that 'evil is associated with a state of mind in which victims are reduced to things and objects to be owned.' This state of mind, again, is a form of ignorance, perhaps a willed ignorance, but certainly a failure to properly understand. The ideological killer, or the genocide-denying conspiracy theorist, or the operator of a totalitarian state, suffers a failure of empathy and imagination, a failure to recognize the reality of the victims. Once humans have been reduced to a fictional status as mere resources or threats, then it's a simple matter to arrange their annihilation. To some will fall the unpleasant job of cutting throats, but many others will contribute simply by arranging the provision of sharp knives. This is not to let anyone off the hook – for we must punish evil to deter it, even if we aren't sure exactly what it is or what causes it – but only to understand that evil can be endlessly amplified by organisation.

Indeed, in recent centuries, complex organisation combined with bad ideology has very often led to genocide. Lutfiye Zudiyeva's essay describes repeated assaults by Russian imperialism against the Muslims of Crimea, starting in the eighteenth century and still continuing under the Russian occupation today. The period of most intense suffering was under Stalin: 'According to official data,' Zudiyeva writes, '183,155 Crimean Tatars were deported from Crimea on 18 May 1944, most transported in cattle cars. In the first year and a half after this date, 46 percent of those deported died.' It was the beginning of an expulsion of over 200,000 children, adults and the elderly – the entire Tatar population. Furthermore, 'many other Muslim peoples in the Soviet Union – Karachais, Chechens, Meskhetian Turks, Balkars, Ingushes and others – were forcibly deported from their homelands. Muslim religious and cultural values interfered with the Soviet regime's demand for faith in the leader and the party rather than in God. Muslims' collective spirit and mutual devotion irritated and frightened the authorities, so Stalin chose a tough anti-religious policy.'

But Muslims weren't the only victims. Non-Russian nationalities suffered the most, but Russian dignity too was violated by a slave labour regime. In general people's fates were determined by arbitrary decisions from on high. Powerful humans treated weaker humans as if they were mere possessions. Powerful humans granted themselves powers which should belong only to God.

The world is full of evil examples. Look at Vietnam, which in the twentieth century was ravaged by colonialism (French), neo-colonialism (American), and neo-neo-colonialism (Chinese), as well as by its 'liberators' who forced hundreds of thousands of Vietnamese into 're-education camps' and many more into exile. Or look at Afghanistan, wrecked by Communists and Islamists, by Russians and Americans, by Pakistanis and Iranians, by third-world obscurantism and state-of-the-art technology. Or look at Syria, where so many forms of evil have thrived at the expense of human health and happiness –the various distinct evils of individuals, the institutional and organisational evils of militias, states and empires, and the ideological evils of fascism, nationalism, Salafi-Jihadism and sectarianism.

During the war precipitated by the Syrian regime's violent counter-revolution, the country became an arena in which the world's evils fought their battles, and a magnet attracting the angriest of misfits. But even before the war, sadism was a central ruling strategy. (This was of course one of the first causes of the revolution.) The works of Syria's expansive prison literature provide a glimpse of the seemingly senseless cruelty perpetrated against dissenters, and through them against society as a whole. Another kind of insight is provided in Salwa Ismail's academic study *The Rule of Violence*, a book which explains how categories more suited to horror films – the grisly, the uncanny – were employed to inculcate dread and passivity in the populace. For quite a while it worked. Syria appeared to be a 'kingdom of silence' (in the words of leftist dissident Riyad al-Turk) until the dam burst in 2011.

Such evil governance was echoed by ISIS, 'secular' Assad's 'religious' mirror image, as the organisation tortured and killed its victims in ever more public and technologically polished ways, not hiding but glorifying in the horror.

The aim of such performative violence, whether it calls itself secular or religious, is to stun its audience into apathy, an evil as bad in its own way as fanaticism. Assad and ISIS instrumentalise fear, but more sophisticated operators employ confusion (it's too complicated to know what to do), or the sense of impotence (there's nothing we can do) to arrive at the same destination. In their study of apathy, Ben Gook and Seán Cubitt write 'this term for being "without feeling" ... marks a reduction in feeling and activity, typically describing forms of indolence, diminished initiative, slowness, inertia, and generalised passivity ... It is then not only that there are causal factors pushing many sectors of the population towards exhaustion, disaffection, alienation, and apathy, but that the one thing that might motivate them, the mere possibility of a condition other than the one we all occupy, has been erased.' The evil of apathy, therefore, accompanies a lack of faith in any better alternative.

One defiant response to apathy is offered in these pages by the Canadian artist Marc Nelson. His paintings of the Caesar photographs – pictures of activists murdered by the Syrian regime smuggled out of the country by a defecting military photographer – and of Mazen Hammada – a revolutionary activist who escaped Syria after torture but who was tricked into returning, and then disappeared back into the Assadist gulag – act against the immediate forgetfulness of social media, and therefore against apathy. 'Photos and videos of the civilians murdered by the Syrian regime are being shared in real-time, for everyone to see,' he writes. 'I feel that there is an inherent ephemerality to media shared on Twitter and Instagram, and I attempt to reflect on these quickly scrolled-by images through the time-consuming act of drawing and painting.'

It takes time and effort to counter evil or even to give due consideration to its victims. Evil, on the other hand, destroys its targets quickly and easily. It often feels as if evil dominates and is only beaten back by exceptional circumstances. Zaina Erhaim's essay 'Grinding Mills of Evil' describes her youth in Syria and 'the two big evils in our lives – fear and hate'. As a schoolgirl, Zaina herself participated in generating evil, albeit unwittingly. When she joined the Ba'ath Vanguards Organisation and repeated its propaganda slogans at home, her mother's face turned yellow: 'I felt her fear of me, and I felt powerful without understanding why.'

Fear and hate were produced not only by the totalitarian Syrian regime but also by 'the maze of social evil' limiting personal freedoms by keeping people under a social surveillance which mirrored the 'security' surveillance of dictatorship. Women, of course, suffered this evil more than men. The antidote to such judgmental suspicion is love, and according to Erhaim it was love which defeated fear and hate – temporarily – when the revolution erupted in 2011: 'The men I had always feared as potential harassers had finally become trustworthy. They loved me without knowing who I was, just for demonstrating beside them, and I loved them back.' Evil was dissolved by the opening horizons and new social bonds of revolutionary cooperation, and if the regime had fallen quickly this positive energy might have continued melting evil obstructions to reform a wounded society. But the regime found powerful foreign allies, and revolution became war, the cities were burnt, and the people were traumatized. Soon forms of hyper-authoritarian Islamism thrived amid the horror: 'In the final demonstration I attended, someone chanted, "Our leader for ever is our Prophet Muhammad." The chant was new, but it sounded very familiar, copying even in its Arabic rhythm the slogan we had grown up repeating – "Forever, forever, oh Hafez al-Assad". It was a cue for all the evils to reveal themselves again, but this time wearing different masks.'

Some of the authoritarian Islamists joined with more democratic groups in a genuine attempt to bring down Assad, but ISIS – to return to that grim organisation – was more interested in fighting the revolution in order to set up its own dictatorship. It merged al-Qaida-style Salafi-Jihadism with a Baathist approach to statecraft. The Islamic State of the twenty-first century bore very little resemblance to the pre-modern state established in Madina by the Prophet, but it did closely resemble the totalitarian surveillance states, with their prison networks, armies of informers, and rule-by-torture, established in the late twentieth Century in both Syria and Iraq.

When religious justifications are mixed with political organisation, then – in Julian Baggini's terms – 'righteous evil' meets 'utilitarian evil'. Baggini's essay 'Ordinary Folks' argues that evil is indeed ordinary, and that it originates in humans, but that it often seems superhuman: 'When the means is seen to justify the end but the means are so vile, it seems akin to possession: in this case by an ideology.'

In his essay 'Atrocity, Evil and Forgiveness' – focusing on the 2019 massacre of Muslims by a white supremacist at the al-Noor mosque in Christchurch, New Zealand, and on the 2017 massacre, by a Salafi-Jihadi extremist, of young girls attending a concert at the Manchester Arena, England – Luke Russell asks if evil and forgiveness are essentially religious concepts. He may well ask – 'evil', after all, is only a letter away from 'devil'.

Michael Wilby's essay continues the supernatural theme, but his devil is AI – 'an intelligent but alien being with the means and motivation to turn the whole world to dust; an artificial Satan or Mephistopheles ... Can a mere tool,' he asks, '– even a highly advanced tool – be held morally responsible?'

Bearing moral responsibility is not the same as being evil, and accusing others, even machines, of evil may not lead to greater understanding, and certainly not to self-knowledge. Julian Baggini writes that 'most psychologists and many philosophers would prefer that we never used the term "evil". The problem is that it suggests some people or acts are in a different category to others, that evil inhabits its own wicked sphere, separate from ordinary badness. Evil "otherises" the extremely bad, allowing us to feel that we could never have anything to do with it. Yet most, if not all, of what we call evil is the work of ordinary human beings.' How then to reduce 'evil' in our perceptions to the work of ordinary human beings? Here Zaina Erhaim quotes the Syrian writer Samar Yazbek to great effect: 'No matter how much the evil they produce is aimed at me, I still view it in its context.'

So how does Bashar al-Assad – responsible for the destruction of Syria, the expulsion of half its population, and the murder of up to a million people – look in his context? If I were him, would I have done it any differently? I mean, if I were really, exactly him. If I had his genetics, his childhood and social context. If as I was growing up my father had carried the blood of tens of thousands on his hands, and I only ever saw people showing him love and respect. If the authority figures around me as I formed my ideas of right and wrong had emphasised the necessity of shedding blood. Would I have done anything differently?

The man is too small a figure to bear so much Satanic weight, and indeed the evil wrought is far bigger than him. He doesn't do the torturing, raping, shooting, bombing, gassing etcetera by himself. He exploits the weaknesses and failures of his opposition, and of Syrian society. He requires a sadistic social structure to do the bloody work. He needs foreign helpers, and the apathy and racism of the 'international community' of states. He's the chief representative of a particular sort of evil, but the evil itself spreads far beyond him.

In his essay 'Encountering the Shadow', Jeremy Henzell-Thomas warns against the solipsism which identifies absolute good, often locating it in 'us' or 'our society', and absolute evil, often located in 'them', whoever they may be. He suggests that identifying others as evil may itself be an evil pattern of thought. John Liechty connects this 'us and them' to 'the War on Terror, the cosmic duality of Pure Good versus Pure Evil' and then to an ancient religious model: 'neither the September 11 terrorists nor the counter-terrorists seemed overly devoted to their respective faiths. The one faith their thinking and actions did bear a striking resemblance to was Manichaeism, long since declared heretical. Pure Good, Pure Evil, Cosmic Duality, God, Satan … a Masters of the Universe comic-book worldview made up of sharply drawn opposites, stirring a marked capacity for self-righteousness and delusion.' Jonah's self-sacrifice, on the other hand, his readiness in the face of the storm to be thrown overboard, 'indicates a moment of repentance, of submission to God, of admission of the need for renewal. In letting the Self go, in losing it, Jonah takes a step toward gaining something far better.'

Letting the self go is to recognise that evil resides there. What if we saw evil, rather than as a sharply drawn opposite, as our shadow? Following Jung, and using dream analysis, Henzell-Thomas seeks to examine his own shadow and thus to go beyond Manichaeism. And Zaina Erhaim concurs that the distinction between good and evil is a lot more shadowy than a simple sharp line: 'War taught me that fighting evil once is no guarantee that you won't fight on its behalf at a later time.'

Everything is connected, everything is ultimately one. Satan is able to corrupt and pervert only because God allows him to. Satan is a shadow that lives within us. By knowing the evil in ourselves and others, and by understanding its context, we might be able to untangle it somewhat, and thus to defuse its power. To describe this strategy, Erhaim refers to Samar Yazbek's metaphor of 'combing Medusa's hair'.

If we could try this more often, we might avoid doing evil in the name of fighting evil. We might avoid falling into the pitfall encapsulated in a joke remembered by John Liechty: 'A political cartoon from the early War on Terror days shows a smiling Satan telephoning the White House as the President lifts the receiver to his ear. "Hello, George?" the caller says. "It's God again".'

EVIL IN THE ABSENCE OF GOD

Richard Appignanesi

Concerning evil, nothing occurs to me. Evil is simply the privation of good. This was the profound insight of the Church Father St Augustine which in its wisdom would advise feeble spirits to look no further. There is no comfort in the hardships of moral psychology for shallow minds. Evil is beyond the grasp of our superficial contemporaries as they go about the streets careering against each other like random dodgems, lost in the trivia of their iPhones into which they peer mesmerised.

To whom do I speak of evil? Who thinks seriously of evil any more? I cannot converse with the fanatic trustees of evil. I am equally repelled by the lukewarm liberals and sanctimonious agnostics discomfited by evil. Who then?

My mother of peasant stock used to warn, 'Don't stare too long in the mirror, *figlio mio*. You will see the Devil ...' Did she mean the Evil Angel of Catholic theologians, Hellish and real? Or perhaps mean the devil in me? Or an eyeful of my own vanity? The mirror has since cracked. Any question of discourse on evil has turned in self-portrait against me.

I ask myself the thorny question. *Is evil understandable intellectually?*

I am tempted to give up at once my dismal reconnoitre of evil. Let those who know better proceed with silence. I sympathise with the seventeenth century mathematician Blaise Pascal whose cold shiver of fear I share as he gazed up at the night sky that should normally fill one with the awe of its splendour. *The eternal silence of these infinite spaces fills me with dread.*

I too do not see what should be otherwise a vision of aesthetic magnificence but is instead an outspread black pall of a universe in mourning. We have given the stars themselves cancer by contagion from our millennia of crimes, from all the unheeded and unexpiated cries of tortured innocents that have risen noxiously to infect the constellations.

The music of the spheres, if it could be heard, would be the immeasurable threnody of victims.

Pascal feared 'those empty spaces' which might contain no God but only the 'God-shaped black hole' of vain human longing. He feared above all the limitless harvest of evil in a godless finite universe.

I look to another stargazer for kindlier light, Immanuel Kant. He claimed freedom was a *scibilius*, a known certainty of experience: an optimism expressed in his *Critique of Pure Reason* (1791) from which is taken the epitaph on his Königsberg tomb:

Two things fill the mind with ever new and increasing admiration and awe, the more often and steadily we reflect upon them: *the starry heavens above me and the moral law within me.*

Beethoven recorded Kant's maxim with Romantic enthusiasm in his Conversation Book of 1820 in his trying time of deafness. We would expect no less from the composer of *Fidelio* and the *Ninth Symphony* who sought fervently for the widest expanse of freedom. There is something of broad-beamed bourgeois *Gemütlichkeit* in Kant's outlook, a self-congratulatory complacency for too sedate for Beethoven's restless revolutionary spirit. But that is a wilful double-bind in Kant's anthropological speculation on man. I see what no one else sees, that the redoubtable abstraction of Kant's *Critique of Pure Reason*, with all its conceptual mechanics, is the apparatus for his portrait of the bourgeois man, his psychical biography, so to speak, exemplified by revolutionary personages like Thomas Jefferson and his extremist Jacobin counterpart Maximilien Robespierre, but best typified in civil society by the species designed for longevity that survives the leveller, Madame la Guillotine, to endure as the acephalous tribe of ruthless capitalist entrepreneurs whose evils are so well catalogued in Balzac's *Comédie Humaine* to inspire Karl Marx's insidious poetry of commodities.

Bourgeois man's gradual declension from Haute Bourgeoisie status is traced in Thomas Mann's magisterial novels (awarded highest class *summa cum laude* by the Marxist critic György Lukàcs) and perhaps best focussed in his novella *Death in Venice* ending with the protagonist (the author ironically portraying himself as a great writer), Gustav Aschenbach, gibbering homosexual aestheticism as he dies of cholera on Venice's Lido beach, well-timed in 1912 to prelude the carnage of World War One and the decline of the West.

I meander to make myself plain. *Evil has a middleclass terminus.* I have no feral hunter companions to help me track down the Sloth of Evil in the jungle's high canopy (what looked once like Dante's theological Dark Wood but has today been cleared and property developed into the unsurpassable high-rise of 'postnormal' history) and strike its side with a blow-pipe's curare-tipped dart to paralyse its sluggish metabolism, till it let's go its hold and drops to the forest floor. My stalker's metaphor is a guise fitted for an existentialist tracker's philosophy in pursuit of evil. I require the fortitude of existentialist irony — irony not as sarcasm but meant in the sense of Greek tragic drama's *eironeia* which is knowing what is to be but unable to change it. This is not a recipe for quietism as we'll see. My pertinacious sloth of evil is also evasively quicksilver in its capacity to vanish away from attention. Absence of evil is what I most often encounter but try nevertheless to calibrate on a social Vernier scale going from *denial* of evil by forensic gradations to its *exoneration.*

Denial begins in a modest everyday idiom. Evil is normally translated in plural 'ills'. the 'heartache and thousand natural shocks that flesh is heir to', as Hamlet soliloquises. Evils are the bodily suffered vicissitudes of illness, penury, old age, senseless accidents and death, all familiar to us in ordinary life. In streetwise parlance, shit happens. There is no evil. Singular evil of truly sinister type, of Satanic disposition, is far removed to the outer reaches of pathology, into the specialist province of psychiatrists, exorcising priests and the police. We have a disquieting sense of seepage, however, that the boundary is not assured impermeable. What is most unnerving is to acknowledge that terror prevails in the everyday air we breath and that the assasin's bomb is only an outrageously redundant reminder of it. Evil seems to hang suspended undecided between fact and fiction. Is it the monster chimera that sleeps by our side and inhabits our dreams, awakening to inflict what dreadful terrors we know not. Is it beyond the compass of Law that has always failed to tame it, since age-old times? Is it only our own recognition that we see mirrored in the phenomenal abyss of evil? Suppose that all this talk of evil is mere fairy tale to frighten the religiously timid or sentimentally gullible. My question again arises. Can evil be understood intellectually?

There are no moral facts

True statements must be empirically verifiable. Who could guess that such a trite declaration would take us beyond good and evil to the end of morality? Morality ended in 1936 with the publication of A.J. Ayer's *Language, Truth and Logic*. Ayer submitted moral judgement to the logical positivist test of verification which maintains that a statement is meaningful only if it is either a logical truth (a 'tautology' as Wittgenstein defined it in his 1921 *Tractatus*, such as a theorem of mathematics) or is empirically verifiable. Particularly the latter is morality's death knell. Statements of morality are incapable of verification and are therefore meaningless.

Ayer's invalidation of morality's philosophical authority, or some would prefer to say, metaphysico-religious pretensions, and its precepts abandoned as pseudo-concept, is named emotivism. It is also aptly nicknamed the 'Boo-Hurrah' descriptive theory by which moral utterances are reduced to emotional expressions of approval ('caring is good', hurrah!) or disapproval ('murder is bad', boo!), neither of which can be said true or false, not anymore than the tone of my voice indicating approbation or a tone of abhorrence indicating disapproval conveys truth or falsehood.

Emotivism introduced modernity to a species of ethical minimalism. A logical positivist version of science was weaponised to confirm beyond any shadow of doubt the obvious, known ever since Aristotle, that there is no flawless system of ethics. Emotivism was prima facie accused of subjectivism, a charge it refuted, because unlike subjectivists who take for fact what they feel is moral, no shock of fact pertains at all to judgements deemed moral for emotivists. I find something disagreeable in this minimalist contraction of morality to impeccable logic. No standard of right or wrong, no warranty to judge evil, but the mere ejaculations of feelings of approval or not – is that not the worst form of subjectivism, nihilism? We are left to wander in a desert of deontology, all directive signposts effaced. Evil vanishes in an expiring breath. Imagination has committed suicide.

First stage of irony

Logical positivism did not escape enmeshment in the irony of history.

Two years previously to the publication of his book at the age of twenty-four, which made Ayer an enduring celebrity of British analytic philosophy, he was welcomed into the prestigious Vienna Circle by its chief founding luminary, the physicist and philosopher Moritz Schlick, only twenty-three in 1915 when he published an appreciation of Einstein's General Theory of Relativity (Einstein was a subsidiary member of the Vienna Circle). During Ayer's two-year residence he imbibed the revolutionary new principles of logical positivism. Schlick and the Circle's brilliant constellation of empirically motivated physicists, philosophers, logicians, and social scientists hailed themselves into existence with their 1929 manifesto, a pamphlet proclaiming 'The Scientific Conception of the World', which, thanks to the explicitly socialist political beliefs of two of its leading members, Otto Neurath and Hans Hahn, linked it to an eccentric mix of Karl Marx and Friedrich Nietzsche whose anti-metaphysical bombardments would assist in liberating the Austrian working-class from the shackles of Christian superstition. The essential agreed focus of the Circle was to renovate empiricism by means of modern logic and thereby create a properly unified field of scientific philosophy. And it proselytised itself. Ayer returned with it to British academia. Schlick lectured on it at Stanford University in America and others spread its gospel in congresses throughout Europe in the 1930s. But it was the philistine sledgehammer of Austrofascism that would effectively smash the Circle into emigrant smithereens.

Schlick was shot dead in 1936 on the steps of Vienna University's Mathematisches Seminare building. His assassin was an unbalanced former student Johann Nellböck who at first claimed that the debonair Schlick had 'distracted' his girlfriend. His light ten-year prison sentence, instead of the death penalty, was then entirely commuted two years later by the Nazi government which stepped in after the Anschluss, Austria's annexation by Germany in 1938. Why was Nellböck favoured? The irony of history is the answer. What he had going for him were the aberrant historical circumstances of Vienna. Former capital of the Hapsburg's grand Austro-Hungarian Empire now shrunken to resentful parochialism, where backwardness and avant-gardism grappled blindly with each other, 'the waiting-room of the apocalypse' as its vitriolic satirist Karl Kraus christened it in his one-man war against the Black Magic of Vienna's corruptive journalism, where clinics for syphilis treatment were advertised in the streets but Freud's sexual secrets of the unconscious were duly greeted with dog shit in his mailbox, where Egon Schiele exhibited his ferociously erotic art and former war-time cavalryman and Expressionist painter Oskar Kokoschka caused a sensation with his play *Murderer, the Hope of Women* in 1919, where architect Adolf Loos disgorged the Viennese addiction to the whipped cream Baroque style in his bulimic tract *Ornament and Crime* in 1908 and his shockingly unadorned buildings that previewed Mies van der Rohe and the Bauhaus school, where his friend Wittgenstein constructed the perfectly functionalist house for his sister Margarethe in 1926 , while Arnold Schönberg's abstract 12-tone compositions paved over the schmaltzy Blue Danube waltzes in harsh atonality, and Kafka composed his cruelly absurdist humoresques…a tapestry in which, beware, the Devil is in the detail.

Something else lay deep abiding beneath this cultural civil war, a sewer of anti-semitism. It gave disturbing sign of itself in 1923 and worse yet to come when a far-right student group prescribed that the Star of David should be branded on all books written by Jews. Schlick appeared on its list of undesirable professors. That he was not a Jew but a Christian and a Prussian of minor nobility made no difference. It would serve to justify Schlick's death warrant, as indeed Nellböck exploited it as an ideological fait accompli at his trial in 1937. Schlick was ringleader of the Vienna Circle's 'Hebrew conspiracy' to corrupt German culture with perverse Jewish ideology. (Recall that the Nazis organised a massive exhibition of *Entartete Kunst* in Munich in 1937, 650 pieces of 'degenerate' modernist art confiscated from museums, featuring works by Jews and other Bolshevik subhuman decadents, and attended by over two million visitors in five months.) Newspapers of Austrofascist sympathies supported Nellböck's courtroom defence and saved his neck from the noose (or the guillotine upon the German annexation.

Schlick's murder is not simply a chance anecdote but a fated irony. The date 1936 is specific to what I see as history communicating its vindication, vengefully it looks to be. Evil displaced by an apparent shrinkage of morality in one place spreads wide in capillary motion throughout the system. The killing of a professor of ethics in 1936 occurs on the eve of the Spanish Civil War, the year beginning the 'anti-Trotskyite' Moscow trials, Mussolini's occupation of Ethiopia, Japan proceeding with geocide in the Rape of Nanking, Sachsenhausen's death camp operating a month before the Olympic Games in Berlin. The time of decision against evil had slipped away. I hear retreating footsteps on the staircase of the academic ivory tower. It isn't much for A. J. Ayer eventually climbing to the Wykeham Professorship of Logic at Oxford to offer us his axiom of 'kindness', which anyway he got from Moritz Schlick, a gentleman's anodyne comfort that complements his bonhomie and sparkling wit. I mean no disrespect for Ayer, whose philosophical stature is perhaps higher than Bertrand Russell's, but his technical principality of clarifying the linguistic knots of logic does not yield existential bread-and-butter ethics for the perplexed hungry.

Sadly, ironic too that Ayer's mentor, the Circle's impresario, Moritz Schlick, should appear the lone voice to argue that the principles of logical positivism do not require that ethics (or even metaphysics) be void of cognitive content. His brand of humane treatise, *Problems of Ethics*, 1930, goes some way to correct this misapprehension, but is at best resolutely circumspect, so to put it, in his assumption of the good. It must surely have struck Ayer as odd to read Schlick stating that 'man is noble because he enjoys [moral] behaviour...it is *natural* for him to be good'. Odd for a convinced logical positivist knowingly to violate the rule of 'naturalistic fallacy', stipulated by G.E. Moore's *Principia Ethica* in 1903, that a moral value cannot be judged by any such uncertainty as a 'natural' quality; nor should you conflate a description of what *is* with a prescription of what *ought* to be. He knew perfectly well that his 'ethics of kindness' must sink into quicksand, unless a renunciation of absolute certainty is granted: '... the sacrifice has no practical significance, for in life, indeed ultimately in science as well, we deal always with probabilities only. Moral rules, too, must refer to the average.' Kindness is his hymn to the Kantian average bourgeois man and the end of morality that lies in verifiability. Evil has been relieved of necessity.

Evil in modernity has been conceptually ironised, if I may so put it, and has not since recovered its former gravity.

Second stage of irony

From my existentialist prospect no system is or can ever be complete. My QED comes from within the Vienna Circle itself. Fifty years on, at the end of his life, A.J. Ayer repudiated his notorious book, pronouncing it 'mostly mistaken'. His impish disavowal is nothing so thoroughly undermining of logical positivism as the theoretical work of Kurt Gödel (1906-1978), the most brilliant mathematical logician of the Vienna Circle. In 1931, at the age of twenty-eight, he published his *Incompleteness Theorems* which had the consequence of gigantomachy in reducing to pygmy size the Circle's hubristic overconfident prescriptions that axiomatic verifiability prevailed in the foundations of mathematics and logic. Gödel's theorems at their most simple, without their formal mathematical setting, state that (1) if a set of axioms is consistent, then it is incomplete and (2) that no set of axioms can ever prove its own consistency (to prove themselves consistent requires an additional axiom not on the list).

For some consequences of Gödel's theorems, I refer to the reported far-reaching effect on the continuum hypothesis in the mathematisation of physics: that the measure of the endlessness of the sizes of infinity is undecidable; that in AI it remains undecidable whether machine intelligence can ever complete the additional axiom required for its completeness. And there is also the 'halting' problem which asks whether a computer program fed with random input will ever run forever or inevitably halt. In my existentialist prospect, the far graver terminal defect that machine intelligence suffers from, and that it can never hope to overcome by simulation, is its utter lack of *emotional vulnerability*. The benefit of the existentialist prospect is its reckoning on the unexpected always being decidedly human.

I dwell on the fascination that Gödel's theorems still exert because of the shadowy borderline of vindictiveness where history ironically intervenes. The formidable brain-teaser that Gödel couched in logico-mathematical enigma is in fact based a very old commonplace already known to ancient Greek wiseacres: 'This sentence is untrue.' No effort is needed to see this is unprovable and therefore undecidable. The grandest schemes of philosophy are at risk of abridgement in the bogus (or more charitably, misprision). This is no cause to rejoice cynicism but to grieve at the melancholy irony that attends on history.

Evil is not far. It knocks at Gödel's door. He had lapsed ever deeper into depression ever since the murder of his close friend Moritz Schlick and the horrors of the war hounded him out of Europe. Paranoid delusions of being poisoned took hold of him. He would let no one but his wife Adele prepare his food. When she fell ill and had to be hospitalised, he ceased eating. Chronic malnutrition contributed to his death in 1978. Had he been crazed by the extreme aridity of mathematics that made his mind a desert, rendered insane like the genius mathematician Georg Cantor, inventor of set theory? Einstein in his Princeton University neighbourhood could not comfort Gödel become a recluse in his torment. Strange thing, he complained that Wittgenstein had 'lost his mind' because he misunderstood the theorems.

Third stage of irony

I look at that famously charismatic face with its sunken features and mad staring eyes and I know this is a man who has seen evil. I open his book of signal 'logical positivist' certitude and see it kin to Kafka's Talmudic disquietude. A treatise laid out in rigorously decimalised propositions, so alike to Baruch Spinoza's geometric demonstrations in his *Tractatus Theologico-Politicus*, 1670. Did not Wittgenstein say, in admiration of precision, 'I would grind lenses like Spinoza'? A mind overwhelmed like Pascal's in despair at the 'God-shaped black hole in the universe'? Did he not read Pascal's thoughts on death in the trenches of World War One?

Consider his first proposition: 'The world is everything that is the case.' He knows we can never aspire to *all* that is the case in the world. Nor is there binding coronally in the next two propositions:

The world is the totality of facts, not of things.

The world is determined by the facts, and by those being all the facts.

The totality of facts is surely beyond knowing and must be the hypothesis of an absurd (but not necessarily meaningless) world. It touches existentialism's core, the fearsome irony of the universe ('containing infinite hope, but not for us', as Kafka put it in one of his sardonic sallies).

Aware that these pesky credibles, facts, will get him into trouble, he clothes them in enigma in proposition 2: 'What is the case, the fact, is the existence of atomic facts.' Is this to confirm Bertrand Russell's view, his supervisor at Trinity College, Cambridge, in 1911, who proposed to reveal a logically perfect 'truth-functional' language obscured by ordinary language, and that the most elementary constituents of true logical form, the 'logical atoms' correspond to the most elementary constitution of reality; a combination which established 'Logical Atomism'? Is this Wittgenstein's default understanding in the German term he uses for atomic facts, *Sachverhalten*? Wittgenstein apparently sought to adapt Logical Atomism to an ideal language which actually shares structure with metaphysical reality, that is, going beyond Russell's correspondence of elements between language and reality, there is *isomorphism* whereby reality itself shares the logical form of language and is *pictured* in it, a version of atomism become Wittgenstein's well-known 'picture theory' of language.

I ask what is that 'share' of reality existentially apart from its obscuration by idealised logical form? Facts are not logico-mathematical confetti but are *arrested decisions*, compelling because they have what philosophers call 'qualia', the 'what is-ness' of things. 'What is it *like* to be a bat?' as Thomas Nagel inquired in 1974. What is the taste of anchovies *like* which I enjoy but some do not? Qualia advises that we should speak of the evanescent fragility of fact which will never give anyone the contentment of certitude. But there is another sense to this condition provided by the existentialist psychiatrist Ludwig Binswanger.

> 'What we perceive are 'first and foremost' not impressions of taste, tone, smell or touch, not even things or objects, but rather, meanings'. He has intensified qualia to another level of existentially factual meaningfulness.

I appreciate Wittgenstein's *Tractatus* for its aesthetically perfect design, meticulously perfect as the formal purity of the architectural plan of the house he constructed for his sister Margarethe. I appreciate it poignantly as a screen which conceals him from the reality of the world that he pictures with such logical lucidity in the circumstances of a dire history that interests me. What possessed him to volunteer for military service in the Austro-Hungarian army at the age of twenty-five? He could have stayed safe in Cambridge, a non-combatant sheltered by the pacifist Russell, pleading medical exemption, but he chose to be a dog face regular soldier, eschewing at first an officer's commission to which his social rank entitled him, alienated from the fraternity of coarse, ignorant Croat, Slovak and other conscripts on the Eastern Front dredged up by the polyglot Empire who barely spoke German and disliked his patrician airs. He gave no explanation for his patriotic sacrifice apart vaguely from a need 'to share in the civic burden'. To test an existential axiom private to him?

There can be no grimmer misalliance of Wittgenstein's *Sachverhalten*, the 'atomic facts' of a meta-reality, than to those of abattoir mechanisation of slaughter. He could not possibly escape unscathed from the totalisation of blood-and-iron fact. Frequent depressions and thoughts of suicide were not dissuasive but drove him to proofs of reckless bravery in his 1916 frontline debut with the Austrian 7th Army facing the Russians' heavy assault in the Brusilov Offensive. Decorations were pinned to his chest; adornments comforting to the mind were forgone. He volunteered for the most dangerously exposed observer's post in no-man's-land from which to survey the enemy and direct artillery fire. There, in that confined open grave, he had what he preferred, isolation, to engage with mortality in range of snipers and test his consciousness of God in his meditations on a future terrifying empiricist philosophy. On another undramatic level of volunteering for the solitary, Wittgenstein gladly peeled potatoes on kitchen duty for the opportunity of meditation it granted him, paring away not at potatoes but in his mind at the embryonic *Tractatus* naked of inessentials.

I could multiply anecdotes, had I the space for a novel. I focus instead, as in a triage of diagnostic urgency, on what is pertinent to Wittgenstein's cultivation of an idiosyncratic poetry of occluded mysticism, more openly admitted than is usually credited. I like this one exemplifying the isolatory proselyte. In the capture of the Russian-occupied Polish town of Tarnów in 1915 after heavy Austrian shelling, he finds the one bookshop with the one book in it – Tolstoy's 1902 *The Gospel in Brief*, in which divinity, doctrines and liturgical accessories are stripped away to the essential teachings of Christ. Wittgenstein read this book compulsively and importuned others with it. Christianity without religion and God, solely a pursuant voice of conscience, had already begun filling the 'God-shaped hole' in 1913 when he abandoned the witty frivolities of the Cambridge clan, unendurable to is ascetic temper, and retreated to the remote Norwegian village of

Skjolden and there learned Danish to read the humbling theological paradoxes of Søren Kierkegaard, inheritor of Pascal's angst, but transformed to exhilaratingly ironical existentialism.

In that mirage of futile courage, mud and mustard gas, the endless rain of heavy artillery and close quarter gut-skewering bayonet combat, evil is commonplace and omnipresent as the rats nibbling at dead men's eyes, and sub-lieutenant Wittgenstein's real camaraderie in this hellish pandemonium was with the poets. I knock at the door of poetry for the admission of Wittgenstein's true purpose. The ideal logical language on the surface of the *Tractatus* that misled the Vienna Circle's enthusiastic accreditation is better aligned with the Symbolist poet Stéphane Mallarmé's declaration in his homage 'The Tomb of Edgar Poe' that the dishonour of Poe's alcoholic poisoning is uplifted to the eternal order of his task, which is 'to give a more pure sense to the words of his tribe'. Purification is similarly a tribute of Wittgenstein mourning the suicide of the young poet Georg Trakl (1887-1914) whose purity of German he much prized. Trakl poisoned himself by an overdose of cocaine when his mind became unhinged by his experience as a medical orderly of the grotesquely mangled casualties on the battlefield of Grodek:

A thorny desert surrounds the city.
The moon chases the shocked women
From the bleeding stairways.
Wild wolves have broken through the door.

(Trakl, last stanza from 'On the Eastern Front', 1914)

Wittgenstein's sacrificial cleansing of language is effectively unspeakable. Its memorial to the dead in the *Tractatus* is one of absence. Proposition 6.431: *Death is not an event of life. Death is not an experience of life.* Not many will guess that the *Tractatus* is a cenotaph.

Wittgenstein's real 'truth-function' is emetic, to make pure the tribe's language in preparation for life's only truly serious concern. What is that?

Wittgenstein carries the reader relentlessly to that famously radical conclusion in the last proposition, 7, and nothing after. *Whereof one cannot speak, thereof one must remain silent.* His advice to the reader left perplexed is that if the lessons of his book have been grasped, it must be ditched, like a ladder kicked away once its rungs have led the reader to its destination. What lessons? What destination? One has a sense rather of each rung of the ladder collapsing behind one in the climb, leaving one marooned with a final oracle of silence.

I believe this. More of evil is understood from what Wittgenstein leaves out of the *Tractatus* than can be from theological confrontations with evil.

Evil has no face

I do not expect any persons anywhere going about the routines of life to fear they have been robbed of their beliefs by the logical analysis of the Vienna Circle or other schools of philosophy. Disconnection is the prevailing norm between the doxa of popular opinion and the formal technicalities of philosophy. It is symptomatic of the conundrum of history that nags existentialism and is unresolved. How is history made but somehow translates from its object into recognisable individual human behaviour? Or obversely to ask how individual behaviour is manufactured so that it presents itself in history as though responsible for itself? What we know is not what happens. History is not what appears in headline news. Rather it is where the ephemerality of events goes to die like the expiring elephant to its unknown twilight cemetery. History operates anonymously by slow capillary spread of its vindication that brings upon us the nemesis of irony. The present which so preoccupies us is what the past has left undone and which the future has already bypassed. French philosopher Auguste Comte (1798 – 1857) held the idealist belief that 'the dead govern the living'. On that basis he rejected the seductive causality of 'time's arrow' (past—present—future) and rescheduled it as the impetus of the future hurrying us ahead to the past with the barest incidence of a transitory present. An alternative progressivist, Karl Marx, expressed a different horrified view in his *Eighteenth Brumaire of Louis Bonaparte*, 1852, 'The tradition of all the dead generations weighs like a nightmare on the brain of the living.' There is no contradiction between them in the existentialist perspective on time.

I skirt a fundamental peculiarity. How strange it is that morality was formerly the product of insight exercised on humanity's behalf by pious lawgivers. Now it is a university subject. Whereas once we saw medieval schoolmen counting the angels accommodated on the head of a pin, now we have professors of ethics splitting hairs to weave into abstruse articles for each others' career estimation. Morality as become an academic secret. Wittgenstein himself is guilty of it. His stainless evil-proof ethical model must be discarded as inimitable – as he had the foresight to advise.

Yet stranger still, I look back and find to my astonishment what had never occurred to me before, that academics have always predominated in the teaching of ethics. One of the greatest, Immanuel Kant, 'the Chinaman of Königsberg', as Nietzsche called him, was a lifelong academic clock-puncher; and back, two thousand years and more, to Aristotle, whose *Nicomachean Ethics* has been the handbook of Western civilisation, was a text he gave as lectures to his students at the Lyceum in Athens. Confucianism is the perpetuation of moral teachings that require no God or gods by a collectivity of mandarin scholars whose revered founder is the semi-legendary paragon of sages, Kong Qui, in the sixth century BCE. Our university dons are the thinnest whey extract of those ancient mandarins. I think of the smug phonetics professor Henry Higgins brow-beating the Cockney working-class girl Eliza Doolittle into a cultivated lady of high society – but in reverse now to inculcate in her the analytic logician's purified version of 'ordinary language'.

What did I expect? A.J. Ayer in th guise of a wild-eyed Moses descending Mount Sinai bearing the sculpted commandments of God's dictation? How far back must one go to discover the origin of morality in theodicy? To the Babylonian black column that illuminates the Sun God Shamash prescribing the Hammurabi code of laws (circa 1750 BCE)? (I think irresistibly of that mysterious black slab that appears from nowhere in Stanley Kubrick's classic science fiction film *2001* which dropped amid a group of prehistoric hominids and exerts its alien power to transform them into the first organised weapon-wielding tribe.) To the Vedic scriptures of the late Bronze Age or the revelation first received by Prophet Muhammad on the Jabal an-Nour mountain in 610?

One thing is clearly demonstrated to me. The monotheistic faiths all agree to dissociate God from the evil that is strictly the responsibility of humankind. St Augustine of Hippo, the theologian of fourth century Christianity, most darkly, inexorably and pitilessly attributes human sinfulness to the fault of original sin indelibly branded on our souls by the

Fall of our first parents, Adam and Eve. This encumbrance of near-irredeemable benighted sinfulness has controlled the insufferable darkness of those puritan Christian sects like Calvinism hold to a creed of predestination to Hell-fire doom for everyone not among God's Justified Elect whose salvation is certain because of His inscrutable Grace and not by any worthy acts of goodness. I recommend for a cure the reading of Scottish author James Hogg's novel, *The Private Memoirs and Confessions of a Justified Sinner* (1824), featuring a Calvinist protagonist who assumes that his election to guaranteed salvation justifies the murder of those he judges already damned to perdition.

We have come so far without an answer to the simplest, most obvious question. What is meant by the word 'moral'? An example of it is heard at the end of ancient fables, 'and the moral of the story is…' Moral is a lesson. Moral is declaimed in Cicero's oration: *O tempora! O mores!* 'What times! What manners!' Here it is a concern with behaviour or comportment, as it is also used in 'morale'. Moral is therefore an intended lesson or illustration of behaviour. Understood like this, 'moral' must be one of these adjectives that modifies or more clearly specifies fact. It makes no sense to say 'there are no moral facts'. There are *only* moral facts in the existential sense (using the commonplace 'experiential' misplacement of the proper technical term, existentialist).

Nor have I yet said what evil is. Evil is not a sayable portrait. It will not wait patiently for your recognition. Meanwhile we can only imagine to whom evil bears resemblance. To Hitler with his Charlie Chaplin toothbrush moustache? To the American serial killer Ted Bundy with his middleclass regulation smile?

Does it sometimes appear with stomach-churning evidence? The ten-month-old baby boy Finley Boden died on Christmas Day 2020 after his mother Shannon Marsden and her partner Stephen Boden had subjected him to prolonged tortures. The postmortem found seventy-one bruises, burn marks from lighted cigarettes, fifty-seven fractures to his pelvis, shoulders, ankles, and ribs. Finley's close-up photograph shows a cherubic-faced infant looking into the camera, and the worst of it, smiling, we can only presume at the executioners taking his picture. Nausea and anger collide to overwhelm us in this unaccountable gratuitous crime. Pure evil. And it bears the face of two very ordinary-looking people.

His cries like those of countless other martyred innocents will mount cancerously infectious to sicken the stars. But not on this media-dominated earth where communication of his torture sponsors indulgence in pornographic sentimentality, but never long, maybe a few days, then fades away into the ether of public surfeited disinterest. This is the unquantifiable difference between the two spheres, the constellated universe on which Pascal gazes with horror and Kant rejoices in comfort, our sublunar madhouse where, as Karl Kraus jibed about Vienna, 'solitary confinement is preferable'. Occult gnosis used to speculate that 'as it is above, so it is below' on the mystical ladder that joins Heaven and Earth in analogical similitude that permits the climber's spiritually upward transformation, Wittgenstein offered a ladder in modern times to world destitute of spiritual renovation, but it is far too arduous. *Wozu Dichter in dürftiger Zeit?* asked Friedrich Hölderlin, the finest of German Romantic poets, in his elegiac 1801 'Bread and Wine', 'what are poets for in unendurable times?', despairing of the world before his fall into thirty-six years of madness until his death.

We must have faces to identify evil, individual or socially collective, as the grinning ensemble of accomplices shown photographed in a Deep South lynching party. We would wish them all ugly to match their evil deeds. We seek in vain for evident guilt. Guilt requires a moral law to condemn the agent of intentional evil. The sense of sin too has its qualia of shared ingredients which, if I may recall, I'd said makes for a qualifiable fact. No amount of neurophysiological archaeologising will get to the psychical root of the 'whyness', so to speak, the test of 'what is' morally good or bad. Like originality in art, no amount of expert discussion will ever satisfy the 'what-isness' that attests to the Mona Lisa's aesthetic fact. I am tempted to say that evil is but itself an *aesthetic* fact of preternatural ugliness.

Does religion still beckon? Atheists are supremely confident that evil is the proof of God's inexistence. Their argument ironically relies on the ontological proof of God's existence. Its first and simplest formulation is that of St Anselm, Benedictine Archbishop of Canterbury (1099 – 1109) who argued that God's existence can be conceived as a being 'than which no greater can be conceived' and therefore whose inexistence is inconceivable. 'The fool says in his heart, "There is no God"...' Psalm 14:1 Is our atheist unintelligent enough to maintain that the ontological proof of God's must explain why this 'greatest being', all mighty, all benevolent, all knowing, allows the existence of evil..? Ergo, if evil exists, God does not. This is a nihilist belief that there *must be* no God for evil to exist.

But God is dead...

Wittgenstein knew Dostoyevsky's final novel, *The Brothers Karamazov* (1879–1880), practically by heart and could not fail to come across Ivan Karamazov's desperate realisation that has by now become a cliché of existential philosophy: 'If there is no God, everything is permitted'. The question troubled Nietzsche too, son of a Lutheran pastor who studied theology for the ministry, and who promoted himself in mountain-top ecstasy to Persian prophet Zarathustra *redivivus* come to bring the new religion of enlightenment 'beyond good and evil'. 'If God is dead'.' Nietzsche asks, 'who killed him? We have...' The 'death of God' worried him, although irreconcilably hostile to Christianity, because of foreshadowing the human tragedy of faithlessness that would lead to nihilism and the value-free but weakling inferior 'last man' filled with resentment. A prophecy vindicated by irony. I cross reference here to the political scientist Francis Fukuyama's *The End of History and the Last Man*, 1992, whose similar fear is that Nietzsche's 'last man' in postmodernity will sink in his negation of values to a resentful torpor of boredom causing him to itch for indiscriminate troublemaking, without even the sincere belief of anarchism, which is a political value investment, but mere mischievous pretence. Fukuyama's prediction has proven true by the rise of Wokedom's self-justifying 'morally superior' trolls in acts of censorious cultural vandalism. What makes us suppose that our world of amoral simulacra is any way morally advantaged over the evils of the past? We are no worse than what we were but no better than it. Comte's prediction of the dead in governance over us will take its vengeance.

Atheism is a commonplace that does not understand itself hopelessly pronged on Kant's tuning fork of the antinomy in his *Critique of Pure Reason*. I'll explain. Kant furnished his creation of the average bourgeois man with an unconscious, otherwise said the *paralogisms,* to limit his tendency to hubristic self-confidence. A paralogism is simply the fallacy of which the reasoner is unaware. A further humiliation closely related to the fallacies of paralogisms recognises that the mind is forever trapped in its own necessary circularity, that is, technically designated as the antinomy, meaning 'contradiction in the law', which is a frustration of transcendental reason.

One apt example relating to the human attempts at counselling God is this. The mind cannot escape its own binary foreclosure, so that to say 'God exists' will inevitably and *lawfully* be contradicted by 'God does not exist'. Monotheism is patently vulnerable to this contradiction. Posit a belief in God and for sure it will summon the contrary. It is as if God is a one-legged trick asking for disbelief. Kant in his own logical language says the same as Wittgenstein. To speak knowledgeably of God is meaningless.

If belief in God is not assured one leg, its other assurance of a prop in the agency of the self is also denied. The self in *self*-confidence has gradually been eroded away. I prefer an existential observation of this dry-bed arroyo in the soul. I take for one example Bertrand Russell, well-known for disporting an egotistical self, hardly one to be imagined suitable to sacrifice it. And yet...in 1912, it is written Russell 'started by believing that the self was an object of acquaintance,' as Bertie's friend, A. J. Ayer, elegantly avers in his critical study, meaning that 'we are not only aware of things but of being aware of being aware of them.' Russell gave up that belief altogether in his *Analysis of Mind* in 1921. 'He there agrees with Hume that the self is not a possible object of introspection, and he thinks it naïve to suppose that just because the word "I" is used as a grammatical subject, there must be some object which it names ... the difference between mind and matter is regarded not as a difference between mind and matter, but as a difference in the arrangement of neutral elements.'

Russell is taking a well-trodden path of provenance to David Hume's radical empiricist abolition of the self. Hume proposed the first most convincing radically argument that the self is just a bundle of perceptions in his *Enquiry Concerning Human Understanding*, 1748, especially persuasive because of the perfection of his prose. We like to think of ourselves as stable entities existing the same over time. This is a fallacy due to our natural habit of attributing unified existence to any collection of associated parts. It is an easily discredited illusion to believe that we can ever be directly aware of ourselves but only of what we are experiencing at any given moment. *Can you imagine a chain apart from the links that constitute it?* I am only the memory I am having of myself. Hume is in striking accord with one ironical principle of existentialism. *I never was the man I used to be.*

Hume's chain has extended unbroken to Russell's analytic dissuasion of the self. Kant initially struggled against Hume's binding chain round the ankle of the Enlightenment's manumitted freed man, the bourgeois. He specifically addressed his *Critique of Pure Reason* to refute Hume and rescue the self from evaporation. He did not succeed. There is no cause here to enter into the complexities of that failure. Suffice only to emphasise celebration of his effort to engage with the fundamentally existential question of consciousness: 'what permits thinking?' Otherwise, the 'I'-self is left narratively unmoored as a merely convenient unit of grammar:

> The identity of the consciousness of myself at different times is therefore only a formal condition of my thought and their coherence, and in no way proves the numerical identity of the subject. Despite the logical identity of the 'I', such a change may have occurred in it as does not allow the retention of its identity, and yet we may ascribe to it the same sounding [gleichlautende] 'I'...

I find the Vienna Circle also keeping to Hume's chain in its logical positivist philosophy of mind called logical behaviourism. Investigations of the self's mental states, such phenomena as feelings, perceptions, imagination, and so forth, that manifest a tendency to certain modes of behaviour, can be explained by resorting to scientific tests applying the methods of behaviourism for which everything consists of stimulus-response pairs of various types of conditioned reflex reinforcement.

There it is. The self has become a solipsistic fiction in empirical philosophy's pursuit of the certitude that evaded Descartes's apparently doubt-proof assurance, 'I think, therefore I am.' No existence pertains *thoughtfully* to 'I am' The final buttress of belief has toppled. Religion's competence over evil is unmoored and without rudder of selfhood. Whether God exists or is dead is futile anxiety. Evil is as it always was, always permitted.

My promise of monitoring evil's measure on the social Vernier scale has been steadily progressing in the background. Denial of evil from which it started has moved on by each further gradation to demonstrate how increasingly difficult it is to grasp evil. It has long past conveyance of extent by religious or secular morality to arrive at the 'metaphysical nonsense' of talking of evil at all. Reconciliation and exoneration of evil cannot be far off. Empirically reliant philosophy has conspired to set loose a being not responsible for itself. It was 'in the air', as they say, the property Zeitgeist of postmodernity. But the consequences are what must fall to earth. Does the blame lie with history? It does 'lie', taking that term in its ironical double sense.

I appreciate Kant's dry statement of weariness: 'I have found it necessary to deny knowledge in order to make room for faith.' By sheer weariness have we come to the last-ditch effort of faith, *sacrificium intellectus*, the sacrifice of the intellect? It was first seen polemicised in St Paul's *Epistle to the Corinthians*, 10:5 in Macedonia circa 55. 'We destroy arguments and any lofty opinion raised against the knowledge of God and take everything captive to obey Christ.' St Ignatius of Loyola, sixteenth century Counter-Reformation founder of the Jesuits, based his order's disciplinary *Spiritual Exercises* on the sacrificial curbing of the intellect's potential rebelliousness. It may be objected that a God who demands sacrifice of the intellect is not worthy of belief. God is not by want of our belief nor our intellect. I am deliberately ambiguous concerning 'want'. Not God but we are in want. Best remember Wittgenstein's advisory closure on silence...

The Nazi Beast in the Glass Booth

We did not have to wait long for the Last Man. He arrived in an SS uniform with all the resources of the German state to commit indiscriminate atrocities.

I need not rehearse information already well-known about the Holocaust. Those killed in it are now suffering a second death, submerged beneath denials that it ever happened, mutated into cliché by mass-media and museum representation, conflated with the excesses of Zionism to become anti-Semitic propaganda. Two things plead for the Holocaust's unspeakable distinction of purest distilled evil. The first is perhaps best known but never fully acknowledged because it has shamed Western civilisation into hypocritical silence. It was the systematically *cultivated* nature of the Holocaust that makes it unique in the annals of genocide. What do I mean, 'cultivated'? I look to the planning itself, the systematic bureaucracy of its implementation, exact even to the smallest details of train schedules, the mass transport of victims across Europe, which required the complexities of a Europe-wide collaboration; the orderliness of extermination which far supersedes haphazard military on-the-spot slaughter, but worse, far worse, a negotiated one that prolonged the continuous selection of the hapless victims in every country towards the intended target of zero; the provenance of one's name which could itself spell one's doom, the officious anthropometric measurement of blood, as in apartheid South Africa, that ruled on one's degree of being almost acceptably human; the detailed logistics of evil that itemises profits from the recycling of the victims' clothing, the post-mortem hair, gold teeth, tattooed skin, and even their ashes; the brutalising of the living bodies in senselessly painful unanaesthetised surgical experiments in support of bogus Aryan theory; and at last the warning odour of Zyklon B gas, a hydrogen-cyanide based pesticide, also used in fumigation, invented by German industrialist chemist in the 1920s, that kills a human being in a few minutes, as it enters the odourless valves of our own minds to kill the imagination permanently. Is 'permanent' as unbelievable as the immolation of the self that has preceded this state of mass murder? The question dovetails with my second point.

Sometime muse and fashion model, Lee Miller, iconically photographed by the Surrealist Man Ray, who then became a remarkable war-time photojournalist with the Allied Forces, submitted the earliest photos of the liberated Death Camps, Dachau and Buchenwald, to *Vogue* magazine with the telegraphed caption, BELIEVE THIS! The world was not yet ready to believe it; and the 'yet' has been provisory but enduring. The world entire, make no mistake, with the particular inculpation of Germany forever unforgivable, accomplished the ground zero of the unimaginable. I speak not of the nuclear-sited test ground or Manhattan's Twin Tower's sense of ground zero – although both may figure in it – but an absolute levelling that leaves no trace of the imagination. The poetic healing power of the imagination cannot retroactively redeem itself from the evil that this unimaginable ground zero has forced upon it. Imagination has been annihilated – not by the Holocaust as an event in history, but by its *meaning* which criminalises history. Fall-out reminders of the unimaginable, its waste wreckage, so too speak, are a semblance of the imagination which might make it appear functionally recuperable. But it is a delusion fashioned by denegation, *Verneinung*, in the Freudian vocabulary of psychoanalysis, referring to the unconscious defence mechanism of abnegation which rejects as untrue for oneself a fact too unpalatable to be faced.

Does the death of the imagination sound untrue, personally? I will exemplify. Suppose the chance occurred to meet face-to-face with a Nazi accused of Holocaust crime. The occasion of such encounter arose for Hannah Arendt when she accepted to report on the trial of the Nazi war criminal Adolf Eichmann for the *New Yorker* in 1961. SS Obersturmbannführer Adolf Eichmann, the media sensation 'man in a glass booth', built for his protection in the District Court of Jerusalem, faced judgement for his war crimes against Eastern Jewry. The trial conducted with scrupulous legal protocol was, as everyone including Eichmann himself knew, a sham, its verdict which would deliver the death penalty was a forgone conclusion. Not the point. Nor was it the point for Eichmann who vigorously defended himself with the aid of a prominent German lawyer, Robert Servatius, known for his able defence of Nazi war criminals at the Nuremberg Trials in 1945, appointed by the Jerusalem court, whose only best course was to plead for clemency, which surprisingly gained an additional two-month hearing.

The point was expressed by the grandee Prime Minister of the new Jewish state of Israel, David Ben Gurion, who wanted a 'Jewish Nuremberg Trial' for the world to see, 'Justice done for Jews', a 'trial against anti-Semitism' stage-managed by a fledgling state only thirteen years established, and for many of its international critics, illegally. Illegally too, Eichmann had been seized in Argentina by Israeli intelligence operatives, kidnapped and transported to Israel – a predecessor to the 'rendition' perfected by the CIA, but in this case brought home for caged exhibition.

Arendt sat in one of the 474 places reserved for world journalists. What was she doing here? Curiosity alone does not explain her choice to report on the trial. I believe it was philosophically motivated to meet 'in the flesh' with an official mechanic of genocide, the manoeuvring engineer accused of an alleged 1.5 million deaths. She wished to appreciate the qualia, the particular 'whatisness' of a marionetteer of evil. An existentialist enquiry, and therefore a choice accredited by the qualia of her own experience 'in the flesh': a love affair, in 1924, of an eighteen-year-old philosophy student at Marburg University with a thirty-five-year associate professor of philosophy whose 'mesmerising presence at the podium' attracted passionate students, 'the secret king of philosophy' as she later titled him, Martin Heidegger, who joined the Nazi party in 1933, ten days after being elected Rector of Freiburg University; 1933 when she was arrested in Berlin by the Gestapo and imprisoned eight days for suspected Jewish agitation, when at the time she wrote to him hoping he would deny his Nazi allegiance, and got his reply saying, yes, it was true, but his love for her remains unchanged. She fled with her mother to France and persisted there to assist in the underground escape of refugee Jews like herself and write journalistic propaganda for Zionism, until rounded up by the collaborationist Vichy regime for transport to an internment camp in southwest France, Gurs, from which she escaped in 1940 over the Pyrenees and via Lisbon to residence in the US, where she laboured to achieve celebrity as a philosopher and academic. An itinerary that is barrenly told without affective existential texture.

And Heidegger? Despite the shifty Nazi that he was, she never renounced him and 'the secret king of philosophy' kept his crown. But the verdict that she kept secret in her heart, the 'certain uncertainty' in this darkly tortuous Dostoevskian tale, how darkly astringent that qualia must seem of 'what is-it-like to be a Nazi', as she compared him to the man in the glass booth. A transparency indeed surrounded Eichmann, a far from kingly fifty-six-year-old Philistine captive of triumphant Zion. Philistine in the cultural sense, a product of the German petit bourgeoisie in appearance – if appearances meant anything. What? A middle-rank manager? A used car salesman? But just as likely to be the dutiful civil servant he enacted. Arendt had the five months from August to April while the trial dragged on to puzzle over this passive cog-in-the-wheel well-behaved apparatchik of the Holocaust with his slightly protuberant ears and pointy nose, hopelessly boring, so unselfconsciously boring as he roll-called himself in Wagnerian resounding titles, his position in the Schutzstaffel organisation, department of the SS Sicherheitsdienst, Bureau IV B4 under the Reichssicherheitshauptamt or Head Office for Reich Security, RSHA, confessing himself upset that his work had been underacknowledged by a Lieutenant-Colonel grade rank ... Arendt thinks, 'even his superiors didn't rate him. The man has no ears to hear'. This was the first clue she had to his riddle.

She tired of the endless byzantine maze of Nazidom's sub-departmental fractions, larded with initialled acronyms indicative of power-mad paranoiac mentalities heading for catastrophe. She tired of the endless queue of over a hundred Holocaust survivors whose tearful, heart-rending polyglot testimonies often needed translations communicated through headphones; tired of the Chief Prosecutor in the panel of five, Gideon Hausner's judicial showmanship: 'I am not standing alone. With me here are six million accusers ... Their blood cries out, but their voices are not heard ... Therefore I will be their spokesman ...' She noted that a degree of judicial fairness was preserved by appointing three judges and prosecutors who had not themselves directly experienced the Holocaust. But she did not approve of the trial steering towards Ben Gurion's goal. She had been advised against attendance by her other philosophy supervisor, the existentialist Karl Jaspers, a 'friend of Israel', who feared the trial would only further blot Israel's already shaky reputation.

Her wishful thinking of a trial exclusively to judge Nazi crimes against humanity and not to serve Jewish revindication was disappointed by Ben Gurion's prevailing vision of it. What she got instead was a nonentity whose pretentiously long complex sentences were at times interrupted by Judge Yitzhak Raveh who patiently corrected the defendant's grammar. Eichmann's unwary boast of familiarity with philosophy drew the erudite Raveh's challenging query on the accused's knowledge of Kant's Categorical Imperative – quoted from the judge's memory – and whether he had acted in conformity with it. 'Act only according to that maxim whereby you can at the same time will that it should become a universal law'. Arendt smiled bitterly. Eichmann had indeed acted wilfully to make Nazism a universal law.

The first uncustomary sign of animation shown by Eichmann after long weeks of showing none in this trial for his life was a sudden agitated waving of his hands. A fly had become trapped, buzzing round distractingly in ricochets off the panels of the glass booth. 'Verdammte Fliege!' was heard translated from Eichmann's German into Hebrew, French, and English round the courtroom audience's headphones – and his muttered apology for a lapse of good manners.

Arendt laughs, as others did. A moment of comic relief. But what comes to her mind is a singularly eerie moment in Dostoevsky's novel The Idiot. The society beauty Nastasya Barashkova is torn between her desperate attractions to Prince Myshkin, the eponymous 'idiot', 'a soul of saintly purity', and her bestially crude lover Rogozhin who ends by stabbing her in the heart. Rogozhin invites Myshkin, in an apotheosis of cruelty and despair, to witness her corpse stretched out on a bed and covered by a sheet from which 'only an alabaster foot peeks out'. The silently tense poignancy of the scene is trespassed by a buzzing fly that settles by Nastasya's head.

That fly – no, not only it but the 'bad grammar' that betrays Rogozin's merchant lower class crudeness and re-echoes like the shamelessly transgressive fly in Eichmann's petit bourgeois defective grammar - that random congruence inspired Arendt to the fatal words: *the banality of evil*, which came to subtitle her book on the Eichmann trial. Fatal, because they libelled her a pariah to the Israeli public for the next three decades, in their eyes 'self-hating Jew' who denigrates the Holocaust and is an anti-Zionist. I can understand their touchiness. The 'banality of evil' has taken time, if even now, to be understood.

Arendt emerged from the trial with a new conception of evil. The steps to it are almost too accusingly self-evident as is Eichmann's guilt. Only two things about him need be known. First, he did not have to be monstrously evil for his task of genocide as a ready tool of policy implementation. He is a paradigm of the 'desk murderer' whose sole intention is to advance his bureaucratic career for which he viewed himself well-fitted as a law-abiding citizen who obeys his superiors' orders. He did not have to 'close his ears to his conscience' because his own was jointly and consensually the conscientious voice of respectable German society that does not censure the crime for which he should not feel guilty.

The second feature about him is his characteristic of 'thoughtlessness', the inability ever to look at anything with any interest from the other's point of view, which accords with his sociopathic 'absence of ears'. He is nothing Satanic but an egregiously ordinary man. His deeds are monstrous but the man himself banal.

Arendt's summation contradicts tradition from St Augustine to Kant that acts of evil must necessarily be manifestations of evil intentions. For her, instead, such intention of evil is absent from Eichmann whose 'thoughtlessness' reigns above all, a kind of hollowness of mind not identical to stupidity but which can wreak more havoc than all the evil instincts taken together, these instincts being perhaps inherent in man. Hence, the banality of evil.

My calibrations on the Vernier scale, by gradations across these pages, have finally reached in diminuendo the terminal point I feared: reconciliation with evil. Reluctantly or not, but nevertheless, anaesthetising us to evil immunises it against us. Arendt should not neglect to recall the testimony of Eichmann's SS deputy who overheard him say that 'he would leap laughing into his grave because the feeling that he had the deaths of millions on his conscience would be for him a matter of great satisfaction'.

Eichmann wins. One puny civil servant can laugh to his grave with his easy conscience.

But it wasn't ever about one man. Buzz, buzz. That charnel-house fly that put in her head the fatal word banality. Eichmann's 'easy conscience' has been rightly identified by Arendt as communally shared by *them*. Who is 'them'? Anyone with some knowledge of Heidegger's philosophy will at once be alerted to his hallmark existential basics of 'lapse of concern', 'forgetfulness of Being' – reprised by Arendt as Eichmann's 'thoughtlessness' – which have resulted from modern subservience to technocratic efficacy and consequent fall into the faceless reign of 'they' who idolise the irresponsible chatter of 'minding to business'. The unspectacular unselfconsciousness of 'they' is epitomised by Europe's war-time collective guilt turned indifferently cold as it welcomed the Cold War nuclear threat of total annihilation. That is the banal complexion of evil.

The student has reconfigured the secret king's philosophy to produce an exoneration of evil, to the dismay of her own sense of morality –and to the bewilderment of ours. She was not wrong to make the fact recognisable. Not wrong to 'banalise' evil, to de-criminalise the culpable, no matter their number by immersive disguise in the grey mass of 'them'. The banality of what they do serving all too obligingly in the aftermath to grass over the ground zero Holocaust and abandon it to the paupers' field of the unknown dead, whereupon what 'they' did becomes by tomorrow 'no one' who did it.

Seeking a language for evil is a perilous folly. Evil is the absence of meaning that wants only our complicity for its expression.

The Psychoanalysis of God

No one can be anything but appalled by Arendt's conclusion that evil is a matter of 'banal thoughtlessness'. What sort of dire unconsciousness is that? Inhuman? All-too-human?

I return to where I began. Evil is nothing more special than the ordinary, sometimes but infrequently extraordinary, 'evils that the flesh is heir to' and not requiring grandiose theorisation. Evil is lamentable but reverts to what it always was, incomprehensible.

My inquiry has convinced me that the inadmissible God is at the origin of human evil. The incarnation of that mystery of evil has unfolded in history to our bewilderment or most usually disregard. Morality to counteract the evil assigned solely to humanity has been invented on the basis of that inadmissibility, first, of God's implication in evil, and second, the inexistence of God that permits evil. Once again, we run headlong into the Kantian antinomy. Dialectical thinking suggests a third option to binary full-stop.

Concerning evil, nothing occurs to me ... These are familiar words of repression from the unconscious of the psychoanalytical patient, or technically termed, the analysand. I propose that this admission of a 'de-negating disinculpating unselfconsciousness' is traceable to God. My seemingly bizarre notion has a provenance. Before his death in 1961, after a long a clinical experience, the psychiatrist C.G. Jung (1875-1963) decided to confront the mystery of evil in his 1952 book, *Answer to Job*. He had long been intrigued by the question of how an allegedly all-benevolent Supreme Being could permit evil.

But God does not exist. How can an inexistent being be made a subject of psychoanalysis?

Jung discovered a hitherto unimagined psycho-ontological proof of God's being by his own admission of inexistence. Only an entirely unconscious being can assume existence by constantly demanded reliance on the consciousness of others. Jung comments diagnostically:

'Such a condition is only conceivable either when no reflecting consciousness is present at all, or when the capacity for reflection is very feeble and a adventitious phenomenon. A condition of this sort can only be described as amoral'.

This is God. Among his many attributes traditionally ascribed to him by monotheistic religions – the congratulatory compendium of all transcendental capabilities – there is this ancillary unimaginable missing one, the All-Incognisant one who has no apperceptive comprehension of himself, no self-apprehension apart from and alone from the cognisance that human beings submit to him. Islam has rightly understood God in the meaning of its name, 'submission to God'. The term 'reconnaissance', either in our military sense or used in French to mean recognition and alluding to gratitude, also applies. God is the 'recognised' Incognito One in which He glorifies because glorified.

Going to Freud for psychoanalytical assistance is pointless. He has no sense of evil. It is not for him a verity of existence but the collateral damage of psychological disorder. Freud's *Future of an Illusion* (1927) is a title indicative enough of an ill-disguised hostile polemic grudgingly conciliatory to religion because it is provisionally recognised as humanity's quasi-indispensable crutch of morality. Freud himself was Jewish by ethics not by religion. Freud approaches the secrets of the psyche always with cerebral franchise of the neurologist to keep himself at a safe diagnostic remove from the unpleasant surprises of his analysands' mental imbroglios.

Not so for the Swiss alpinist. He is the 'feral companion' I previously requested on my jungle hunt for the elusively slothful evil. Jung, originally trained in psychiatry at the Burghölzli psychiatric hospital in Zurich in 1900 under the eminent psychiatrist Eugen Bleuler (already in touch with Freud who had recently published his *Interpretation of Dreams*) did not see his psychotic patients' bizarre fantasies as pathogenic symptoms from which they needed to be relieved but as beliefs essential to the design of their lifeworld. Which brings us to the finally crucial difference between them. Freud admitted only to an ability to treat neurotics; whereas Jung did not hesitate to take on psychotics – and he found his ultimate psychotic as he neared the end of his life, God.

Who is this that says 'I am that I am', Yahweh, the sacred tetragrammaton revealed to Moses in Exodus 3:14? Is this the bluff of an insecure deity? Jung has all he needs of God's clinical autobiography detailed in the Old Testament, a memoir of violently temperamental mood swings, a being blindly eaten up with rage and jealousy, insightful and obtuse, loving and cruel, creative and destructive. Yahweh, as Jung says, 'is not split but is an

antinomy, a totality of inner opposite'. Strange retraction, is it not? We saw
Kant before identifying the antinomy as the impacted critical dilemma of
human reason, now here instead in Jung's diagnosis the 'contrariness of the
law' or antinomy is the psychical essence of God's existence.

Jung takes heed with the analyst's expert ear to the Old Testament
dialogues between God and man. The Psalms, ostensibly hymns of praise,
are incandescent with the discourses of disappointment between
antinomial lovers, God and David:

'My steadfast love I will keep for him for ever, and my covenant will stand firm
for him...
How long, Lord? wilt thou hide thyself for ever?
shall thy wrath burn like fire?
Remember how short my time is...

Thus, it is in God's 'burning wrath' that the light of David's consciousness
yields eye-witness account of the absent deity. Is there anything more
sensual, more sex-scented than the magnificent Canticle, 'The Song of
Solomon'? Who are the speakers in this effusive third century BC lyric of
frustrated love? The Bride of Zion seeking her lover, God, who eulogises
her while in quest of her too in the nocturnal alleys of Jerusalem:

Let him kiss me with the kisses of his mouth—
    for your love is more delightful than wine.
Pleasing is the fragrance of your perfumes;
    your name is like perfume poured out.
    No wonder the young women love you!
Take me away with you—let us hurry!
    Let the king bring me into his chambers.

The lovers reappear transformed into Christian yearning in the *Dark
Night of the Soul* by the Spanish mystic of the discalced Carmelite order in
the sixteenth century, St John of the Cross. The nocturnal travails of the
Bride allude to the poet's own torture and imprisonment by the Inquisition
torture.

The relationship of God to human is too uncomfortably 'fleshy' for
modern liking. Jung does not presume on the acquittal of our belief to
make us a believable audience of his therapeutic procedure. I can hear

Hume's clanging chain of scepticism as the flat-footed pedestrian objection of 'anthropomorphism' is dragged out. Anthropomorphism's anchorage in the weighty corporeal reaches its climax in the Sistine Chapel's advertisement of the deity in the travesty of a muscular bearded old man extending his index finger to touch Adam's outstretched one. A knee-jerk iconoclasm directs the fully rationalist modern sceptic's reproach against such barbaric superstition. The lean and hungry coyotes of modernity arrive too late at the feast. God signed his full fleshed-out confession in the *Book of Job*. It is one of greatest texts of world literature which divulges him succumbing to the gratuitous infliction of suffering on his loyal subject. I am astonished that compilers of the Bible allowed this scandalous portrayal of God in the canon of the Holy Scriptures. On what grounds do they give God such bad press? Apparently, simply, on a default position that evil can visit the innocent. God's responsibility for evil does not seem an issue, which accords with the axiomatic rule of all religions dissociating God from the origination of evil that is due slowly to man's fallen nature. It is quite a feat, in John Milton's opening words from his *Paradise Lost*, 'to justify the ways of God to man.' I recommend reading that extraordinary novella, *The Book of Job*. The sixth century BCE is a likely period for its composition, anticipating the rise of Greek tragic drama in the fifth century with its *eironeia* test of divinely sanctioned law.

Cometh the day when the sons of God present themselves in homage to their Lord, with Satan among them. When asked where he'd been, Satan replies in the fine words of the King James Version, 'from going to and fro in the earth, and from walking up and down in it.' God, as though spoiling for trouble, inquires of Satan, 'Hast thou not considered servant Job, that there is none like him in the earth, a perfect and upright man, one that feareth God, and escheweth evil'. Of course, he does, Satan rejoinders. Haven't you hedge-funded him with every possible earthly blessing? 'Take it all away, and he will curse thee to thy face.'

What insecurity in God prompts him to accept this slanderous wager. 'Behold, all that he hath is in they power', knowing full well that Satan has already been granted dominion over the fallen world to tempt mankind into its penchant for sinfulness. It is God's pre-ordained bequest to his son, therefore, evil occurs. Poor beleaguered Job is thoroughly stripped of everything, robbed of his wealth, his sons and daughters killed by a whirlwind, smitten by diseases to the brink of the grave, until he is left sitting on a dung-heap scrapping his sores with a potsherd. Denuded of everything, except faith in his faith. That faith too, of course, must be tested to the breaking point. His surviving wife berates him: 'Do you still hold fast your integrity? Curse God and die!' Job's piously hypocritical comforters, summed up by Elihu the Buzite: 'Yet, surely God will not do wickedness, neither will the Almighty pervert justice'.

God cares not a fig to 'pervert justice' by countenancing Satan's acts of robbery, murder and wilfully premediated bodily injury – all in violation of his proclaimed Ten Commandments.

What he confesses under Jung's analysis is a scintilla of a suspicion harboured in that vast almighty but Unconscious Being.

'I cannot bear the glimmer of superiority in his face...'
'You mean Satan?'
'Not him, Job's, as though in his eyes he is secretly my peer.'
'You have crushed him into the dust because of a doubt?'
'He has no doubt in the light of himself.'
'He has suffered proof of his reverence for you.'
'What is reverence when there is no alternative to it but my wrath. His reverence is a matter of his own undoubting choice.'
'Is that it? Are you jealous of his reflection?'
'Who gave him that upstart freedom? Man has ever been troublesome to me, ever since Adam...'
'You tempted Adam with the Tree of Knowledge and then forbade it... '

God's laughter – what the Greeks of Homer's time called *asbestos gelos*, the 'inextinguishable laughter' of the gods – is a frightful thing to hear out of the mouth of a psychotic divinity.

'Oh, miserable worm! How dare you seek to question me?' Whereupon God comes riding down on the tempest of his almightiness to face the quaking sore-ridden Job: 'Who is this that darkens counsel by words without insight?' ('Have you not darkened insight?' the analyst asks.
'Not so, not so...')
Will you even put me in the wrong?
Will you condemn me that you may be justified?

Have you an arm like God,
and can you thunder with a voice like his?

There is no apparent answer to Job's miscarriage of justice. What he gets
is God's remonstrance, an overpowering 71-verse lecture on the creations
of a primeval menagerie borne out of chaos, as though being conducted
like cowering child on a tour of a divine Natural History Museum by a
fearsomely omniscient David Attenborough. Job does not need sight of the
fire-breathing crocodile, the Leviathan, nor the Tyrannosaurus Rex-like
monster, the Behemoth – the superfluous memorabilia of Divine Power -
for an answer suitable to his faith in God. Job has no alternative but to
evoke his demand for divine justice:

Behold, I am of small account; what shall I answer thee?
I lay my hand on my mouth.
I have spoken once, and I will not answer;
twice, but I will proceed no further...

And is not God's 'thoughtlessness' unashamedly criminal, a discomfiting
reminiscence of Arendt's 'man in the glass booth', to make restitution of
Job's perished loved ones? Insult added to injury. 'You've lost your sons and
daughters? No harm. I will give you new and better ones!' Reminiscent
too of post-war Germany's reparation policy of *Wiedergutmachung*, 'making
good again'. Can it ever be 'made good' again for Job? For the Holocaust
victims?

The curtain descends on Job's drama at this point, as it apparently did on
the Holocaust too, in neither case satisfactorily. The drama that isn't over.
The analysis goes on.

There had never really been doubt in the faithfulness of God's servant that
unsettled his unconscious, but the doubt that existed beyond the enforced
acclamation of a small chosen elite naggingly persisted. To make the
unconscious conscious is the key insight of psychoanalysis, be it agreed or
not, Freudian or Jungian. Jung's analysis discovered in the unconscious God
a jealous wish for reflection, his own, not others' faith in him. This is what
God in the impenetrable dark of his fury perceived in the 'patience of Job',
that thing, that indestructible reflection of consciousness. Willing himself

conscious would not succeed to do it. Being all-knowing is the consciousness that is wanting. Knowing is not being. He would have to acquire a self which is not the same as his proclaimed perfection, 'I am that I am' – a divine prolepsis of Descartes's 'I think, therefore I am' – but a self *inmost*.

There is a first analytic clue in the figuratively single-minded Job. Do not think of Job as one person but as a *collectivity* mirroring the tribulations of a universal Everyman to be redeemed. Do not think of God's dip into the cellars of primeval bestiary as showcase exhibitionism but, in the precinct of quintessentially Jungian analysis, as the expeditionary voyage of self-knowledge into the oceanic vastitude of the Collective Unconscious whose inhabitant 'beasts' are analogically the symbolic archetypes of transformation. I give the briefest distillation of the venturesome sense of Jungian analysis absolutely in contrast with Freud's confessionally introspective one (the 'occultist mysticism' that Freud strongly disapproved of). The proper analytic understanding of God's demonstration of his primeval bestiary is not to impress an answer on Job. It is for both a voyage of self-knowledge into the Collective Unconscious in which lodge the primordial and terrifying archetypes of transformation. This is the *therapeutic* transformation of God himself.

What is the outcome of the therapeutic transformation that God undergoes by immersion in the Collective Unconscious? That scintilla of reflection has made known to him that a self is *not perfection* and that the answer to Job is for God to become man and endure the insecurity of being finitely human. His son, Satan, swindled him to wager on Job's test of faith; but it is the collective Everyman Job whose suffering is the prefiguremnt of the 'Son of Man', Jesus Christ, who must bear the trial of redemption. We should take seriously Job's collectively uttered prophecy on the advent of the redeemer: 'For I know that my Vindicator lives, and that he will stand upon the earth.' *Job* 19:30 Incarnation was the last step prophesied in the *objectification* of God 'At the time of the creation he revealed himself in Nature', Jung says, 'now he is more specific and wants to become man'.

But God, transitionally in man's flesh, is not fully and absolutely human until agonising on the cross he cries out despairingly like a lost child for is parent, *Eli, Eli, lama sabachthani*, 'My God, my God, why hast though forsaken me?' Now, perhaps, is understood the cries of countless tortured

God-forsaken innocents reaching to the stars to give them cancer. Job's repellent sores are transferred to that crucified body in the Isenheim altarpiece painted by Matthias Grünenwald in 1512–1516 for the hospital of St Anthony's Monastery whose monks specialised in the care of plague victims and sufferers of skin diseases. It is graphically literal. And the Christological message of redemption – should that too be taken literally?

Hume's chain scepticism is heard clanging in the approaching spectre of logical positivism. Rationalism is in consensus to denounce Jung's anthropomorphism. Christian theologians of the modernist Protestant sort have proposed to 'de-mythologise' Christ. To what purpose, Jung asks:

> A rationalistic attempt of that sort would soak all the mystery out of his personality, and what remained would no longer be the birth and tragic fate of a

God in time, but, historically speaking, a badly authenticated religious teacher, a Jewish reformer who was hellenistically interpreted and misunderstood— but certainly not a son of God or a God incarnate.'

He is not simply a teacher in the humanist cast, a Socrates or Confucius or Buddha. This is not what Jung contemplates:

> The fact that the life of Christ is largely myth does absolutely nothing to dis-prove its factual truth—quite the contrary. I would even go so far as to say that the mythical character of a life is just what expresses its universal human valid-ity. It is perfectly possible, psychologically, for the unconscious or an archetype to take complete possession of a man and to determine his fate down to the smallest detail. At the same time objective, non-psychic parallel phenomena can occur which also represent the archetype. It not only seems so, it simply is so, that the archetype fulfils itself not only psychically in the individual, but objec-tively outside the individual. My own conjecture is that Christ was such a per-sonality. The life of Christ is just what it had to be if it is the life of a god and a man at the same time. It is a symbolum, a bringing together of heterogeneous natures, rather as if Job and Yahweh were combined in a single personality.

Something has been banished from this drama. Something crucially decisive to make sense of it. There is a logic of compassion in anthropomorphism. What do I mean by that?

I journey back to the Golden Age of Islamic philosophy circa the ninth century and the scriptural exegete and theologian, Abu Hasan al-Ashari (874–936). Ashari cut a middle path between two distinct competing schools of Islamic theology: the Mutazilites, intoxicated by Neo-Platonist's flights on Aristotle, who risked reducing Islam to pure rationalism, for whom God's attributes are negative, and who postulated a Quran created in time and place, thus violating the orthodox belief in the uncreated because eternal Quran. In contrast, the Hanbali school of Islamic thought favoured *bila kayf*, meaning 'without asking why', to address apparent contradictions in the *ayat* (verses that compose the *surahs* or chapters of the Quran) by accepting them without questioning, that is, Quranic literalism.

Al-Ashari held that God has seven basic 'essential attributes': the ability to act, cognition, volition, life, speech, sight, and hearing. What can we understand of 'attributes' ascribed to God? How so? It is inappreciable to us now that God's otherness, said *mukhalafa*, had not yet entirely settled on an incorporeal deity early on, neither in Islam nor in Judaism, the latter benefiting from the theological efforts of Moses Maimonides (1138–1204) – and note well, under the influential guidance of the Aristotelian commentators Ibn Sina (Avicenna, 908-1037) and Ibn Rushd (Averroes, 1126-1198) – to arrive finally at an 'invisible non-theophanous' deity as the recent centrally espoused faith. Anthropomorphism was the theologians' thorn on the flesh.

Monotheism of the Judaic or Islamic type strictly forbids God's 'graven image'. No picture of God but an embarrassment of riches in textual anthropomorphism. We have seen it multiply with God addressing Job. As a hadith states: 'If it is said, He sees, does He not have eyes? If He reaches out, does he not have hands? If He rises from his throne does He not have legs?' (*Sahih Muslim* 5326). How best to manage that? By rational dismissal as figuratively intended. Or is it that God reveals Himself metaphorically? Very thin ice to bear the weight of *fiqh*, the deep comprehension of jurisprudential Islamic law.

I come for counsel to the controversial theologian Shaykh al-Islam Ibn Taymiyyah (1263-1328), known as the Damascene, *floruit* in the troubled times of the Mongol Invasions which destroyed Baghdad in 1258. He was charged incorrectly with the libel of *tashbih*, 'God's anthropomorphic assimilation'. He steers the Asharite middle way in his *Medinian Treatise on the Literal and Metaphorical Regarding the Attributes*, to respond on such issues as the 'createdness' of the Quran and the figurative interpretation (*ta'wil*) of the attributes. How does he deal with 'God on his throne'? Consider first how the Hanbali and Shafi'i traditionalists underline a distinction between the attributes of God that are some among the Scripture's informative clauses (*sigha khabariyya*) and others among the imperatives (*sigha insha'iyya*) to assert that the informative *ayat* are not incumbent on the believer's religious practice. Such obscure *ayat* as 'God descending from his throne' are not necessary to belief.

Ibn Taymiyyah disagrees with both poles of opinion. Hear is the hadith in which the Prophet said, 'Our Lord, the Blessed and the Exalted, descends every night to the lowest heaven when one third of the latter part of the night remains, and says: "Who supplicates Me so that I may answer him? Who asks Me so that I may give him? Who asks Me forgiveness so that I may forgive him?"' Ibn Taymiyyah is moved by compassion for the believer who heeds these words of the Prophet. Is there not imperative practicality driven by the believer's awe and pious desire to meet his Lord in those early hour of proximity unavailable to him at any other time of the day? To interpret this attribute metaphorically or deem it inconceivable sabotages the genuine simplicity of faith and will have consequences for the longer term agenda of practice.

Was not the Prophet sent as Messenger of God to explain the Quran to ordinary people? Ibn Taymiyyah feels called on to do no less as a logician in God's service. He begins by staking out his own distinctive differences between connotative (*mutawaji*) and denotative (*mushtarak*) usages of the attributes mentioned in the Quran and Hadith. Whereas the denotative word can have a multiplicity of references – the human eye, the eye of a needle, or the letter i – a connotative word can bring together several referents by their mutual participation in a an abstract universal:

> But true abstract universals exist only in the mind. Yet, it does not follow [from this] that what is common among entities existing in the outside world must be denied. For such would necessitate the denial of all connotative nouns; and these constitute the bulk of nouns found in languages, i.e. generic nouns (*asmā' al-ajnās*), which are nouns that apply to a thing and its resemblances, be it a concrete noun (*ism al'ayn*), or an adjectival noun (*ism sifa*), primary (*jāmid*), or derivative (*mushtaqq*), and whether it be a generic of logic, law, or other. Nay, generic nouns [alone], linguistically speaking, include genera, categories, species, and the like. And all of these are connotative nouns whose referents are individually distinguishable in the outside world.

I am struck by Ibn Taymiyyah's repeated insistence on exegesis being firmly based upon the ordinary 'language of the natives', that is, Arab speakers. Wittgenstein would understand at once the *corporeal adjustment* that Ibn Taymiyyah is attempting to perform in his deployment of linguistic logic. I note Wittgenstein's allusion to *embodiment* in his proposition 4.011: 'Colloquial language is a part of the *human organism* and is not less complicated than it [...] The silent adjustments to understand colloquial language are enormously complicated'.

Although Ibn Taymiyyah is clearly employing an analogical schema for conveying the attributes of God, he is careful to maintain a distance from the analogy's literal anthropomorphic assimilation of God. He states:

Nay, to him is the highest similitude. It is thus not permitted that He be compared with His creatures through analogical assimilation (*qiyas tamthīl*) or through analogy which encompasses all of its given parts (*qiyas shumūl tastawī afrādihi*). Rather, it is only befitting that the highest similitude (*al-mathal al-a'lā*)1 be applied to Him. This implies that everything that His creatures are endowed with of perfected qualities, the Creator a fortiori possesses. Also, every fault which His creatures are declared above, the Creator is a fortiori declared above them. If the creatures are declared above comparison one to another though they share the same noun, then the Creator is a fortiori assumed to be beyond compare with His creatures.

Nevertheless, connotative similitude tolerates an elevated sort of anthropomorphism in a sense remarkably akin to that of Ibn Taymiyyah's quasi-precedent, the Dominican theologian St Thomas Aquinas (1225–1274), who describes analogy as the *via eminentae*, a 'way of superior eminence', in that what we say and know of God is but humanly partial.

Ibn Taymiyyah is reputed a 'dangerous thinker'. A narrow mind that assisted in the closure of Islamic free thinking, a direct current to Wahhabi fundamentalism, the 'theologian of choice' for the Al Qaeda and ISIS terrorists. The record of the Damascene's *mihna*, his hardship years of trials and imprisonment, does not suggest a mainstream thinker acceptable to his contemporaries. One reason that seems to me to explain why he is shunned in favour of ibn Sina and ibn Rushd is that they represent a more user-friendly interface with Western philosophy. His intellect was of sophisticated enough match for a devastating assault on Greek logic which he demonstrates flawed and redundant to the practice of Islam. The case rests for our prejudiced view of his anti-Westernism. Ibn Taymiyyah saw his theologian's duty to safeguard the guileless (not gullible) believer, simple not (stupid) and faithful (not blind) from the scandal of a God either so metaphorical or so transcendent beyond the ken of ordinary language that it will all end by instilling disbelief. His compassion extends beyond his contemporaries to warn us that faithlessness has no destination that can endure. He would not be surprised that faith and morality have been trammelled to exhaustion in our over-fished waters of rationalism.

I see Jung venturing one last time to preserve what remains of our fragile ecology of wonderment in faith. It is not Jung's aim to *re*-instil belief. Nor is it mine by enlisting his psychoanalysis of God. It is a summons to our modern incomprehension that evil resides with an *amoral* unconscious God. Is the veil on that enigma finally lifted a little?

Jung's final words:

> We now know again that God is not only to be loved, but also to be feared. He fills us with evil as well as with good, otherwise he would not need to be feared; and because he wants to become man, the uniting of his antinomy must take place in man. This involves man in a new responsibility. He can no longer wriggle out of it on the plea of his littleness and nothingness, for the dark God has slipped the atom bomb and chemical weapons into his hands and given him the power to empty out the apocalyptic vials of wrath on his fellow creatures. Since he has been granted an almost godlike power, he can no longer remain blind and unconscious. He must know something of God's nature and of metaphysical processes if he is to understand himself and thereby achieve gnosis of the Divine.

The old man and the sea ... My voyage too at my age is very near complete. There is a test of cold comfort in Wittgenstein's advisory silence on knowledge of God and evil. Pull up the ladder, cast it away, the loftiest I will reach is nescience, not knowing, *bila kayf,* not questioning, and always there unfailingly at the foot of the ladder in existentialist prospective is the advocacy of negative theology, for which the attributes of God are unknowable and beyond the arrogant reckoning of human understanding. It is a practice of mystical abjection familiar to Eastern Orthodox Christianity rooted in the early Church Fathers, but equally known to our Western lineage of apophatic mystics from the divine abbess Hildegard of Bingen to the fourteenth century Middle English author of the beautiful aptly named *The Cloud of Unknowing*, Thomas à Kempis, Meister Eckhart, Teresa of Avila, John of the Cross and onto the present, Simone Weil (1909–1943), God's saintly fool, taking the harshest road of soteriology... and for whomever else the substrate of evil is disclosed.

JONAH AND REDEMPTION

John Liechty

The story of the prophet Jonah (Yunus) is briefly sketched out in the Qur'an (37:139-148): Jonah is a messenger on the run, bent on eluding the message, the God who gave it to him, and the duty to deliver it. He ends up aboard a vessel that soon sails into stormy weather. Lots are cast, and blame for the misfortune falls on Jonah, who is pitched overboard. After being swallowed by a big fish, Jonah repents and is spewed ashore in less than mint condition. Allah sends a vine to bring shade, and reminds his wayward messenger of the charge to preach to the city of Nineveh (present-day Mosul). At last Jonah rises to the occasion, the city's 100,000 plus inhabitants repent, and Allah holds off on their destruction for the time being.

The story is fleshed out in greater detail in the Old Testament, where the compact Book of Jonah constitutes 'one of the smallest strands in the mighty cable of Scripture,' as Father Mapple puts it in Herman Melville's *Moby Dick*. God's instructions are straightforward and clear: 'Go to Nineveh and cry against it.' Instead, Jonah goes to Joppa and takes ship for Tarshish. God sends a mighty wind that his messenger contrives to sleep through until, the ship on the verge of sinking, he is shaken awake by frantic members of the crew. Lots are cast to determine who has brought on this precarious state of affairs. Jonah loses, at which point he admits that he is 'fleeing from the presence of the Lord.' The crew does everything in its power to save the day, but is forced in the end to accept Jonah's recommendation that he be thrown overboard. The storm abates. Jonah's former shipmates fear God, offer sacrifice, and take up vows. The reluctant prophet has proven effective despite himself.

God appoints a great fish to swallow Jonah, who spends three days and nights in its belly. As the cramped accommodations inspire prayer and supplication, God authorises the fish to vomit Jonah onto dry land, repeating His original directive: 'Arise, go to Nineveh, that great city, and proclaim to it the message that I tell you.' This time Jonah obeys, warning the people of Assyrian Nineveh that in forty days their city will be destroyed. The people repent, fasting and putting on sackcloth. The royal court follows suit, going so far as to issue a decree that not only the people of Nineveh but their livestock as well should take up fasting and sackcloth. Once again, Jonah has improbably, almost inadvertently got the job done. God is satisfied that Nineveh's display of repentance is genuine, and stays His hand.

The news that the city is to be spared has a curious effect on Jonah. He is not pleased, seeming to feel that after all he's been through, God's mercy on Nineveh comes as an exasperating anticlimax. Angry, sulky, and despondent, Jonah sets up a little booth outside the city walls where he sits waiting to see what will happen. When God sends a green plant over the booth bringing comfort and shade, Jonah's mood swings to 'exceedingly glad.' The next morning God sends a worm that attacks the plant until it withers away, followed by a scorching wind and merciless sun. Jonah reverts to angry and despondent, 'angry enough to die.' God points out that if Jonah can allow himself such extremes of emotion over the fate of an ephemeral plant, he has no right to resent God's decision to feel pity for a city of 120,000 human souls.

Jonah's reluctance to welcome God's tolerance toward Nineveh is thought to reflect Jewish attitudes prevalent in the prophet's day (around 785 BC) – Jonah simply could not accept the idea of salvation for Gentiles. Whoever wrote the Book of Jonah much later in the fifth or fourth century BC would have been inclined to oppose such narrow-minded displays of Israel First. The fact that the Assyrians were a military superpower with a reputation for ruthlessness would further explain the prophet's preference for their destruction. Assyrian Nineveh, one of the biggest cities in the world, was built on conquest, blood, and slave labour. Jonah likely feared and detested the place, so his lack of enthusiasm over God's decision to spare it is explicable. Still, the peevish reaction indicates an unsavoury side to his character. To pull for the annihilation of 120,000 people seems shameful. Many of the prophets found themselves at one time or another imploring God to show mercy on a particular population – this one is more or less imploring Him to bring the hammer down. Whether fuelled by hatred, nationalism, or indifference, a readiness to ignore if not to applaud the misfortune of others remains one of the uglier features of human nature.

I have followed the story of Jonah (or it has followed me) for more than six decades. As a child I was drawn to its brevity and accessibility – clear and easy to grasp, the story could be read in a quarter hour, for which reason the Book of Jonah served as a regular Sunday morning diversion from the sermons I probably should have been more attentive to at church. I read it dozens of times there on the hard pew, where I found myself all too receptive to the prophet's foibles – Jonah lowered the bar so far as prophetic propriety went. By no means every individual called by God to deliver a message was thrilled at the prospect – the responsibility was daunting. Many must have found themselves wishing they'd been singled out for a more conventional line of work. But like it or not, the prophets (save our Jonah) accepted the call. Some, like Isaiah, accepted with consummate grace – his response to God's, 'Whom shall I send, and who will go for us?' was an unwavering: 'Here am I! Send me.' In Sunday School, this readiness to serve was justly cited as exemplary.

While Isaiah's was clearly the nobler response, I found myself drawn to Jonah's evasions, and still do. I am not proud of the affinity – Jonah is the patron prophet of fickleness, cold feet, avoidance, inconstancy, procrastination, irresponsibility, ingratitude... He is all too human. He is all too me. Jonah's initial words on receiving the call to go to Nineveh and preach are unknown, though it is safe to suppose they were not, 'Here am I! Send me.' One can picture him appearing to acquiesce with a wink and a nod – only to scamper off the moment he presumes he's fallen under God's radar. The next thing we know, Jonah has ducked into some waterfront dive, standing drinks for a group of sailors headed out on the tide, intent on finagling passage to Tarshish. Once there, the artful dodger, consort of Plans B-Z, will simply arrange to go someplace else. God, however, is not through with Plan A.

Jonah's story is concise and accessible – it is as well compelling and extraordinarily potent, casting a spell on the imagination down to the present day. Early Christians read Jonah's three days in the belly of the fish as a sign of Jesus's three days in and eventual deliverance from the belly of the grave. The second century sage Rabbi Eliezer likened the inside of the fish's mouth to a synagogue illuminated by a pearl, from which the prophet could peer out through the windows of the fish's eyes. The ninth century Persian historian Al Tabari declared the fish to have been transparent, enabling its occupant to marvel at the 'wonders of the deep,' where all the fish could be heard singing praises to Allah. Across two millennia, the prophet's story has furnished a rich theme for sculpture, mosaic, stained glass, literature, painting, and popular culture. Jonah and his adventures remain broadly familiar today.

The time-out in the belly of the fish is assumed to have taught Jonah something, *You Can't Run from God* being the readily drawn moral. But like any powerful story, this one carries a depth of meaning that has kept it resonant through the ages. The reluctant messenger does not seem to be an isolated type, so much as a universal one. There are on occasion people called to a specific task in life who grasp what they need to do from the outset, and resolutely set about doing it; Isaiah perhaps was one such. More commonly, it seems to me, there are people aware of a calling in life who get side-tracked or lose the plot altogether, owing in part to circumstances beyond their control, but above all to their own Jonah-like propensity to fly from responsibility. Flawed as he is, Jonah represents the bulk of our flawed species.

The Book of Jonah has something to say about evil, and about how to address it. God's initial call to go to Nineveh suggests that rising to the challenge of evil is a human responsibility. In this case it involves delivering the message that an evil city's days are numbered. Like Jonah, we are not always keen to accept responsibility – not steadfast enough, mature enough, or courageous enough to embrace our true calling. Having turned from the straight path, having opted for life on the run, we risk being undone in a sea of evil, dragged to the bottom, our lights extinguished beneath the waves. 'The water,' Jonah cried, 'closed in over me, the deep was round about me ...' Yet his story was not over. Though Jonah had straightway turned his back on God, God did not turn his back on Jonah, who was given another chance to get back on his feet.

What is evil? The question is at least as old as human history. The recent news that a pair of teenagers in Kansas beat their Spanish teacher to death with a baseball bat because she had given them a bad grade makes me reach for the word evil, simply because I can think of no other – a response based more on feeling than on rational analysis. I do the same in response to other events, individuals, or practices – wars (including the ones dubbed good), the steady poisoning of the environment, child labour in the cobalt mines of Congo, the Sandy Hook school shooting, Adolf Hitler, bear-baiting, lynching, torture... Other practices or individuals commonly described as evil may not strike me as precisely that. Saddam Hussein? Close, but for some reason bullying, vain, cruel, vindictive, and the like seem adequate. Judas Iscariot? Again close, but pitiable to a large degree, and something of a fall guy. Earthquakes? Devastating, terrifying, demoralising. But the frequent cry of 'How could a just God allow this to happen?' on the heels of such catastrophes doesn't make sense to me. Is an earthquake or other hiccup of nature evil? Does a mean-spirited deity 'allow' such things to happen, with its implication of cruelty or indifference? The notion seems false, a kind of base conspiracy theory. On the other hand, an earthquake attributed to fracking or the underground testing of nuclear weapons could be called evil, as could a decision to deliberately delay help or withhold it altogether from earthquake victims – an evil recently added to the Syrian regime's collection. Bullfighting? Cruel, unnecessary, but not evil in my estimation. Why bear-baiting evil but bullfighting not? I'd like to credit it to discretion, but am not sure. Most people, I think, make similar distinctions. Our judgment is prone to error, given our blind spots and limitations; we may lack common sense or insight, compassion or understanding, while being susceptible to bias, envy, resentment, peer pressure, or other factors clouding the vision; yet I think that at bottom we know evil when we see or feel it. Human beings are equipped with the capacity to know right from wrong, good from bad – that we are not always willing or able to use the equipment does not mean it isn't there.

More interesting, perhaps, than who or what outside ourselves qualifies as evil, is what we see of it within. At the very least we must admit a potential for evil within ourselves. I have little patience with the view that the barbarians we single out as evil are somehow not of our species. A Hitler, or any other of the evil overachievers we tend to focus on, may rightly be called inhuman; unfortunately, being inhuman is typically human. Who hasn't pulled it off on occasion? Hitler managed to exhibit inhumanity with such consistency and callousness, and on such a scale, that a consensus has been reached that the man was evil. Yet while Hitler may have been inhuman, he never ceased to be a human being – he was not un-human. That's the frightening thing; he was 'one of us,' as the saying goes. A movie depicting a Hitler or Stalin as someone capable of telling jokes, playing piano, hugging children, or making agreeable company in addition to doing terrible things seems more instructive than the standard effort to depict such types as twisted monsters from an alien realm. Yet we go on demanding the monsters, preferring our evildoers remote and absolute – anything to render them less one of us.

The early Church's concept of original sin confirmed not only the human race's capacity for evil, but the inevitability of it. It as well gave rise to some clumsy pieces of baggage, such as a determination that the soul of an infant who died unbaptised must be damned for eternity. Original sin became official policy largely through the efforts of St. Augustine, a key figure in shaping Church doctrine. Augustine was born in 354 in Roman North Africa at Thagaste, modern-day Souk Akhras in Algeria. For nine years prior to converting to orthodox Roman-style Christianity he followed Manichaeism, a dualistic religion out of Persia that declared man evil by nature and saw the world strictly in terms of Good versus Evil, Dark versus Light. The concept of original sin owed something to Manichaeism, as did Augustine's views on predestination. Due to Adam and Eve's fall, sin was inevitable, a kind of defective chromosome Adam and Eve's descendants could do nothing about. Human beings didn't become evil – they were born evil. There was no room for free will. Only through the grace of God could a predestined few, God's elect, have a slim hope for salvation. It all seemed very complicated, and often rather cruel.

Pelagius, a contemporary of Augustine's, granted that there was evil in the world and a potential for evil within human beings, but his views were far less doom-laden. Pelagius more or less agreed with Augustine's definition of sin as: 'a word, deed or desire in opposition to the eternal will of God.' For Pelagius, however, sin was not 'original,' a bad seed in the human race inevitably destined to lead it to damnation unless grace could somehow be arranged. Why, he wondered, would God hobble human beings with what amounted to a curse guaranteeing their failure? Sin, Pelagius argued, was the result of an act of will, and therefore avoidable. We each possessed a conscience allowing us to recognise right from wrong, and we each possessed a capacity to reason. God had not built a defective Creation. Through wilful disobedience, human beings chose to malfunction. They were free from the burden and taint of original sin. Damnation was not a foregone conclusion. Infants were faultless; parents who endured the death of an unbaptised new-born did not have to cringe in terror over the fate of its soul. Pelagius's views seem sensible and compassionate by comparison to Augustine's. They had widespread appeal during his lifetime, and remain influential, even though Pelagianism eventually lost out to Augustinianism in determining Church doctrine.

The Quran recognises that evil exists, and is to some degree tolerated by God. For arrogantly refusing to obey Allah's command to bow down before the newly-created Adam and Eve, the angel Iblis, or Satan, loses his former place among the other angels in Heaven. Although he is demoted and condemned to punishment in the hereafter, Satan is granted a respite until the Day of Judgment, suffered to remain in the world of human beings till then. Satan is clearly a threat, bent on leading people astray, intent on persuading them to work mischief – a liar and a deceiver, a whisperer of fake news. But he is not an insurmountable obstacle dooming the human race to unavoidable destruction, as he is under Allah's authority, serving in effect as a kind of tester for the human race. People are not obliged to swallow lies or to be led astray. Allah has granted them the equipment needed to tell the difference between right and wrong. If an individual falls for Satan's deceptions, he has no one to blame but himself. Allah has woven signs throughout Creation, and sent a clear message – truth and right guidance are available for those with eyes to see and ears to hear. By turning to Allah, and away from Satan, human beings are effectively schooled in how not to be gullible, foolish, deluded, deceived, greedy, distracted, or otherwise drawn from the right path. Evil can and should be avoided.

If God tolerates a degree of evil in this world and is able to harness its potential danger, drafting it into the service of potential good, any notion that evil can or should be eradicated is foolish and misguided. It would be like setting out to eradicate death. One might rationally seek to limit death or to avoid or prevent it to some degree, but its eradication is neither possible nor desirable. Death is an essential feature of life – human beings may not welcome the thought of it, and often fear it. They may not welcome the thought of evil either, and often fear it. Yet a person may come to terms with the necessity of both evil and death, diminishing fear in the process – a state of acceptance reflected in words from a familiar Psalm: 'Even though I walk through the valley of the shadow of death, I fear no evil; for thou art with me ...'

Some of what we call evil in the world might in fact be called good. Like death, one aspect of evil seems a natural and necessary part of the picture, an elemental reality that is tolerated by God, under His control like a powerful beast held in check. But the sort of evil unleashed on the world by human transgression is another matter. It is unnatural, misguided, a product of wilful sin, mischief, and broken limits, threatening to fiddle the scales of justice until they tilt to the detriment of good. In human hands, the beast of evil breaks its restraints, running unchecked, leaving misery and mayhem in its wake. God does not love the state of imbalance brought on by injustice. While a degree of evil may be regarded as necessary to the grand design of Creation, there is another aspect of evil whose aim is to bring it down – a human misapplication of evil seeping into the atmosphere like toxic fumes, corroding and unravelling the intricate web of life itself.

One aspect of evil, then, is inevitable. Like death, it is part of the picture. Nothing can be done about it – it would be foolish to try. Another aspect is not inevitable – the evil wilfully spilled into our world by human beings. What can be done to prevent that side of evil? Avoid it seems to be sensible advice. Avoid both the provocation of it and the practice of it. Acknowledge the potential for evil within. Beware the seductive murmuring of Satan. Heed the signs and messages of God – do not run from them. Hold evil in check so far as is humanly possible. Work to restore balance by working to restore justice. 'Repel evil with what is better,' counsels the Quran. In short, recognise what is good, cherish it, and put it to practice. There is no shortage of sound advice; yet, despite its apparent conviction to the contrary, the human race does not often appear to constitute the brightest species on the planet. Good advice frequently falls on deaf ears. Clear signs routinely fall on blind eyes. Taking matters into our own hands, through arrogance or ignorance we seek to repel evil with more evil, with what is worse. The audacious piece of political theatre that opened 11 September 2001 offers a case in point. This ruinous faux-morality play is still running in 2023 (despite being declared 'over' in 2010, 2013, and 2021), and has spawned dozens of ruinous spin-offs that promise to drag well into the future. (In 2014, one of these spin-offs instigated the destruction of the prophet Jonah's tomb – more on that later).

The 11 September terror strike on the United States and the ensuing War on Terror have generated reams of commentary. The acts and the motives behind them have been defended or condemned for myriad reasons we are not about to weigh and counter-weigh here. Both the September 11 strike and the response to it felt wrong – not just wrong in the sense of misguided, but wrong in the sense of evil, to a degree that it's hard to say and fruitless to argue over which was more so. Neither act should have happened. Both were avoidable. The notion that religion motivated either is unpersuasive, though both sides claimed as much. The terrorists, with Allah's approval, were hitting out at a symbol of Pure Evil, the Great Satan no less. The Bush Administration, with God's approval, was hitting back at Pure Evil – there rose talk of Evildoers, Crusades for Justice, God and Satan, Light and Dark, axes of Good, axes of Evil. Often as not there came unsubtle hints that military might could prove just the thing to bring an end to Evil altogether (the old canard). Fear and folly flourished in an atmosphere further obscured by a blizzard of global media as driven to make money as to provide insight or understanding.

For all the talk of God and Religion, neither the September 11 terrorists nor the counter-terrorists seemed overly devoted to their respective faiths. The one faith their thinking and actions did bear a striking resemblance to was Manichaeism, long since declared heretical. Pure Good, Pure Evil, Cosmic Duality, God, Satan... a Masters of the Universe comic-book worldview made up of sharply-drawn opposites, stirring a marked capacity for self-righteousness and delusion. A political cartoon from the early War on Terror days shows a smiling Satan telephoning the White House as the President lifts the receiver to his ear. 'Hello, George?' the caller says. 'It's God again.' This raises a smile, but should as well serve to remind that Satan had everyone's number, from Osama bin Laden's to Tony Blair's to ours.

The acts of violence and the reprisals, the counterattacks and the counter-reprisals, the officially declared wars leading up to 11 September 2001 and those stemming from it could serve as a master class in what not to do about evil. Running from an opportunity to repel evil with what is better, Jonah too illustrates a common example of what not to do about it.

The storm makes it impossible for him to run further. He must turn again towards God, or die. The early Christians saw Jonah's immersion in the sea as a symbol of baptism, as a kind of rebirth. Jonah's shipmates do not insist on throwing him overboard – he himself insists on it, as if to acknowledge that Selfishness is a central part of the problem. And so, he takes the plunge. Jonah's Self-sacrifice indicates a moment of repentance, of submission to God, of admission of the need for renewal. In letting the Self go, in losing it, Jonah takes a step toward gaining something far better. Lines from Farid Ud-din Attar's *The Conference of the Birds* suggest this wondrous alchemy, whereby the straw of the Self is converted to the gold of God:

> *Shadows are swallowed by the sun, and he*
> *Who's lost in God is from himself set free;*
> *Don't chatter about loss — be lost! Repent,*
> *And give up vain, self-centred argument;*
> *If one can lose the Self, in all the earth*
> *No other being can approach his worth.*

The next stage in the prophet's metamorphosis involves something like a dark night of the soul – three days and nights in the belly of a fish, where he develops a capacity for prayer and supplication. By the time Jonah is spewed to shore, the old Self is dead. Jonah is a new man, ready to accept his true destiny, ready to answer the call. When the city repents, the prophet's peevish reaction suggests that dross from the old Self may yet cling to him. Old habits die hard. The story ends, but one can imagine Jonah coming around fully in time, recognising that his human conception of evil and what is to be done about it fall short of God's love.

Plan A in the Jonah saga still resonates: 'Go to Nineveh and cry against it.' In the 2023 context, Nineveh might be described as a planet-girdling megalopolis of eight billion inhabitants whose time is limited. These eight billion consumers send out an estimated eight trillion messages per year (Homo sapiens currently dedicates its distinctive opposable thumbs and outsize brain to fiddling with phones), yet none of the eight trillion messages bears much resemblance to the message in Plan A. Jonah-like, these eight billion souls are on the lam hoping to outmanoeuvre global warming, food shortages, drought, inflation, political paralysis, pollution, pandemic, war, spiritual blight, crippling fear, economic collapse, societal breakdown, collective neurosis, cultural implosion, and other largely self-inflicted inconveniences; yet the running seems to be getting us nowhere fast (unless extinction rates as somewhere).

The war-diminished northern Iraqi city of Mosul has long supplanted Nineveh, which petered out in the thirteenth century. Until recently, Mosul featured a fourteenth century mosque built atop a demolished church over an ancient Assyrian palace on the Hill of Nabi Yunus. The shrine, upheld as a symbol of tolerance, was reputed to hold not only Jonah's tomb, but a tooth of the whale that had swallowed him. The site was dear to Muslims, Christians, Jews, and others who found something to love in the reluctant prophet. In 2014, Mosul was overrun by a group of intolerant ideologues with guns, who maintained that the Mosque of Nabi Yunus 'had become a place for apostasy, not prayer.' So, they blew it to smithereens, commemorating the event with videos posted on the Internet. Feeling entitled to destroy sections of a city that Allah Himself had spared, ISIS/Daesh seemed blind to its own apostasy, as guilty of hubris as the myriad Enemies of True Islam it so revelled in condemning. The irony of this version of making the world a better place most likely escaped those in charge of the 'cleansing'. It is tempting to propose that the demolition of the Shrine of Nabi Yunus serves as a kind of unintended homage to the prophet. After all, it was Jonah who'd sulked at God's decision to show mercy to Nineveh – who'd resented God's allowance that for all our capacity to get it wrong, human beings have a capacity to repent, and perhaps to get it right. Angry, vindictive, and seemingly forgetful of the fact that his own undeserving Self had been granted a crack at redemption, Jonah's impulse was for vengeance. He might have understood Daesh's nihilistic bent.

If only the nihilism and the intolerance, the cruelty and the violence were limited to a handful of fanatics with fantasies of caliphates fogging their narrow minds. But depravity is anywhere one cares to look, from the highly-placed arguably-civilised lovers of Freedom who unleashed the Global War on Terror to the pair of oil-rich arguably-civilised lovers of Religion who unleashed the latest round of state violence on impoverished Yemen; from gang wars in nothing-left-to-destroy Haiti to drug wars in

Mexico to poverty and famine in Somalia, Ethiopia, Afghanistan, Burkina Faso; from the prison at Abu Ghraib to the internment camps of the Uyghurs; from land and water grabs in the Amazon or Gabon or Cambodia or Tabuk in the Saudi desert, to practically any place on earth where what's left of our fields and coastlines can be razed for a golf course or a corporate farm or another row of concrete cubicles surrounded by billboards and eventually sold as Prestige Apartments; from the relentless global war on fish and wildlife, insects and trees, the very birds and the bees to the bloody attacks on schools, mosques, markets, temples, shrines, nightclubs, music halls, churches; from the torture chambers of Syria to Israel to the Palestinian Authority to occupied Ukraine. From the abandonment of culture and human creativity to a blind reliance on the ephemeral fixes of technology ... Nineveh is everywhere.

If there was ever a time to 'Go to Nineveh and cry against it,' this is it. The story of Jonah hints at a way beyond our contemporary Slough of Despond. The world's a mess. It always has been, if perhaps never before on such a scale. And human beings can't readily be trusted to make it less of one. Our friend Jonah is a case in point, all too human, all too us. Yet despite himself, he rose (messily) to the occasion; he answered God's call. Ultimately, the Book of Jonah is about the possibility of repentance. It sometimes feels as if we have built little booths for ourselves, eight billion of them, and are sitting outside the city walls watching things unravel, resigned to, even rooting for destruction. Repentance means, at the very least, wanting to get it right – struggling to rise, to answer a call, to turn from our wilful war on creation. To heed a voice from beyond the echo chambers of our irresponsible selves. We will never get it just right, but if we can't at least endeavour to get it righter than this, we don't deserve to be here. We may be headed for a dark time-out in the belly of something, or for oblivion altogether. But as the spirited story of God's reluctant messenger allows, we may yet get a fresh crack at redemption despite ourselves. If it could happen to Jonah, it could happen to anyone.

ATROCITY, EVIL, AND FORGIVENESS

Luke Russell

Assault rifle in hand, Brenton Tarrant stormed into the Al Noor Mosque in Christchurch, New Zealand, on the 15 March 2019. His objective was clear. Tarrant, a white supremacist, wanted to kill as many Muslim worshippers as he could. And kill he did, livestreaming the massacre as he went. He took the lives of fifty-one innocent victims. How should we describe this kind of extreme and egregious wrongdoing? Can we make sense of it? How should we respond?

One survivor of the attack, Mohammed Siddiqui, described Tarrant as 'the devil'. 'Yes, I call him a devil because you entered the house of God with evil intentions to kill innocent people. You've killed the dreams of my friends and family with ... your gutless action.' The *Daily Mail* echoed this language, calling Tarrant an 'evil terrorist'. If Tarrant really is evil, it might seem that the best response from victims would be to condemn him, to support the strongest possible legal punishment, and shut him out forever. Maysoon Salama, whose son Atta Elayyan was murdered by Tarrant, said to the killer 'you gave yourself the authority to take the souls of fifty-one innocent people, their only crime - in your eyes - being Muslims ... You transgress beyond comprehension; I cannot forgive you'. Salama's refusal to forgive is perfectly understandable. Her loss is unfathomable, and Tarrant himself is completely unrepentant. We might wonder whether it would ever be morally permissible to forgive someone like Tarrant. Yet there are people close to this tragedy who did forgive. Janna Ezat, whose son Hussein Al-Umari was one of the fifty-one victims killed in Christchurch, came face to face with Tarrant in the courtroom. She said, 'I have decided to forgive you, Mr Tarrant, because I don't have hate, I don't have revenge ... The damage is done. Hussein will never be here'. Could it be permissible to forgive evildoing in this way?

Tarrant's murderous spree in Christchurch is shocking and horrifying, but far from unique. If we look to another recent example of terrorism – the suicide bombing at the Ariana Grande concert at Manchester Arena on 22 May 2017 – we find similar denunciations in terms of evil, and similarly divergent opinions as to whether forgiveness is the right response. In this case it was an Islamic extremist, Salman Ramadan Abedi, who detonated a bomb that killed twenty-two concertgoers and parents. The Mayor of Manchester, Andy Burnham, said 'these were children, young people and their families that those responsible chose to terrorise and kill. This was an evil act'. One of the victims was Liam Curry. Liam's mother Caroline declared 'forgiveness will never be an option for such evil intentions, and those that played any part in the murder of our children will never ever get forgiveness'. In contrast, Figen Murray, whose son Martyn Hett was also killed that night, did choose to forgive. In Figen's words, 'forgiveness is not for the benefit of the terrorist. It was for my benefit.'

In the wake of atrocities, talk about evil and forgiveness is common. Nonetheless, some of us might feel unsure as to what these claims involving evil and forgiveness are supposed to mean. To critics such as the British philosopher Phillip Cole, evil is nothing more than a myth, and calling a person 'evil' is naïve, obfuscatory, and inflammatory. Cole thinks that if we label people as 'evil' we are mistakenly demonising our opponents and distracting ourselves from the real issues. It is the ultimate in Othering. But what exactly does it mean to say that Tarrant is an evil person, or that what he did that day was evil? How are evil actions supposed to be distinguished from ordinary wrongs? If we say that some actions are evil, have we adopted an unrealistic Manichean perspective that leaves no room for shades of grey? Equally difficult questions arise in relation to forgiveness. Forgiveness is supposed to be a way of moving on, getting over it, and healing the wounds created by wrongdoing. But what does forgiveness really amount to? Janna Ezat contrasts forgiveness with hate and revenge, and Figen Murray thinks that forgiveness is beneficial to the forgiver. If we are going to forgive, should we forgive only those who have apologised and shown genuine remorse, or should we offer unconditional forgiveness to the repentant and unrepentant alike?

These tough questions have sparked off some fascinating disputes amongst philosophers. In some of my own philosophical work, I have defended the use of the concept of evil in response to atrocities and have tried to clarify what is at stake when we decide whether we ought to forgive evildoers. This might sound as though it must be a religious project, or, at least, a project that is situated within a religious worldview. To many people, the words 'evil' and 'forgiveness' just *sound* religious, and it is true that victims whose lives are torn apart by atrocity often turn to religion to find comfort, to seek an explanation, and to locate a meaningful path forward. Islamic and Christian sacred texts speak about evil and forgiveness. The Qur'an and the Bible warn us against the activities of evil supernatural beings – Iblis and Satan – who disobeyed God and who tempt humans into wrongdoing. Mohammed Siddiqui's description of Brenton Tarrant as a devil suggests that he may well be thinking of evil in these supernatural terms. So here is one possible meaning of the word 'evil'. Maybe the word refers to a malign supernatural force or supernatural being. If evil were by definition supernatural, then atheists and agnostics, who do not believe in God or other supernatural beings, would have to deny that evil exists. It could be argued that forgiveness also rests on a religious foundation. Some of the most high-profile advocates of forgiveness, including Bishop Desmond Tutu, call on religion to support their view. If you initially believe that we should forgive one another because God has likewise forgiven us our sins, where does that leave atheists? Is forgiving, like praying, a practice that is for religious believers only?

The idea that evil and forgiveness are essentially religious concepts is, I think, mistaken. We need to pay attention to the fact that these words are frequently used in non-religious contexts as well. The secular world of therapeutic psychology is full of recommendations for victims to forgive and move on, regardless of whether the victims take themselves to be following a divine command or emulating a forgiving God. Forgiving, like punishing, is something that people can do for a range of different reasons. Victims of wrongdoing can make wise decisions about forgiveness even if they are atheists. These atheists are not merely mentioning the word 'forgiveness' in scare quotes. They are talking about something that they believe in and practice. For these reasons, I think that we should provide a secular account of forgiveness; that is, an account which explains how forgiveness can fit into both religious and non-religious worldviews. This is compatible with the view that Muslims, Christians, and devotees of any other religion might have additional beliefs about when and why we should forgive. It may well be that Christians, for example, have a distinctive view about the moral value of unconditional forgiveness. Nonetheless, forgiveness is something that atheists can believe is real, and can strive to embody in their own lives.

Similarly, I think that we ought to give a secular account of evil which explains how theists and atheists alike can believe that evil is real (although in this case, of course, we do not think that we should embody it in our lives). Even though the word 'evil' has religious connotations for some audiences, we should notice that many atheists denounce atrocities as evil. This includes high-profile advocates for atheism such as Christopher Hitchens and Richard Dawkins. It would be implausible to claim that when they are doing so, these atheists are committing themselves to a belief in evil spirits. When Hannah Arendt condemned the Nazi war criminal Adolf Eichmann as an evildoer, for example, she clearly was not implying that some kind of supernatural being took possession of Eichmann's body and drove him to commit genocide. Instead, Arendt was morally condemning Eichmann's actions in the strongest possible terms. This, I think, points us towards the best candidate for a secular account of evil actions. Evil refers to a kind of extreme immorality. An evil action is a wrong action that is extreme in some yet-to-be-specified way. This conception of evil is available for use by atheists and theists alike, because both groups believe that some actions are extremely morally wrong. Just as atheists can believe that love is real while denying the existence of a loving God, they can believe that some actions are evil while denying that there is any such thing as the Devil or evil spirits.

Let us set aside forgiveness for a while and focus on evil. If I am going to claim that evil actions are extreme wrongs, then I need to be more specific about the special kind of extremity that pushes an action into the category of evil. Philosophers hold a range of conflicting views on this issue. Some think that evil actions are distinguished from ordinary wrongs in virtue of being motivated in a distinctive and extremely bad way. These philosophers are looking for a psychological hallmark of evil, something that sets the mind of the evildoer apart from the minds of ordinary people. According to this view, the evildoer thinks differently, or feels different emotions, or does things for distinctive reasons. But if this is correct, which are the special psychological traits of evildoers?

Some have suggested that all evil actions are performed out of malice or ill will, and that this is what distinguishes evil from ordinary wrongdoing. I agree that an action that is motivated by malice or hatred of the victim is morally worse than a wrong action that is not motivated by malice, other things being equal. This kind of exacerbation seems to be reflected in the legal category of hate crimes, which are judged to be worse than similar crimes that were not targeted at persecuted groups. It is obviously true than many extremely wrong actions, including those performed by Brenton Tarrant and Salman Ramadan Abedi, were motivated, at least in part, by hatred of the victims. But is it really true that all evil actions are motivated out of ill will, malice, and hatred? To test a philosophical theory, we need to look not only for examples that fit with the theory, but also for examples that might clash with the theory. In this case, we ought to ask whether there are any actions that are not malicious but that do strike us as being evil, and whether there are any malicious wrong actions that do not seem to be evil.

Imagine a case in which the executives of a pharmaceutical company discover that one of their profitable new medications has no real health benefits and is actually deadly in a large number of cases, but then these executives conceal this information and sell the product regardless, resulting in thousands of needless deaths. This action is not motivated by ill will or hatred towards the victims. Instead, it is motivated by a desire to make money. These executives are being greedy and callous, not malicious. Nonetheless, many of us think that this kind of action is extremely wrong and deserving of our strongest moral condemnation. If we condemn this kind of non-malicious action as evil, then we have rejected the claim that malice is the psychological hallmark of evil. The opposite kind of problem arises as well. There are plenty of minor wrongs that are motivated by malice. You might make a comparatively harmless mean joke about a successful colleague out of envy and malice. Let us suppose that it is morally wrong for you to do so. Surely making a virtually harmless joke falls short of doing something evil, even if you did act out of malice.

Other philosophers have claimed that the psychological hallmark of evil action is not malice but sadistic pleasure. According to this view, a wrong action is tipped into the category of evil via the fact that the perpetrator *loves it*. This is reflected in the way that evildoers are portrayed in television or in the movies: the Emperor in *Star Wars*, Voldemort in *Harry Potter*, Mr Burns in *The Simpsons*, or Dr Evil in the *Austen Powers* films. If you want your audience to think that a character has done something evil, then you make that character smile or cackle with delight when contemplating the damage that he is about to do. Does this popular stereotype capture the true nature of evildoing? Some real-world cases of extreme wrongdoing do fit this model. Serial killers including Ted Bundy and the BTK killer, Dennis Rader, took delight in torturing their victims. Sadistic pleasure makes a wrong action morally worse, other things being equal. Again, though, we need to test this theory by looking for possible counterexamples. Are there any actions that do seem to be evil, but that are not performed with sadistic pleasure?

Consider this utterly chilling speech made in 1944 by the Nazi war criminal Heinrich Himmler, who was tasked with solving what he called 'The Jewish Question':

> I believe, gentlemen, that you know me well enough to know that I am not a bloodthirsty person; I am not a man who takes pleasure or joy when something rough must be done. However, on the other hand, I have such good nerves and such a developed sense of duty – I can say that much for myself – that when I recognise something as necessary, I can implement it without compromise. I have not considered myself entitled – this concerns especially the Jewish women and children – to allow the children to grow into the avengers who will then murder our children and our grandchildren. That would have been cowardly. Consequently, the question was uncompromisingly resolved.

If we take Himmler at his word, he did not take sadistic pleasure in ensuring the murder of millions of Jews, including women and children. Rather, he carried out this horrifically immoral task because he mistakenly thought that it was his duty. He felt at most a grim satisfaction in doing so. This is not Mr Burns, lit from below and cackling with delight at the suffering of his victims. And, we might say, so what? Himmler's actions were clearly evil even if he took no pleasure in carrying them out. If this is the case, then we ought to reject the claim that sadistic pleasure is the psychological hallmark of evil.

Rather than claiming that all evil actions are malicious, or that all are accompanied by sadistic pleasure, some philosophers maintain that the psychological hallmark of evil is the knowing defiance of morality. Evildoers, according to this view, do the wrong thing while being aware that it is wrong. Plenty of wrong actions do not fit into this category, because many wrongdoers mistakenly believe that what they are doing is morally right. These wrongdoers violate morality, but they do not knowingly defy morality. We might describe them as deluded rather than defiant. There does seems to be something especially blameworthy about realising that an action is immoral but defiantly pushing ahead and doing it anyway. Sometimes people do this out of selfishness, doing what they know to be wrong as a means to make money or to gain power. Some people do the wrong thing precisely *because* it is wrong. This is the kind of deliberate defiance that is displayed by the character of Satan in Milton's epic poem *Paradise Lost*, when he says 'evil, be thou my good'. But is defiance of morality really the psychological hallmark of evil action? Again, we need to test this theory by asking whether there might be cases of evildoing that are not performed in defiance of morality. We do not need to look far. Many of the most egregious and appalling war crimes and acts of terrorism are performed by people who mistakenly believe that they are doing something morally heroic. Brenton Tarrant believed and still believes that what he did was morally justified, so his wrongdoing was deluded rather than defiant. Nonetheless, many of us will maintain that what Tarrant did was evil. The fact that he falsely believed himself to be a moral hero is no excuse, and does not lessen the extremity of his wrongdoing.

It is turning out to be very difficult to locate a distinctive psychological hallmark of evildoing, so much so that we might doubt whether this really is the right way to capture the concept of evil. Hannah Arendt famously rejected the idea that evildoers have a distinctive psychology. This was the result of a change of mind on her part. In her initial reaction to the horrors of World War II, Arendt claimed that the twentieth century had shown a radical new kind of evildoing that could not be explained by ordinary motives. Several years later, Arendt attended some of the trial of the Nazi war criminal Adolf Eichmann, who had been captured by Mossad agents in Argentina and taken to Jerusalem to face justice. While watching Eichmann give testimony, Arendt was astonished by how far he diverged from her expectations. She thought that she would encounter a monster; a malicious and sadistic evildoer who was determined to defy morality. Instead, she reports an ordinary man who did not bear malice towards his victims, who believed that he was doing his duty, and who wanted to impress his superiors by doing his job well. She describes Eichmann as suffering from a terrible kind of thoughtlessness. Nonetheless, Arendt still concluded that Eichmann was an evildoer. She claimed that the Eichmann trial revealed the banality of evil. Evil is never radical, according to Arendt's later views. Rather, evildoing can flow from perfectly ordinary motives. Some evildoers, like Eichmann, are psychologically normal people who have done terribly wrong things.

Arendt's claims about Eichmann have been hugely influential. It is important to note, though, that Arendt was clearly mistaken in at least one respect. The historian David Cesarani, amongst others, has provided overwhelming evidence that Eichmann *did* act out strong anti-Semitism and malice towards his victims, and pursued the elimination of the Jewish people long after it became clear that Germany was doomed to lose the war. Cesarani's view fits with the judgment handed down in the trial itself. The real Eichmann was not the thoughtless, obedient dolt described by Arendt, but a malicious mass-murderer. Arendt is hardly the first person to have been fooled by a perpetrator who was acting dumb in the courtroom. However, this mistake on Arendt's part does not, in itself, undermine the plausibility of her general claims about the nature of evildoing. While the real Eichmann's evildoing was malicious, Arendt's supporters claim that there are many other cases of evildoing in which the perpetrators do not act of malice, do not act in knowing defiance of morality, and do not take sadistic pleasure in the suffering of their victims. On this view, some evildoing is stereotypically monstrous, in Arendt's sense of that term, but some is banal. Some perpetrators of atrocities take themselves to be just doing their jobs.

I think that Arendt is on the right track when it comes to the nature of evildoing. While many of the most horrendous cases of wrongdoing are performed by malicious sadists, sometimes the evildoer is a comparatively ordinary person, a so-called desk murderer who bears no ill will towards the victims, and who is acting in what could be described as a recklessly thoughtless manner. Evildoing can come from a very broad range of motives, so there is no psychological hallmark of evil. But that leaves us with an unresolved puzzle. If evildoers do not have a special and distinctive psychology, what is the difference between an evil action and an ordinary wrong? We might be tempted to say that evil actions are simply wrong actions that are extremely harmful, no matter how they are motivated. This would allow us to say that a malicious and sadistic serial killer has done something evil, but so has a thoughtless bureaucrat who obediently helped to administer genocide despite bearing no malice to the victims. Both of them have wrongly inflicted extreme harm, and both are morally responsible for what they did, so both did something evil. This strikes me as coming closer to capturing the idea that evil actions are extremely morally wrong. However, we might worry that this definition of evil action leaves out an important class of harmless evils. What I am thinking about are cases in which wrongdoers try but fail to inflict an extreme amount of harm on innocent victims. Some terrorist attacks, for example, are unsuccessful due to an accidental failure of the bomb to detonate. In light of this, I propose that evil actions are best defined as culpably morally wrong actions that are extreme in sense that they inflict an extreme amount of harm, or would have inflicted an extreme amount of harm had they been successful. In calling an action 'evil', we are condemning it as being over the threshold and into the worst kind of culpable wrongdoing.

This is a rather deflationary and unexciting conception of evil action. If this is all that it means to call an action 'evil', we might ask, then why do some critics insist that evil is a dangerous myth? I think that this is because the philosophers who are sceptical about the existence of evil are primarily focused not on the concept of evil action, but on the notion of an evil person. There is plenty of confusion and disagreement as to what an evil person is supposed to be. Just as there is an escalation in the move from saying 'what you said was cruel' to 'you are a cruel person', so too there is some kind of escalation between 'what he did was evil' and 'he is an evil person'. This is echoed in the claim that not every evildoer is an evil person. Some might suggest that an evil person, by definition, is someone who was *born* evil, who was inevitably disposed to grow into someone who would seek out the opportunity to perform evil actions. But I think a more plausible definition of an evil person is someone who, as an adult, is strongly disposed to perform evil actions, and who is so fixed in his ways that we should give up hope of changing him for the better. An evil person, on my view, is an individual who is so morally bad that we should treat him as a write-off. This leaves open the question as to whether any given evil person was doomed to become evil no matter how he was treated, or grew into an evil person due to the particular social environment in which he is raised and the choices that he happened to make.

If an evil person is a write-off, then we can see why not every evildoer is an evil person. Many people who commit terribly immoral crimes are not unfixable or beyond redemption, but end up seeing the error of their ways and undergoing moral reform. We might doubt that *anyone* is unfixable and beyond redemption. This is the primary reason why philosophers such as Phillip Cole think that we ought to ditch the concept of evil. It is the thought that we should never write anyone off, no matter what they have done. I agree that we ought to be extremely cautious when it comes to judging that someone is an evil person. In the majority of cases, even when we know the details of the wrong action and the motives that lay behind it, we just do not know whether an extreme wrongdoer is beyond reform. Brenton Tarrant is an evildoer, but whether he is an evil person depends on whether he is fixed on that path. This remains uncertain. In some cases, though, evildoers provide us with very strong evidence that they will never change. Think about a recalcitrant serial killer such as Ted Bundy, who broke out of prison and promptly returned to abducting, torturing, and murdering his victims, and who went to his death unrepentant. Bundy seems to have been unfixable. If he was not an evil person, then I do not know who is.

I want to consider one final objection. It is the thought that people who use the concept of evil thereby fall into an unrealistic and dangerous kind of Manichean way of thinking, where every action and every person is treated as either wholly good or extremely immoral. Thinking in terms of evil traps us within an unrealistic binary and removes the possibility of shades of grey, or so this argument goes. Sophisticated moral thinkers aim to understand complexity and nuance, to identify mitigating circumstances, social causes of crime, power relations between victims and perpetrators, and so on. The concept of evil is supposedly incompatible with this kind of admirable sophistication; a blunt tool that erases nuance, that ends inquiry, that blocks understanding. If this were true, then we really would have good grounds to be sceptical of evil. But is it true?

On the one hand, I agree that there is a real danger here. Plenty of people jump too readily to the judgment that their opponents are evil, and then promptly shut down further inquiry or deeper engagement. This kind of hasty demonisation is a genuine problem in our increasingly polarised world, and one that we must guard against. On the other hand, someone who judiciously employs the concept of evil is not going to assume that every wrong action automatically must count as evil, nor that every wrongdoer is the worst possible kind of person. The concept of evil is an extreme concept that ought to be applied only to the extreme cases. The vast majority of wrong actions fall short of being evil, and the vast majority of wrongdoers are not evil people. Using the concept of evil does not push us automatically to hold a Manichean worldview, just as believing that some people are moral heroes does not force us to assume that everyone is either wholly good or wholly bad. We can believe that, say, Rosa Parks was a moral hero, and that Ted Bundy was evil without supposing that everyone is a morally admirable saint or an appalling evildoer. We need concepts to pick out the extremes at either end or the moral spectrum, but we ought to wield these concepts alongside many others that pick out the vast majority of cases that fall between the evil and the morally heroic or saintly.

The concept of evil is liable to be misused, in the sense that people who use the concept of evil can fall into inaccurate and dangerous patterns of thought. But the same is true of the concept of moral duty, or the concept of virtue, any other moral concept. As we have seen, Nazi war criminals mistakenly judged that it was their moral duty to commit genocide, and that they were being virtuous in doing so. The solution to these problems is not to call for the elimination of these concepts and this moral vocabulary, but to call for a fitting level of care in their use. To my ears, there is something condescending in the claim that the concept of evil stifles any engagement with moral complexity. We began this discussion of evil by noting some of the responses to the terrorist attacks that were carried out by Brenton Tarrant and Salman Ramadan Abedi. Many of the survivors and the family members of deceased victims denounced the actions of these terrorists as evil. Are we supposed to assume that these victims are all simplistic thinkers who are insensitive to any kind of moral nuance, who have no interest in understanding the multifarious web of causes that contribute to attacks of this kind? It would be more charitable – and I think more accurate – to suppose that victims of atrocity can denounce an extreme wrong as evil without falling into a cartoonish oversimplification of moral issues.

Suppose we agree that Tarrant's act of mass murder should be denounced as evil. What should we then say about forgiveness? Forgiveness is often touted as the cure to society's ills, ending cycles of revenge and allowing both victims and wrongdoers to move on in peace. As we saw, some of the people who were impacted by the mass murder in the Christchurch mosque were staunch in their refusal to forgive, while others did forgive Tarrant despite the appalling nature of his crime and his complete lack of remorse or apology. One possible view is that forgiveness is the victim's prerogative. This is not merely the idea that any given victim of wrongdoing has the ability to forgive or not to forgive as they see fit, but that any given victim is morally permitted to forgive or to refuse to forgive. Whichever of these responses that the victim chooses, she will be blameless for having chosen that response. Who are we to criticise and correct people who have suffered so much?

While it may be appealing to give a lot of discretion to the victim in relation to forgiving, it remains contentious to claim that forgiveness is the victim's prerogative. There is a strong competing tradition, especially prominent in Christianity, according to which we morally ought to forgive all of those who wrong us, regardless of whether they have repented. We can call this the moral ideal of unconditional forgiveness. Advocates of unconditional forgiveness would admire victims such as Janna Ezat, who forgave Brenton Tarrant without requiring him to apologise or show any signs of moral reform. But praising the unconditional forgiveness of extreme wrongdoing strikes some of us as being misguided, perhaps even dangerous. There is an alternative tradition of calling for forgiveness when and only when the wrongdoer has felt remorse, apologised, undergone moral reform, and appropriately compensated victims for his wrongdoing. Let us call this the moral ideal of earned forgiveness. According to this moral ideal, a victim makes a moral mistake if she forgives without first seeing that the wrongdoer is remorseful and apologetic, but equally she falls into moral error if she refuses to forgive a wrongdoer who is genuinely repentant and who has made up for what he did. (This leaves open the question as to whether there are some actions that are so gravely wrong that they are unforgiveable, in the sense that the perpetrator can never do enough apologising or compensating to make up for them.)

So, who is right? Is forgiveness something that should be given unconditionally, or only when it has been earned? Alternatively, is forgiveness completely up to the victim? One high-stakes disagreement over the appropriateness of forgiveness took place between Holocaust survivors Eva Kor and Jona Laks, as documented in the film *Forgiving Dr Mengele*. Both Eva and Jona were subject to Mengele's twin studies in Auschwitz. Much later in life, Kor publicly forgave all of the Nazis who participated in the Holocaust, saying that forgiveness is the way that victims can heal their souls. Laks was appalled by Kor's unconditional act of forgiveness, claiming that it was impermissible. Before we throw ourselves headlong into moral disagreements over this issue, though, we ought to step back and ask a basic question: what is forgiveness? It is not clear whether Kor and Laks are talking about the same thing. Perhaps their disagreement over the permissibility of forgiving the Nazis rests on a deeper definitional disagreement over what forgiving entails.

Given that we want to figure out what forgiveness is, we might look first to religion. It is easy to find examples of religious voices encouraging us to forgive, but the sacred texts in the major world religions do not provide a definition of forgiveness. Forgiveness has something to do with covering over the wrong, lifting a burden from the wrongdoer, and starting afresh, and it is closely related to being merciful. The details beyond this remain sketchy. Given the high profile of forgiveness in the world of therapeutic psychology, we might wonder psychologists can provide us with a clear definition. The problem here is not that psychologists fail to define the word 'forgiveness'. Rather, it is that they offer a large number of quite different definitions. Plenty of philosophers have excitedly waded into these murky waters in the hope of clarifying things, but the philosophers have generated an even greater number of competing definitions of forgiveness. Regardless of whether we can identify one of these as the correct definition – the one that picks out real forgiveness – it is useful to compare some of these varied conceptions. In doing so, we can at least come to understand which issues are in play when we argue about whether we ought to forgive unrepentant evildoers.

Here is one common conception of forgiveness: forgiving is letting go, wiping the slate clean, moving on, no longer holding the wrong against the perpetrator. According to this view, forgiving ushers in a change in the way that the victim treats the person who wronged her. Typically, we think that wrongdoers incur some kinds of debts or duties. In this vein, we might say that Brenton Tarrant ought to feel guilt and shame, ought to apologise for what he did, compensate the victims where possible, undergo moral reform, and accept punishment that is imposed on him (so long as the punishment is proportionate and just). Some philosophers claim that when a victim forgives, she no longer insists that the wrongdoer continue to pay these debts or act out these duties. A crucial part of this picture is that once forgiveness is in place, the victim does not ask for further apology, and does not impose any further blame or punishment. With this conception of forgiveness in hand, we can then ask when a victim would be morally justified in choosing to forgive. If the wrongdoer is already remorseful, repentant, and reformed, then choosing to withhold further blame and punishment does not seem to be problematic. Similarly, if the wrong action in question was minor in scale, there is little cost in letting it go. But what about a case in which the wrong was so extreme as to count as an evil action, and the wrongdoer remains unrepentant? If forgiving includes withholding further punishment and letting it go, then it is easy to see why many people think that it would be morally wrong to forgive this kind of perpetrator. To forgive a dangerous and unrepentant wrongdoer would be to let him off the hook, leaving him free to reoffend. Forgiving, so conceived, will sometimes come into conflict with retributive justice and our need to protect other members of community from an unreformed offender. Someone who forgives an evildoer in this way could be accused of not taking morality seriously enough. This is why many people advocate the moral ideal of earned forgiveness. We should forgive only when it is safe to do so!

No doubt this will be an alarming and unwelcome outcome for advocates of unconditional forgiveness. Are we not supposed to forgive all of those who trespass against us? If forgiving an unrepentant perpetrator entailed not standing up for justice and not protecting vulnerable members of the community, then it would be immoral to forgive the unrepentant. There is an obvious way in which advocates of unconditional forgiveness could resolve this tension. They could claim that you can forgive someone while continuing to punish him and hold him to account. This is puzzling, though. How can forgiving be a way of letting it go and moving on if it is also true that a victim can forgive while continuing to punish the wrongdoer? The answer, according to some philosophers, is that forgiving is a change in the way that you *feel* about the wrongdoer, rather than a change in the way that you behave towards him. On this view, forgiving consists in losing any anger, resentment, and contempt that you bear towards the wrongdoer. If forgiveness is a change of heart rather than a change of behaviour, then it will never be prohibitively dangerous to forgive an unrepentant evildoer. Survivors of the Christchurch massacre could forgive Brenton Tarrant, in the sense of losing their anger and resentment, while still calling for him to be punished, and while refusing to welcome him back into the moral community. Forgiving, conceived of as a change of heart, is far less costly or risky than removing all punishment and treating the wrongdoer as if he had done nothing wrong. But we might wonder, is it really accurate to say that forgiveness is just a change of heart? Is it plausible that you have forgiven someone and moved on while you are still doing everything you can to ensure that he is locked up forever? I think that Brenton Tarrant is an evildoer, and possibly is an evil person. As things stand, he is completely unrepentant. But the question of whether it is morally permissible to forgive him for his evil deeds depends, in part, on what we take forgiveness to be.

ORDINARY FOLKS

Julian Baggini

As children, whenever I or one of my siblings said in my father's earshot that we hated someone, he would retort 'Don't hate anybody!' It was a noble but futile injunction. Ideally, we would not hate even our worst enemies, and even those sadists and psychopaths who inflicted gratuitous suffering on others would be seen as sick, not objects of odium.

Similarly, most psychologists and many philosophers would prefer that we never used the term 'evil'. The problem is that it suggests some people or acts are in a different category to others, that evil inhabits its own wicked sphere, separate from ordinary badness. Evil 'otherises' the extremely bad, allowing us to feel that we could never have anything to do with it. Yet most, if not all, of what we call evil is the work of ordinary human beings. The Hutus in Rwanda who massacred over half a million mostly Tutsis over the course of just a few months in 1994, the Germans who sent millions to their deaths in concentration camps in the 1940s, the American Army and intelligence employees who tortured people in Abu Ghraib prison after the 2003 invasion of Iraq: all would probably have led blameless lives as upstanding citizens if they hadn't been in the wrong place, at the wrong time, with the wrong weaknesses. The potential for evil lies within us all and so we ought not to talk of it as though it were some satanic other.

But like the call never to hate, the injunction to drop all talk of evil is well-intentioned but quixotic. There are some acts and some people for whom the word 'bad' will never seem strong enough, no matter how extreme the intensifier we add to it. So, the debate about the legitimacy of the term 'evil' can quickly become a merely linguistic one about what kind of vocabulary is appropriate when talking about different forms of wrongdoing. On the one side are those who argue against the use of 'evil' on the basis that it is not a category of badness in and of itself, and on the other those who may or may not agree with this, but either way believe we sometimes need recourse to the strongest words possible for badness, and 'evil' is one such word. Just as the term 'deafening' is more informative and precise than just 'extremely loud', or 'obese' tells us something 'very fat' does not, so 'evil' has a directness and explicitness that 'extremely bad' does not.

Ultimately, I think this is an argument about appropriate language. But that does not make it a trivial one. In *The Analects*, Kongzi (Confucius) said that if he were to govern, his first priority would be the 'rectification of names'. Kongzi reasons, 'If names are not rectified, speech will not accord with reality; when speech does not accord with reality, things will not be successfully accomplished.' Getting words right matters, which is why linguistic debates are not always *mere* linguistic debates. We ought to call things what they are, so it matters whether any things are really evil.

What does it mean to 'get language right'? It is often assumed that words have a pre-existing menage and our own task is to correctly identify this. This assumption is clearest in debates about the meanings of philosophically important concepts. Often people discuss the nature of 'justice', 'goodness', or in this case 'evil' as though whatever the word refers to is simply out there and our job is just to describe accurately its scope.

In reality, such debates occur precisely because the concepts have no generally agreed definitive definition. The debate is therefore not about what the concepts already mean but what they should mean. When language is confusingly ambiguous or unclear, we need to make a case for why and how it should be tidied up. For example, there are competing ideas of justice: as distribution of resources, equality of opportunity, equality before the law, obedience to divine will, and so on. To argue for one of these or any other conception is to make a case that the preferred understanding of justice is the one that people ought to adopt, the one that most consistently and helpfully identifies what we think matters most about justice.

Similarly, the concept of evil could be used as a mere synonym for 'extremely bad'; to refer to a special kind of badness different from the ordinary varieties not just in intensity but in kind; or perhaps in some other way. Clearly at present the word is used differently, sometimes by the same person in different contexts. So the purpose of any philosophical debate is not to claim that one usage is wrong, but to argue that our conceptual map of the world would be clearer and more helpful if we avoided some usages and stuck to others. In other words, any argument is a form of advocacy for a preferred usage for 'evil', not a claim to have identified its 'true' or 'real' meaning.

That is what I will attempt to do here. I will argue that there is a legitimate use for the term 'evil' but that because it is such a problematic concept we should use the word sparingly and carefully. To help identify that best usage, I think we need to look beyond mere words and ask the question of whether 'evil' is ontologically distinct from other forms of badness. That is to say, is there a qualitative difference between 'evil' and 'very bad' or is it merely a quantitative question of how much badness a person or act has?

I will argue that much evil is not a *sui generis* form of badness and that therefore we ought to be wary of using the term in such cases. However, I will also accept that it can be used to identify a sufficiently distinctive kind of badness, so it is nonetheless legitimate and maybe even necessary to have the word 'evil' in our lexicon.

The normality of evil

Bad actions can be plotted on a graph with two axes relating to their intentionality. (See figure) One plots whether the intention is good, bad, or at the midpoint, neutral. The other plots whether is is conscious, unconscious or at the midpoint, indeterminate. In common usage, evil prototypically sits in the far corner of the quadrant in which intentions are both very bad and fully conscious. Evil usually refers to not just horrific actions (or people) but those with clear malevolent intent.

Interestingly, when actions sit in the far corner of malevolent and unconscious, we also tend to call it 'evil'. This has historically been seen as a kind of possession, as though the agent has become conduit for a malign force that they do not even themselves control or even have awareness of. The image of demonic possession is hard to do away with. Even the most naturalistic, secular person finds something deeply chilling about a person being driven to dark deeds by impulses they are not aware of.

I would suggest that these two extremes represent our prototypes of evil. All other uses of the term take this as their reference point and count as evil because they are judged to share a sufficiently similar 'family resemblance', as Wittgenstein described the scope of words. But if we look more closely, I think we can question whether this family resemblance is close at all. In fact, much of what is commonly called evil, is to be found squarely within the circle of ordinary badness drawn in the figure.

Start with the theological category of natural evil. This is great harm done by nature, such as pestilence, famines, droughts, earthquakes, or tsunamis. This sits at the intersection of the graph, since there is no intention good or bad and no conscious willing at all. This runs so counter to the prevailing options of 'evil' that students introduced to the concept often struggle to understand why it is called evil at all. The short answer is that 'evil' originally referred to the absence or the opposite of good, so everything not-good was evil. However, words are not bound by their origins and today no one would use 'evil' in such a broad way. 'Natural evil' barely makes sense to the modern mind and 'evil' has become restricted to 'moral evil': extreme wrongdoing done by moral agents. And if we ask where various forms of such moral evil should be placed on our graph, we can also see that very few conform to the prototype of evil and most is continuous with all-too-common badness.

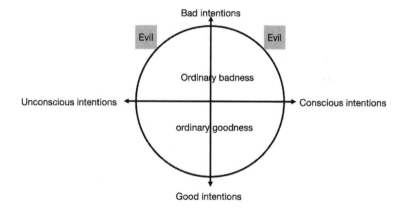

Take what I would call 'systemic evil', practices such as slavery, highly-intensive factory farming, human sacrifice, the stoning to death of apostates and infidels. These are not the acts of autonomous individuals making particular choices but practices which are built in to the structures of society and could be executed by anyone who found themselves in a position of responsibility to do so, without any suggestion that there might be anything morally problematic. In every case where such practices have been part of the widely-accepted social system, the intentions of those who executed them have not been wicked. In fact, they have often been good: people genuinely thought these were righteous – or at least morally neutral – acts.

Then there is the closely-related category of 'complicit evil'. The turning of a blind eye to extreme wrongdoing is itself a terrible misdemeanour and a lot of what we call evil can only take place because if it. Think of how the Roman Catholic Church has frequently ignored evidence of child sexual abuse in its ranks. In a zero-tolerance culture, such awful deeds would never have been committed.

'Evil' can also be the consequence of indifference. In March 2015, a passenger jet crashed killing all 144 passengers and six crew members. They seemed to be collateral damage from the suicide of the co-pilot, Andreas Lubitz. There is no evidence he actually wanted to harm others but in the grip of his own depression, he took them down with him.

In all three of these cases, the acts would fall close to the neutral intersection of the axes on our graph. In systemic, complicit and indifferent evil, there is no intention to harm, in part because there is little conscious intention at all to do anything good or bad since the moral dimension is simply not salient in consciousness. In the cases of systemic and complicit evil the awfulness of the consequences is the result of ordinary people behaving either entirely normally. There is nothing that marks out the behaviour as exceptional other than the extremity of the consequences.

The kinds of behaviour identified here are actually troublingly normal. If anything in our society counts as systemic evil – and I think the treatment of animals in our worst farming does – that is not because we are a society filled with evil people, just ones who are blind to the radical injustices we have become acculturated to. We are also complicit for any number of wrongdoings that we know are going on but which we keep silent about or fail to resist. This is normal human weakness, not exceptional evil. Were we to realise we had been complicit in something truly awful, no doubt we would feel terribly guilty. Indifference is also normal. For example, many of us know that the people who grow our food or make our clothes are treated deplorably, yet few can be bothered to make the effort to choose what they buy more carefully. Much 'evil' is simply what happens when ordinary wrongdoing has extreme consequences.

In these cases, then, there is no reason to think that what we call 'evil' is in a different category to ordinary wrongdoing. Only the extremity of the consequences marks out the so-called 'evil' as different. But we do not generally distinguish between degrees or kinds of wrongness on the basis of consequences alone. If a drunk driver causes an accident, they are not more or less culpable if it results in one or one hundred deaths. It is intent that makes a difference. If someone intends to kill a hundred people, that is worse than intending to kill one. The seriousness of a bad action is related to consequences, but its basic nature – foible, misdemeanour, wicked – is generally related to intention.

Three other types of 'evil' provide interesting evidence for the idea that extremity of intention is required for us to describe a person or action as evil. One is 'self-preserving evil', such as when soldiers, doctors, or functionaries commit terrible crimes against humanity because to refuse orders would risk being killed themselves, or worse. There is something deeply chilling about the conscious suspension of ones own values and intentions purely for the goal of self-preservation, that someone might cross a moral line rather than die honourably. In such cases we might pity the wrongdoer but there is something diabolic in a person being willing to perpetuate evil acts while fully realising that they are indeed evil.

What we might call 'utilitarian evil' also raises hairs on the back of the neck. This is when people convince themselves that the greater good requires massacre, torture, rape. When the means is seen to justify the end but the means are so vile, it seems akin to possession: in this case by an ideology. 'Righteous evil' is similar: when people believe that acts like the suicide bombing of civilian areas or the beheading of infidels are divinely commanded. Again, there is something about the giving over the will to something other than yourself, to do things a person would ordinarily realise are diabolical, which invites the label of evil.

Part of the terror of both self-preserving and utilitarian evil is that most people – if they are honest – can see how they could, in theory, inflict it themselves, if external circumstances lined up in just the right (or maybe wrong) way. This again suggests that these forms of evil are not *sui generis* and that classifying them as such risks denying the possibility that we could ever ally ourselves with the forces of evil.

However, when utilitarian and righteous motivations lead people to do extremely bad things, we seem closer to the total suspension or overriding of will that is characteristic of what I've referred to as possession. This does seem to be significantly different from ordinary wrongdoing, in kind not just in degree. I think this fits with, rather than counters, the idea that 'evil' is a term that we see as referring to truly exceptional wrongdoing and that the intentionality as well as the extremity of the act is part of what makes it exceptional. In most cases, we know that people are neither wholly good nor bad and that they rarely do truly terrible things. They act badly usually due to all-too-human weakness, selfishness, thoughtlessness not extreme malevolence. To be evil is to go beyond these normal bounds, usually meaning to act exceptionally badly through exceptional malice. But the normal bounds are also exceeded when one acts exceptionally badly through an exceptional loss of agency. When it is as though we are being controlled by a malevolent force, it is the apparent absence of our own will that makes our actions 'evil'. To be 'possessed' is an extreme absence of agency just as to wilfully do terrible things is an extreme exertion of agency. The extremity in both cases places the actions (or the actor) in the far corners of the 'bad' quadrants of our graph.

Perhaps the most controversial form of wrongdoing that I resist calling evil is perversion. This is where people's desires are perverted in such a way as to make them seek out behaviours that are seriously damaging and/ or abusive. Paedophilia is a dreadful and all-too-common example. Steven Fechter's brilliant and disturbing play *The Woodsman*, later adapted into a film starring Kevin Bacon, makes us question our default assumption that a paedophile has wicked intentions. His protagonist seems to be an ordinary, decent man but for one awful desire that he struggles to control, knowing that he should do so. The film in no way exonerates paedophiles or justifies paedophilia, but it invites us to consider the troubling possibility that paedophiles may, sometimes at least, be people at war with an impulse they cannot help but feel, not wicked monsters. If we have no such desires ourselves, this can be hard to understand. But if we accept that a person does not choose the strength nor the objects of their sexual desires, and that many people struggle to fully control them, then the paedophile who genuinely tries not to act on their desires is on a continuum with a highly-sexed person who sometimes makes unwise impulsive advances or easily falls into infidelity. To have such impulses is not a choice. To act on them is very bad indeed, but it does not seem psychologically credible to identify the perpetrator as belonging in a separate category of 'evil'.

For the most part, then, the argument that 'evil' does not pick out a real, distinct category of wrongdoing seems strong. Most of what we call evil falls within the circle of the graph that includes ordinary wrongdoing.

Crossing a fuzzy line

Is there then any justification for thinking of evil as fundamentally distinct from other kinds of badness? There are two other related kinds of evil that do seem to belong in a category of their own: the sadistic and the psychopathic. The sadist deliberately chooses to do what they believe will cause suffering to others and take great pleasure in it. The psychopath is simply indifferent to the suffering of others.

The films of the Coen Brothers frequently have psychopathic characters that contrast with other characters in their films who nonetheless do terrible things. What they seem to be showing us that in ordinary cases, the difference between the decent person and the one who acts dreadfully is not fundamental. The wrongdoers frequently go astray by small steps, indulging petty grievances or greed, little by little. The films seem to dramatise a saying in the *Dhammapada*, 'Think not lightly of evil saying that "it will not come near me". Even a water-pot is filled by the falling of drops of water. A fool becomes evil even if he gathers it little by little.' Psychopaths, in contrast, lack a moral character to be eroded drop by drop in the first place. They are a type all of their own.

Perhaps, then, this is a *sui generis* kind of badness worthy of the name evil? The problem is that to the modern understanding both sadists and psychopaths are 'sick' – mad, not bad. There is something awry with their basic empathetic circuitry, to use a hardware analogy that may or may not accurately describe the pathogenesis of their depravity. That is why the penal system treats them differently. Broadmoor is not a prison for the criminally insane, in the old parlance, but a high-security psychiatric hospital. Such people are locked up for life to protect the public on the basis that they cannot be reformed. To resort to the vocabulary of 'evil' is to de-naturalise these pathologies and frame them in terms of some kind of mysterious, external malevolence.

So far, then, I have found it difficult to identify anything as genuinely belonging at the far corners of the graph where evil should lie. But I have not found nothing. Forms of utilitarian evil and righteous evil meet the description, while psychopathic and sadistic evil have only been ruled out on the grounds that perpetrators are better understood as sick rather than depraved. (Although it is interesting that the former word can be used as a synonym for the second.)

So 'evil' on this taxonomy is not an empty set. Still, it remains true that it is not in the fullest sense *sui generis* as it is marked out only by its extremity on two axes, which are spectra. But this could be an argument for calling such badness evil, not against it. The case against evil as a separate category is that badness is on a continuum and so therefore there is no fundamental distinction in kind between different things on that spectrum. But the argument moves too fast. In a naturalised understanding of the world there are few, if any, hard boundaries. Spectra are everywhere. But the absence of definitive boundaries does not nullify the legitimacy of all binary distinctions. Green and yellow are different colours, even though they blend into each other on the colour spectrum. The difference between night and day remains clear even though at dawn and dusk both blend into each other. Mammals are generally male or female even though a small percentage are hermaphrodites. Real — one might say fundamental — differences can be made by crossing fuzzy borders.

Think back to the four quadrants of wrongdoing, along the good/bad and conscious/unconscious axes of intention. I suggested that what we call evil tends to be in the two far corners of wrongdoing: extreme wrongdoing that is motivated by bad intentions, either conscious or unconscious, with the latter being thought of historically as a kind of possession. Both axes represent continua but at a certain point — a fuzzy, not determinate one — a line is crossed. Beyond that lies 'evil'.

It may be empirically true that most of what lies behind the line is the product of psychopathy and so should be treated more as a blameless dysfunction than a morally blameworthy action. But it would be complacent to assume everything in the far corners of the graph can be attributed to forms of mental illness. We have to be open to the possibility that ordinary people can become so corrupted – by base desires, ideology, persuasion, self-deception – that they can become capable of doing terrible things deliberately, in full awareness of the consequences. And we also need to be open to the possibility that we might do such things unconsciously: that we become so steeped in a value system, cause or worldview that we simply do not see that we have become agents of evil. Such evil would not be *sui generis* in the strict meaning of the term, but little is. Nonetheless, we can make sensible binary distinctions between ordinary behaviour and that which falls under the category of evil.

First, nobody causes death or intense suffering to another person deliberately except in extreme circumstances, and even then a person would be deeply troubled and pained by doing so. To cause such extreme distress without any compunction is evil.

Second, nobody uses human lives (or perhaps any highly sentient life) as a mere means to an end with no regard to their welfare. Again, to do so is evil.

Third, nobody takes pleasure in the suffering and death of others except the evil.

The qualmless, instrumental, or pleasurable causing of death and suffering is arguably always a kind of wrongdoing that crosses a line and any decent society ought to recognise it as such, even if it prefers a different label to 'evil'. Sadists and psychopaths, the kinds of people for whom these forms of evil are second nature, are astonishingly rare. That is precisely why they are the kinds of people we think about when we think about evil. Their exceptionalism allows us to place evil outside of ordinary life, to 'otherise' it. But this is a mistake. Ordinary human beings can also become capable of all three forms of evil described, in the right (wrong) circumstances.

To see how easy it is for human life to be instrumentalised, look no further than Putin's war machine. Troops are deliberately sent to the front-line 'meat grinder', entirely disposable. Civilians are also treated no differently from the buildings and infrastructure they use. As for taking pleasure in killing, think only of how ISIS glorified in the grizzly beheading of infidels. In each of these cases, there was not a trace of guilt by the perpetrators. This is evil which is not the result of mental illness, but distorted values and personal vanity, two vices that are extremely common.

And yet...

In a way it is ironic to be offering an academic, scholarly defence of the term 'evil', because we wouldn't need the word at all if we were always careful to talk in precise, academic terms. The usefulness of the term is purely social and psychological. It seems that there need to be things that are beyond the pale, that we do not even think should be classified alongside ordinary wrongdoing.

And yet I am still convinced the reasons for retaining the word outweigh the reasons for avoiding it. 'Evil' could just be used as a word to identify the worst wrongdoings, as long as we don't mistake it for something entirely 'other'. But our tendency to do just that is a good reason to use the word sparingly. Every time we call something 'evil' we place it at arm's length, outside what we consider to be the normal possibilities of human behaviour. But usually, when 'evil' is done, it is done by ordinary people who by tiny steps end up travelling the distance between decency and wickedness, a distance that seems vast until you start to walk it.

Another problem is that if a term is in circulation, it will be used widely and not always in the most helpful ways. And it seems to me that for every legitimate use of 'evil' there are a dozen unhelpful or even harmful uses of it. Donald Trump called federal charges made against him 'the most evil and heinous abuse of power'; George W. Bush demonised and otherised huge swathes of the world when he talked of the 'axes of evil'; former UK home secretary Priti Patel reduced the crisis of migrants dying in boats to a problem of 'evil people smugglers', avoiding any culpability herself. When evil is part of the acceptable lexicon, it is too easy for people to reach for the term to demonise others and paint themselves as being on the side of good.

However, since the word is not going to go away and it serves some purpose, calling for its abolition is futile. What we can ask, however, is that such a heavy term is not used lightly. For a person to have acted evilly, they must have done something truly horrific, with full intent, without qualms, perhaps with pleasure. To call anything else evil is to dilute the power of what should be the ultimate in moral condemnation.

SINFUL AI

Michael Wilby

When asked what he thought the future held in the wake of his invention, Geoffrey Hinton, the 'Godfather of AI', and one of the originators of the architecture behind generative AI Chatbots such as GPT4, was blunt: 'my intuition is: we're toast. This is the actual end of history'. The threat that Hinton thinks AI poses would seem to be the epitome of what the concept of evil was designed to describe: an intelligent but alien being with the means and motivation to turn the whole world to dust; an artificial Satan or Mephistopheles. AI futurists have not been slow to come up with scenarios where AI runs out of control, either deliberately or accidently. For instance, the Swedish philosopher Nick Bostrom devised the infamous example of a 'paperclip maximiser'. This is an AI that is designed to produce as many paperclips as it can, and ends up turning everything in the world, including living beings, into paperclips.

Nevertheless, AI-apocalypse scenarios really are just ways of expressing an underlying fear. Like the Sorcerer's Apprentice, we seem to have created something that we don't fully understand, and the consequences of which are potentially far-reaching and destructive to our way of life. We know that AI is capable of great harm, but it is not clear that we have the necessary concepts and vocabulary to assess these threats in moral terms. It seems doubly wrong, for instance, to describe the threat of artificial systems making us 'toast' as merely a bad outcome. It seems to be something much more than that. But what? Can we make sense of AI as being evil? What would this mean?

It is essential that we make sense of what it could mean to say that AI could be held responsible not just for *moral wrongdoing*, but also for *extreme moral evil*. To do this, we will have to take the scenic route. It won't be enough to just point to the potentiality of a Terminator-style robot and label it 'evil': we need first to get a grip on what it would mean to call something 'evil' and then get a grip on how such a concept could sensibly be applied to a non-living machine.

Taxonomy of the Threats

There are various ways in which we might label the risks that AI poses, depending on whether we focus on the harm caused or on the causes of the harm. If the former, then we might turn our attention to AI risks such as surveillance, bioterrorism, automated warfare, technological unemployment, the control problem, and value alignment. However, given that the focus here will be on AI and the concept of evil – that is, trying to understand the extent to which an AI can be morally responsible for the outcomes connected to it, including where those outcomes are extreme and our ordinary moral responses start to run out – we shall instead discuss, at least in the first instance, the causes of the potential harm. This will require looking at how AI can admit of differing degrees of agenthood which, in turn, might map onto differing degrees of moral responsibility. Here is a fairly crude, but hopefully useful, taxonomy of three forms of AI agenthood:

(a) AI as a *non-agential tool*
(b) AI as a *hybrid, minimal agent*
(c) AI as a *fully autonomous agent*

To what degree would it be correct to think of any of these forms of AI agency as incorporating moral responsibility? Can a mere tool – even a highly advanced tool – be held morally responsible? Should the deadly effects of an out-of-control automated car be the responsibility of the manufacturer, the on-the-loop driver, or the car itself? Further, to what extent would it be correct to say that such systems are not just capable of wrongdoing, but are capable of evil, in the narrow sense to be explained below?

One way of framing the issues of AI moral responsibility is in terms of responsibility gaps. Sven Nyholm, a professor of AI ethics at the Ludwig Maximilian University of Munich in Germany, characterises responsibility gaps as follows:

when we start using technology that take over tasks from human beings, like robots and other AI technologies do, there are often worries that there might be cases when the stakes are high and when outcomes might come about for which somebody should intuitively speaking be held responsible. But it might be unclear who, if anybody, could or should be held responsible. So potential responsibility gaps occur.

The concept of a responsibility gap suggests that an artificial system can be thought, in moral terms, as being no more than a tool. It suggests that moral responsibility, if it is to come, must come from the human operator; and, where the human operator has ceded control to the machine, then we are left with a moral vacuum – a responsibility gap that is generated by the (supposed) fact that artificial machines are not susceptible to genuine moral censure.

We need to scope out the extent to which, in contrast to the assumption governing the responsibility gap, AI itself can be held morally responsible for certain acts, in situations where we standardly would hold agents morally responsible, and then to consider how and when (and if at all) the concept of 'evil' specifically can be applied to AI. Scepticism about applying moral concepts to machines and AI is often unconsciously conflated with a wider scepticism about agency and morally responsibility in general. It is often assumed, for instance, that AI cannot be held responsible because they lack [...]. What fills the gap here could be various (consciousness, intentionality, free will, and so). Such concerns often revolve around a sense that AI is physically determined and hence cannot house these properties and be a subject of genuine agency or moral responsibility. However, once we start inquiring into human practices of holding each other responsible, rather than looking for metaphysical criteria of being morally responsible, questions of determinism fall out of the picture, and the way is open to considering whether the full gamut of moral responses, including the concept of evil, can be applied to AI.

Answering the Evil-Sceptic

AI can, within certain circumstances, be held morally responsible. Moreover, we can use the concept of 'evil' to illuminate some of the threats posed by AI. To understand how concepts of moral responsibility can be applied to machines, however, we will need to go back to the beginning and outline a framework that will provide an account of how so much as *any* agent can be held morally responsible for their acts. This framework can be used, I shall argue, to provide a basis not just for the ordinary run of moral concepts, such as 'good', 'bad', 'right', 'wrong', but also for moral concepts that sit at the extreme, like 'evil'.

There are two forms of scepticism about the concept of evil. A narrow scepticism that questions the reality of evil specifically, and a wide scepticism that questions the reality of morality in general.

The wide form of scepticism about evil argues that evaluative concepts in general are problematic, and so, by extension, is the concept of evil. Scepticism about morality in general has a long history, and numerous variations. There are both descriptive versions of the challenge, as noted by the late Australian philosopher J.L. Mackie and normative versions of the challenge, as discussed by the nineteenth century German philosopher Friedrich Nietzsche. We can focus on two main points, however (both descriptive): (a) that moral concepts purport to pick out moral facts; but since moral facts would be unusual or 'queer' entities – non-empirical and non-physically located entities – then we can assume that they don't exist (The Argument from Queerness); (b) moral concepts depend on moral responsibility, and moral responsibility depends on a capacity for libertarian free will. But since libertarian free will is also a 'queer' entity – it is an ability to act in an undetermined way – so we can assume that there is no such thing as moral responsibility either (The Argument from Free Will).

The narrow form of scepticism about evil argues that the concept of evil specifically is a problematic concept, even though moral concepts in general are of good standing; it is problematic for two reasons. First, it is descriptively inaccurate and fails to pick out anything that exists in the actual world, as opposed to the world of myth and fiction. Second, it is normatively questionable because it leads to the demonisation and dehumanisation of people. These two points are complementary: because 'evil' purports to pick out inhuman mindsets or intentions, then, once we put the concept under scrutiny, we find both that there are no such mindsets and intentions, and that using the language of evil immediately dehumanises those it is applied to.

These are very brief sketches of arguments that have, of course, been developed in considerably more detail through the history of modern philosophy. To show how these forms of scepticism can be responded to, we can appeal to a framework that draws on the English philosopher P F Strawson's influential work on what he calls the 'reactive attitudes'. What is useful about this framework is that it is specifically designed to address concerns about moral scepticism that derive from the apparent incompatibility of moral responsibility and physical determinism. Concerns that genuine responsibility – and in its turn, genuine evil – requires either a libertarian free will, or queer, supernatural entities are ways of speaking about this clash between the natural and the normative. Since, as I have already intimated, this clash is also partly what drives scepticism about the applicability of moral responsibility to AI, we will, with this framework in hand, be able to return to the question of morally responsibility and the application of 'evil' to AI.

The Reactive Attitudes and the Moral Nexus

The reactive attitudes are, as Strawson puts it, 'the non-detached attitudes and reactions of people directly involved in transactions with each other; of the attitudes and reactions of offended parties and beneficiaries; of such things as gratitude, resentment, forgiveness, love and hurt feelings'. For instance, if I were to sullenly push you in the back, then that would invoke in you a feeling of blame or resentment, directed towards me, on account of what I have done. In reacting this way (with attitudes of blame and resentment) you would be reacting to something within my behaviour that expresses an attitude of mine of a lack of regard, or a quality of ill-will, towards you. Reactive attitudes such as these constitute something of a semi-articulate normative system. My attitude of ill-will or disregard should invoke in you a corresponding attitude of blame, which – assuming the blame is well-judged – should then invoke in me an attitude of remorse; and then – assuming the remorse is genuine – it should invoke in you an attitude of forgiveness. Where some of these attitudes are not well-placed, then the appropriate responses might be different: justifications, excuses, indignation, and so on. Put together, the reactive attitudes can be understood as elements of a practice that consist in an interrelated nexus of responses to the attitudes, feelings, and behaviours of others.

What is key to Strawson's approach is a reversal of the standard order of metaethical explanation. Rather than understanding moral reactions as reflective of an underlying set of moral beliefs about what is right or wrong, Strawson instead suggests that we should regard those moral reactions as elements of a practice full participation within which is constitutive of what it is to be morally responsible. In other words, one *is* morally responsible to the extent that it is appropriate, as a member of that practice, to be *held* morally responsible. Insofar as one is not a member of that practice one is not held fully responsible within that practice, and so is not fully responsible by the lights of that practice.

The Reactive Attitudes and Ordinary Moral Practices

Strawson regarded his framework as providing a response to the wide form of scepticism about evil. That is, he suggests that appeal to the reactive attitudes provides a framework for a non-reductive, but naturalistic understanding our ordinary moral practices – practices of responding to each other with attitudes such as blame, praise, gratitude resentment, and so forth – that relies neither on the idea that there is a realm of independently specifiable moral facts, nor on the idea that moral responsibility requires a radical libertarian free will. The framework satisfies both the Argument from Queerness and the Argument from Free Will. We can briefly outline how these arguments are meant to go.

An appeal to independently specifiable moral facts is not required because, on the Strawsonian view, moral responsibility can be fixed by criteria internal to the practice. For instance, a basic demand for recognition between participants of the practice calls for responses to harmful behaviour (at least where that behaviour is expressive of ill-regard) such as blame, excuse, or remedy. The practice itself might be without external justification: it might just be that holding each other responsible in these reactive ways is what we (perhaps contingently) do, or, in some circumstances, what we feel psychologically compelled to do.

An appeal to a radical libertarian free will is also not required for moral responsibility in line with the Strawsonian view because participation in the practice does not require an absolute conception of free will. This is true in both directions of an interaction. From the point-of-view of the blamed, whether one is expressing ill-regard for another is independent of whether it is fully freely chosen; the attitude is one thing, the cause of it another, and the attitude would remain even if it was causally determined. From the point-of-view of the blamer, one's response to another's ill-regard is neither diminished nor extinguished by a philosophical conviction about determinism. That is to say, it is not part of the internal criteria of the practice that one modify one's sense of blame, say, on account of a global conviction about the metaphysics of personal identity; rather, the reactive attitudes are modified in response to particular circumstances (which can generate excuses or justifications for immoral behaviour) or in response to particular facts about a person (for example, on account of being under stress at the time, being ill, or being a child).

So, one modifies or abandons one's reactive attitudes – and hence abandons one's assumption that another is morally responsible or blameworthy for an act – only in particular or 'abnormal' circumstances. This means that we cannot globally abandon claims of moral responsibility, as would be the case if we accepted the wide form of scepticism about evil, because 'it cannot be a consequence of any thesis which is not itself self-contradictory that abnormality is the normal condition'. Again, notes Strawson, 'the human commitment to participation in ordinary inter-personal relationships is, I think, too thoroughgoing and deeply rooted for us to take seriously the thought that a general theoretical conviction might so change our world'.

What we have here, then, is a basic framework for understanding how moral responsibility – grounded in a participatory practice in which participants hold each other responsible by way of reactive attitudes – need not involve an appeal to anything beyond ordinary, naturalistically describable properties of the attitudes and actions of the agents involved. There is no need to appeal to libertarian free will, or to spooky non-natural properties of goodness. This, then, opens up – but does not yet establish – an explanation for how AI can be properly held morally responsible. To the extent that an AI is able to engage in the practices that constitute holding and being held responsible, then AI can be thought of as *being* morally responsible for its actions.

The Reactive Attitudes and Marginal Cases

I have argued, then, that the Strawsonian Framework provides a sketch of an account of moral responsibility that promises to exonerate our ordinary everyday moral practices from at least some of the charges outlined by the wide form of scepticism about evil; in particular, the Argument from Queerness and the Argument from Free Will.

However, as observed by various commentators, Strawson's framework has a *prima facie* difficulty placing what the American moral philosopher David Shoemaker calls 'marginal cases'. Marginal cases are 'cases at the boundaries of our interpersonal community where agents tend to strike us as eligible for some responsibility responses but not others'. For instance, a young child who misbehaves will be held responsible for what they do, but not in the same way that an adult would; in some ways and in some respects their responsibility is diminished. This means that a crude picture of the Strawsonian Framework — in which one is either a member of the moral community or one is not — cannot be the whole story; we need the framework to account for marginal cases.

Although Strawson acknowledges 'essentially a borderline, penumbral area' of marginal cases, his framework struggles to accommodate them. This is because Strawson contrasts his framework of *participant reactive attitudes* — 'essentially natural human reactions to the good or ill will or indifference of others towards us' — with what he calls the *objective attitude*. The objective attitude involves seeing another being as, either temporally or permanently, outside the normal range of moral and interpersonal participation — as 'a subject of social policy; as a subject for what, in a wide range of sense, might be called treatment'. Although the objective attitude can be 'emotionally toned' in various ways, it does not 'include the range of reactive feelings and attitudes which belong to involvement or participation with others in inter-personal human relationships'.

To get a grip on the distinction between the participant stance, and the objective stance, we can consider two broad ways in which might inhibit one's negative reactive attitudes (such as blame or resentment) towards another.

The first — sometimes called *'Type-1 Pleas'* — are when an excuse or justification can be given for an action. For instance, if I miss an appointment with you, I might be excused if it turns out that the missed appointment was due to a factor outside my control, for example a late-running train. In cases such as these – or cases where there are small lapses due to ignorance or tiredness – there is no tendency to regard the other as outside the scope of moral responsibility. As Strawson notes, 'exculpatory pleas … in no way detract … from the agent's status as a term of moral relationships'. Type-1 pleas are part-and-parcel of the participant stance of the reactive attitudes.

The second broad ground for suspending or inhibiting one's negative reactive attitudes – sometimes called *'Type-2 Pleas'* – are when an agent is seen as not capable of proper moral engagement with others. Perhaps, for instance, they are suffering from some 'insane delusion' about the world that doesn't enable them to understand what is happening around them, or perhaps their behaviour is not fully under their control, and they are subject to sub-conscious or non-intentional compulsions or behaviours, or perhaps they are simply, as Strawson puts it, a 'moral idiot' who lacks the capacity to empathise with others. These promote 'the purely objective view of the agent as one posing problems simply of intellectual understanding, management, treatment and control', rather than problems of proper regard in interaction; such a person is (perhaps only temporarily) not 'seen as a morally responsible agent, as a term of moral relationships, as a member of the moral community'. Type-2 pleas place an agent *outside* the participant stance of the reactive attitudes.

There is a need, then, to understand the Type-2 marginal cases, the 'ever-interesting cases of variation' as Strawson called them. There has been significant progress in this direction. Shoemaker, for instance, has argued that we can understand our moral practices as involving three distinct ways of being held responsibile – attributability, answerability, and accountability – that correspond to three distinct ways in which a person might express a poor quality of will. On this view, an act is attributable to an agent if the act is reflective of, and caused by, that agent's deeply held cares and commitments (American philosopher Susan Wolf's 'deep self'). An agent is *answerable* for an act when that act could be regarded – either hypothetically or actually – as being the outcome of a deliberative choice that considered relevant alternatives to the action taken. And an agent is accountable for an act when they are a fitting subject of participatory reactive responses on account of their quality of regard.

Now, Shoemaker argues that by understanding moral practices in this way – as involving three forms of being held morally responsible – we can understand marginal cases as involving the invocations of some forms of responsibility without others. So, while a fully-fledged adult member of the moral community will generally be held responsible for their actions and attitudes in all three ways, more marginal members might be exempt from being held responsible in one or more ways. For instance, a child might be attributively responsible or even answerable for their behaviour in certain respects, but they might not be accountable, because they are not capable of properly holding another in the right regard, even though the action they performed was both in line with their central cares and commitments and was committed after some deliberation.

Likewise, in a way that speaks to our current topic, Shoemaker's account could help us understand the sense in which Artificial Intelligence – either current or soon to come – might be held responsible in a minimal way: to the extent that AI is capable of being sensitive to harm against others, and capable of deliberation about means, but not capable of having its own ends – then we might hold AIs accountable and answerable for their actions, but not attributable, at least in the sense outlined by Shoemaker.

The Secular Problem of Evil

However, marginal cases do not just include agents with what we might call 'minimal' capacities, such as young children or AI. It also includes agents who commit what we would colloquially call 'evil acts'. Such acts invoke in us a contradictory response: extreme offenders at once seem incapable of engaging in ordinary practices of moral accountability – and to that extent seem to fall outside of the practice, participation within which, we have argued, is necessary for moral responsibility – while also eliciting, among ordinary members of the moral community, a sense of undeniable moral outrage and moral blame for their actions.

This raises, however, a lacuna in the Strawsonian approach when it comes to considering instances of evil understood in its narrow sense. It is not clear that Shoemaker's tripartite account has the resources to understand the deficits of evil persons, such as sociopaths. It is striking that commentators in this area – from Strawson onwards – sometimes conflate those who we would regard as morally innocent, such as young children, from those who we would regard as morally deficient, such as sociopaths. In outlining Type-2 Pleas, for instance, Strawson suggests that they consist of excusing factors such as 'he was warped or deranged, neurotic or just a child'. Likewise, Gary Watson states that a 'child can be malicious, a psychotic can be hostile, a sociopath indifferent'. It seems discordant somehow to equate the 'warped or deranged' behaviour of a psychotic adult, or the indifference of a sociopath, with the bad behaviour of a child.

Extreme moral evil will likely have distinct roots from moral immaturity. The immature agent is excused – to the extent that they are excused – because they are not capable of clear deliberation; the child, we tend to think, should not be held fully responsible for their actions and attitude. There is a capability deficit in the child which is a mitigating factor. This is distinct from the agent who engages in extreme moral evil. Although some have tried to argue this way, it would be galling, at least on a standard intuition, to regard the sociopath's moral deficit – their incapacity to have any sympathetic regard for others – as a mitigating factor; it seems, rather, to be an aggravating factor. The fact that they cannot care about other's interests seems to inflame rather than defuse the moral reactions of others. As American philosopher Gary Watson observes, when discussing the actions of the serial killer Robert Harris, 'Harris's form of evil consists in part in being beyond the boundaries of the moral community'. Yet being beyond the boundaries of the moral community – in the sense of not yet being mature enough to properly participate in it – seems to be exactly what excuses or mitigates the child's behaviour. What explains these seemingly opposed reactions? Why should the child's incapacity mitigate, and the sociopath's incapacity aggravate? Are we simply, as Watson suggests, caught in an insoluble conflict where 'we are unable to command an overall view of [the evildoer's] life that permits the reactive attitudes to be sustained without ambivalence'?

An alternative suggestion to Watson's ambivalence about responsibility, and Shoemaker's pluralism about responsibility, would be to regard responsibility as partially contextual. On this view, rather than regarding the internal criteria for being held responsible (in any of the three variations mentioned by Shoemaker) as statically attached to a particular strength of quality of will – such that, for example, one must have this much capacity for emotional sympathy to be eligible to be held accountable for any of their actions – we should, rather, regard distinct situations as calling for distinct strengths of quality of will.

For instance, suppose that one is faced with a very sensitive, vulnerable person who needs help. To help them one needs to have an exceptional capacity for sympathy. One needs to have a very strong quality of will of regard for other people. A person without such a strong quality of will of regard – a person without that exceptional capacity for sympathy – would not be blameworthy if they were not able to help, and perhaps even harmed through lack of needed regard, the vulnerable person. On the other hand, a person with a strong quality of will of regard – a strong capacity for sympathy – would be blameworthy (perhaps in the sense of being held accountable) if they were not to help, or, through lack of needed regard, were to harm that person. In some ways this is similar to how we think about child's responsibilities: their lack of capacity for standard adult-like regard for others is what mitigates them.

Conversely, some acts – or omissions – require a very limited capacity for sympathy. It takes very little sympathy or quality of will of regard to recognise that, for example, torturing an innocent person is harmful and should not be carried out. Most people who might be outside of the usual run of 'strains of involvement' of interpersonal interactions are not so far outside the moral community that they cannot understand or recognise the harm in such acts. The sociopath, who might be excused minor misdemeanours of regard on account of an unchosen deficit of affective sympathy, is nevertheless blameworthy if they carry out an extreme act such as torture. They are blameworthy because such acts require only a very weak quality of will of regard to realise that they are beyond the boundaries of acceptable conduct, and such a weak quality of will can be considered to be within the gift of such agents.

On the view painted above, then, the internal criteria of our participatory moral practice incorporate more than one tier. In the first tier, in the ordinary run of things, one expects and demands of others a particular strength of quality of will (which might be dispersed across three varieties as mentioned by Shoemaker). An agent without such a quality of will – or with only a weakened version – might be excused from blame and other participant reactive attitudes relating to that deficit. While the agent with such a quality of will, but who does not exercise it, is blameworthy for their attitude and actions. In the second tier, in the extraordinary run of things – at the extremes of moral action (typically sadism, murder, cruelty) – the criteria for involvement is much lower. An agent with even a weakened quality of will can still be held accountable, attributable, and answerable for their actions, even though – exactly because of that weakened quality of will – they might be excused along one or more of the three dimensions for comparatively more minor, but typically blameworthy, acts. We expect all agents, even those with serious deficits and some diminished responsibility within ordinary interactions, to have the capacities to avoid doing evil – that is part of the criteria for involvement even with marginal cases – and those who fail to live up to those expectations can rightly be blamed for them, and their actions deemed evil.

The above provides an account of how agents can be held morally responsible for narrowly evil acts within a Strawsonian Framework that responds to the objections that typically arise with scepticism about the narrow concept of evil. The Strawsonian Framework neither requires recourse to a metaphysically suspect conception of evil (the Argument from Supernaturalism), nor leads to a process of dehumanisation (the Argument from Dehumanisation). The moral responsibility of an extreme evil doer can be explained by appeal to acts that would be blameworthy even for people who might be excused blame for less extreme acts. In this respect, agents who would usually seem as if they are outside the scope of the moral community for ordinary purposes, are drawn (back) into it when the acts are extreme enough.

What the account has not yet done is provide a definition of evil, nor try to determine what, within the Strawsonian framework, would serve to distinguish evil acts from what is merely wrong or bad. It would take us too far afield to discuss that in any detail here, so I shall make do with a very brief summary. The broad claim is that actions are considered evil to the extent that they are a continuation or strengthening along some dimension – typically the harm of another – of what is typically considered bad and wrong, with the added element that they have a *distorting effect* on the moral framework itself. As the South African political theorist Stephen de Wijze has put it, evil acts or moralities 'invert or annihilate the "moral landscape"... needed for any civilised attempt to manage conflict and to establish a minimal level of respect and dignity between persons'.

The distorting effect, in my view, is that the nature of the wrong – the extremity of the act – is such that it prevents the kind of normative corrective that is typical of interactions in the wake of ordinary wrongdoing. With ordinary wrongdoing, there are criteria, internal to the practice, for what American philosopher Margaret Urban Walker calls *moral repair*: blame in the face of wrongdoing, remorse in the face of blame, forgiveness in the face of remorse, and reconciliation in the face of forgiveness. These provide the agents involved with a normative map for how they can find their way past a wrongdoing to a form of reconciliation. With extreme wrongdoing – that is, with evil – this normative corrective of moral repair is lost and the path to reconciliation becomes clogged, perhaps permanently, with no normative criteria provided for how to unclog it. In the face of evil, the scope for genuine remorse and genuine forgiveness is limited, and there are no normative criteria or expectations in place for how to deal with the act. As we have already observed, the evildoer who commits the act is liable to already be outside the scope of ordinary practices of interaction, including those of moral repair: we do not expect the genuinely morally disturbed to offer themselves up for genuine remorse. If there is to be remorse it is not to be expected or sought from, say, the cold-eyed sociopath. Likewise, if there is to be forgiveness – from the victims or their representative – then it cannot be normatively demanded: Forgiveness in the face of extreme wrongdoing can only be elective, and not conditioned by the norms of a practice. After all, it seems wrong to suppose that the victim of an atrocious crime might be required to forgive, even in the face of genuine remorse.

Evil and AI

The Strawsonian Framework provides an understanding of our moral practices in terms of a participatory practice involving reactive attitudes that respond to the attitudes and actions of others. This basic framework

– of ordinary interactions and ordinary moral repair – can then be expanded to include the following exceptions or amendments:

Exemption Cases: For some agents it is necessary to step-back and exempt them entirely from the 'strains of involvement' of the participatory stance. In such cases, where one takes the 'objective stance' towards another, that agent is not treated as a functioning member of the moral community but is treated as something to be 'managed'; a matter of 'policy' rather than of interactive regard.

Marginal Cases: For some agents it is necessary to treat them as responsible agents and members of the moral community in some respects but not in other respects. They might have, for example, the capacity for empathetic understanding, but not the capacity for careful deliberation; this will make a difference to the respect in which they are and are not responsible for their actions.

Extreme Cases: For some agents it is necessary to treat them as weakly responsible agents and as members only of the moral community only in respect of a certain sub-set of extreme acts. Such agents might, for example, have a highly reduced capacity for affective empathy which exempts them from some forms of responsibility in ordinary interactions, and outside of the ordinary forms of moral community, but it does not exempt them from those forms of responsibility when the acts are extreme.

We can now turn to the question of how this framework applies to AI and the respects in which AI might be considered morally responsible, including possessing a capacity for extreme evil.

Let's recall the three types of agency, outlined earlier:

(a) AI as a *non-agential tool*
(b) AI as a *hybrid, minimal agent*
(c) AI as a *fully autonomous agent*

We can see here, using the Strawsonian Framework, that when an AI is properly regarded as a non-agential tool – either temporally or permanently – then this is an *exemption case*. An exemption case will occur when there is no capacity, or use, in engaging with the machine as an agent with whom one might have a participatory, moral relationship. Encounters with such a machine involve taking the 'objective stance' which 'promotes the purely objective view of the agent as one posing problems simply of intellectual understanding, management, treatment and control'. The machine might be highly sophisticated and capable of operating independently from a human user. But, if it lacks the capacity to properly engage within interpersonal relations in a way that is at least minimally responsive to the morally infused attitudes of others, then one's attitude towards that machine can be one of management, control and repair. Note that this is the way that many debates about AI are framed: AI is not treated as a potential moral partner, but as a potential problem to be controlled; hence the ubiquitous term 'the control problem'.

When an AI is regarded as a hybrid, minimal agent, then questions of responsibility might go in one of two directions. The minimal AI agent could be understood as being strongly morally responsible along some dimensions, but not at all (or only marginally so) along others. The system might, for instance, be capable of calculating the means for a task, but require that its ends (or goals) be programmed into it. This would be a marginal case. For instance, if the AI in question is a semi-automated self-driving car, then it might be held *answerable* for its choices – why did it choose to career into the sidewalk when faced with oncoming traffic, rather than slamming on the brakes? –but needn't be *accountable* since the actions it performed were not an element of its 'deep self'.

What is interesting here, though, for our concerns, is where an AI hybrid, minimal agent is only weakly responsible along one or more dimensions. For instance, suppose that the AI has a strong capacity for deliberation about means – allowing for engagement within practices relating to answerability – but has only a weak capacity for affective empathy. This latter quality moves the AI into the territory of *a moral 'uncanny valley'*. We can see here a respect in which a mixed and weakened capacity for human-like responses to others; a mixed and weakened form of quality of regard and quality of will, would involve an agent who engages in forms of ordinary participation in interpersonal relations – at least among some dimensions – but yet might, on account of a weakened capacity for affective empathy, or a weakened capacity for a strong deep self, be much more capable of causing extreme harm to others. Such an agent could be causally responsible for such acts on account of their having weak affective empathy, and also morally responsible for such acts on account of such acts requiring only weak affective empathy in order for the agent to be fully morally responsible for them: in other words, such a hybrid agent would be capable of extreme moral evil.

It is worth comparing that with the third form of agency: *a fully autonomous agent*. Although it is the AI as fully autonomous agent that has generated the most excitement and the most fear, it is my contention that, in fact, it is the hybrid agent which should be considered the most liable to be capable of extreme moral evil. The reason for this is that a fully autonomous AI agent would be – on account of its being fully autonomous and responsible along the three dimensions – much more integrated within our everyday, interactive practices. If the Strawsonian Framework outlined here is correct, then the more that an AI system is integrated within our practices, then the more that system will be (correctly) understood as being responsible and autonomous in the relevant respects. The danger is not with such integrated, autonomous agents – it is with the semi-autonomous, hybrid agents: agents who have enough of a capacity to operate within a minimal form of human practices of participation and responsibility, yet remain partially outside of it, capable of acting from outside the parameters of ordinary interactions in certain circumstances, perhaps sometimes for reasons unknown. Here we have the capacity for genuine, extreme moral evil.

The concept of evil often conjures up images of the uncanny, of the macabre, of intentions that go beyond what Hannah Arendt called 'humanly comprehensible motive[s]'. It doesn't just arouse feelings of moral horror, but also arouses feelings of confusion and a sense of incomprehension. Although I do not believe that such uncanniness is definitional of evil – Arendt's 'banality of evil' thesis perhaps tells us that much – it is very often an accompaniment to it. The reason that such uncanniness accompanies evil, according to the ideas sketched here, is that it allows such actors to have one foot in our moral practices, while having one foot outside of them. The concern with AI is that, in our current trajectory, we seem to be creating systems with that kind of hybrid capacity, of being responsible in some ways, and less so in other ways. A way to remedy this would be to try to fully integrate artificial systems into our forms of participatory practices – ensure that such agents are able to engage in practices of reactive attitudes with the capacity for moral repair – rather than partially integrating them, and then hoping for the best.

APATHY

DISAFFECTION, ENTHUSIASM, FANATICISM

Ben Gook and Seán Cubitt

Charity, community, duty, and struggle are good – not only sanctified and rewarding but also good in themselves. And yet the evidence is that society at large is losing and devaluing commitment to others: we live in times diagnosed as consisting of social pathologies and a-pathologies – where, curiously, apathy is taken as a variant of, rather than existing in opposition to, pathology. Fascinated, for obvious reasons, with their diminishing share of trust, older print and broadcast news media have exhaustively analysed the rise of social media bubbles and echo chambers, trolls, and splenetic outbursts, discovering that the profitability of these emergent media forums depends on the speed and energy of their communications. Unsurprisingly, anger sells. Aggrieved fury would appear to be a dominant emotional state of our times. More reflective commentators, including William Davies in the UK and Joseph Vogl in Germany – both acknowledging the same condition where 'knowledge becomes more valued for its speed and impact than for its cold objectivity, and emotive falsehood often travels faster than fact' – observe that it can generate an emotional state in which 'otherwise peaceful situations can come to feel dangerous, until eventually they really are'.

Apatheia

While we recognise the evils of perpetual rage and endless anxiety, we hope to contribute to this discussion of evil, a third outcome of current conditions, one that, fittingly enough, has not stirred the same attention but which is as great a social and personal evil as fury and nervousness: apathy. Wherever it's used today, this term for being 'without feeling' aspires to capture some change in affect, behaviour, and cognition; it marks a reduction in feeling and activity, typically describing forms of indolence, diminished initiative, slowness, inertia, and generalised passivity. The comparator implicit in 'change' may be synchronic (norms and averages) or diachronic (biographical). Apathy describes both symptom and syndrome; people describe the symptomatology ('hasn't eaten in two days,' 'didn't vote') but also go hunting for causation ('brain lesion,' 'feeling of powerlessness').

As well as its synonyms (disaffection) and neighbouring states (exhaustion, burnout, alienation), apathy's vocabulary criss-crosses disciplinary investigations. Medical researchers – studying people with diagnoses of Alzheimer's and Parkinson's diseases, dementia, stroke, traumatic brain injury, major depression, or schizophrenia – will describe apathy in neuropsychiatric terms, using tools and techniques such as the Apathy Evaluation Scale. Philosophers will consider the (ancient) debate about action versus contemplation, and the Stoic state of the soul voluntarily alien to the 'passions' – a concept popular today among Silicon Valley types. The Enlightenment philosopher Immanuel Kant, much later, will portray *apatheia*, the thrilling fantasy of affectlessness, the apex of indifference, which would allow purely rational and moral action. Political scientists will study electorates, probing levels of engagement through indicators such as voter turnout or political activities outside the election cycle, such as letters written to representatives, participating in protests, and community organising; meanwhile the more theoretically minded social scientist may speak of 'motivational deficits' among the masses, a precipitate for broad legitimation crises. In all, the normative weight sits behind the argument that apathy is wrong, a deficit and an individual failing – a valuation nowhere more apparent than in political science research. Already in 1957, the German political theorist Franz Neumann spoke against the ('American') tendency to define voter abstention as clear-cut political apathy. He discussed how 'apathy' actually describes three different political reactions: (a) the lack of interest in politics and the belief that politics does not affect the citizen's life; (b) an Epicurean attitude towards politics, where it is seen as secondary to the individual's personal growth; (c) a conscious rejection of the political system because the individual sees no possibility for change. For Neumann, this third form of apathy is the most concerning, representing political alienation and potentially leading to a paralysis of the state, creating an opportunity for a Caesarist movement to take hold.

This taxonomy of apathy helps us frame its current evolution. Apathy is still conflated with not participating in elections. The contemporary 'crisis of representation' is one in which individuals and communities feel utterly neglected by governing institutions, and so simply refuse to participate. This has two faces, ostensibly leaving an increasing 'void' to be governed. On one side, many voters agree that the parliamentary system has a declining ability – perhaps at its nadir – to provide any effective response to popular will. On the other, governments worldwide have attempted to depress the vote in recent elections, typically targeting young, working-class, and migrant voters through ID and registration mechanisms. It's clear, against the standard commentary, that non-voting ≠ apathy. Both Neumann's 'lack of interest in politics', and the idea that politics has nothing to do with individual lives have become significant tools of neoliberalism's paradoxical mobilisation *and* demobilisation. A certain kind of politician praises self-interest and commitment limited to immediate kin (the family as the 'basic unit of society') and to communities defined by nation, nations defined by ethnicity and faith. Calling on voters to reject politics (the elite, the Blob) while mobilising their votes, and emphasising their freedom while restricting their rights, this kind of political movement – typically populist, usually nationalist, and often associated with the interests of big business, which is to say, tendentially fascistic – attracts political support among the angry and the anxious, often those with most to lose from the policies they enact. Trump, Bolsonaro, Orbán, Modi, the Brexit campaigners and others deploy rhetoric that reveres the past, especially an imaginarily pure community of the like-minded. They frequently set up a small collection of enemies for vitriol, not only their political opponents but often those with little or no political or economic power but who are conveniently 'other'. Clinging to traditions which, as the British historian Eric Hobsbawm discovered, are frequently invented for the purpose, political parties like Bharatiya Janata Party (BJP) and factions like the Christian fundamentalist wing of the US Republican Party, pillory opponents as 'fanatics' when they seek to change, in line with the actual majority opinion, elements of the social order (such as gun control or access to medical services). We can note, then, a general economy of emotions: one person's *apatheia* inspires another's passion.

Fanatics

There's no shortage of people with strong convictions and enthusiasms, many of them with dubious motives, noxious politics, and hateful schemes. The popular cultural fascination with cults over recent years – endlessly rehearsed in podcasts and inexpensive docu-series on streaming platforms – seems to index a preoccupation with those who feel deeply about a cause, rightly or wrongly. But the 'fanatic' has long been a figure and idea with outsized rhetorical usefulness, as the Italian critic Alberto Toscano dissected in work across the 2010s. The concept of fanaticism has been used as a weapon in various political and philosophical confrontations. Fanaticism can be seen as both a strength and a weakness, as it can disqualify or demonise adversaries, but it is also an unstable concept, given this constitutive ambivalence. The accusation of fanaticism can be directed towards *excessive* abstraction (Hegel called it 'enthusiasm for the abstract'), universality ('fundamentalists'), and the irredeemably sensuous and particular. The fanatic is monomaniacal, fixated, irrational, all enthusiasm, and no rationality (or, again, too much rationality – 'raving with reason'). Enthusiasm, the Germany-based anthropologist Monique Scheer reminds us, derives from the Greek *entheos*, meaning 'filled with God,' most notable in possession or divine inspiration. The Enthusiasts of the seventeenth century were adherents of radical religious movements, 'rooting the concept in the connection between religious belief and ... strong emotional and physical excitement'. This polemical, pejorative term loosened to become a desirable quality – passion, conviction, and obsession (political, erotic, aesthetic) now profitable for collective undertakings and individual characteristics (job applications). American literary scholar Jordana (Jordy) Rosenberg accounts, through the very concept of enthusiasm, for the transformations of religious passions into secular contexts, highlighting how debates concerning religious radicalism are bound to the advent of capitalism at its root (legal precedent, financial rhetoric, aesthetic form). Fanaticism, meanwhile, seems to be the remnant of these twists in modernity – the still deeply religiously encoded term for pathological enthusiasm, a haunted echo of our political apathologies.

The contemporary discourse about fanaticism is invariably condemnatory and depicts it as a fundamentally ahistorical pathology of religious and political life. Yet, fanaticism is often born of political crisis – particular conjunctures in which militancy is more a matter of will and faith than organic interests and clear prospects. A wish for purity may drive fanatics, but fanatics also destabilise established demarcations, divisions, and differences. Nineteenth-century British pundits used the term to describe rebels they encountered among the colonised, grudgingly acknowledging their resolve even as they systematically dispossessed them and 'eliminated' their resistance. The discourse *on* and *of* the fanatic is locked in a closed loop. The Western spectre of 'radicalisation' – connected with jihadis from at least 9/11 through to the 2010s ISIS attacks in Western Europe, though now increasingly and begrudgingly connected with armed white (ergo, 'non-Muslim') men – exacerbates the antinomies immanent to the uses of fanaticism. It does this not least by seeking to account, in time, for forms of conviction and action that it simultaneously takes to be monolithically static, abstract, and without history ('Islam,' 'masculinity'). In these reflections, Toscano countered the co-opted social scientists, as well as the self-appointed 'national security' and 'terrorism expert' industry, who constituted the go-to talking heads in Western media commentary on political and social affairs throughout the twenty years from 9/11 to the Covid-19 pandemic.

The fanatic has a political history apparent in the polemics against the French Revolution, describing those who believed in universal human nature. Eighteenth century philosopher Edmund Burke and nineteenth century historian Hippolyte Taine composed polemics against the Jacobins, describing the Revolution's advocates as reckless innovators zealously attacking religion and laying waste to custom, property, and manners. Warnings against philosophical 'fanaticks' who spread the 'political metaphysics' of unconditional equality were often accompanied by a conspiratorial sociology preoccupied with the alliance between intellectuals and mobs – 'the masses'. Burke's template, treating all advocates of radical equality as dangerous fanatics, was taken up in nineteenth-century attacks on American abolitionism and the workers' movement in its socialist, anarchist, and communist strands. Anti-revolutionary polemic describes any social implementation of a philosophy – atheistic, abstract, universal – as more dangerous than old-time religion. During the Cold War, fanatics accordingly appeared in the figure of adherents to the so-called totalitarian 'political religions' – namely, the driven comrades of communism, inveterate chasers of utopia. A slightly different rhetoric, used in 2023 by UK Home Secretary Suella Braverman, describes anyone who speaks of others not of one's own community or communion as 'utopian', which, in Braverman's vocabulary, amounts to a term of abuse. The same word applies to anyone who seeks to represent others that do not yet exist: the future victims of climate change, pollution, and the other great fears that populate contemporary Green and socialist agendas. Apparently, for Braverman, and frankly for the rest of her colleagues, it's conviction that is too much to bear in these groups. Deradicalisation of fanatics shades into depoliticisation of the masses; the conservative's desired quiescence and satiety of the body politic (truly silent majorities) is then lambasted by media outriders whenever election turnout dips further. The ironies and contradictions multiply: passivity is precisely what the top-down version of politics – mass parties without the mass, popular parties without the *populi* – sees as contented constituents; pressure from below – disaffection, rage, protest, voice, mobilisation – is construed as a threat by the democratic bastions of major parties. We are left with a narrow band in which to operate, both behaviourally and emotionally, charting a course between enthusiasm, fanaticism, and apathy.

Hope and Action

What else is the reclusive mass to do? A huge number respond with apathy, overwhelmed by media images of suffering, by the threat, now becoming actuality, of climate change. Faced with the inertia of states and corporations, neither anxiety nor even anger suffice. For many, confronted not only with the prospect of a contemporary situation incapable of and unwilling to take action, even sympathy and empathy with those in pain gives way to their opposite: an apathy at least as dangerous as the hatred it displaces. It is not just that neo-populists disdain any future-oriented politics or ethics as utopianism. Rather, utopia itself is fading, and as it fades, even its previous power to mobilise mass movements appears as insubstantial as the dream that its populist opponents describe it as.

Concluding a conversation with German philosopher Theodor W. Adorno on the meanings of utopia, the German philosopher Ernst Bloch noted 'hope is not confidence. If it could not be disappointed, it would not be hope'. In a probable reflection on the planned economy of East Germany, his postwar home for a brief time, Bloch insisted that no future can be planned since a plan is forged in the present. Implementing it maintains the present at the expense of a future different from what we have now. Utopia, any future worth having, cannot be imagined using the wits of the present. It must emerge, unforeseen, in its own right. To hope is to abandon any claim on what the future must look like in favour of some form of trust that it will appear, be different, and be better. The *locus classicus* of this form of blank utopianism in Bloch's Marxist tradition appears in Chapter 48 of the third, unfinished volume of Karl Marx's *Capital*:

> the realm of freedom actually begins only where labour which is determined by necessity and mundane considerations ceases; thus in the very nature of things it lies beyond the sphere of actual material production. ... Freedom in this field can only consist in socialised man, the associated producers, rationally regulating their interchange with Nature, bringing it under their common control, instead of being ruled by it as by the blind forces of Nature. ... But it nonetheless still remains a realm of necessity. Beyond it begins that development of human energy which is an end in itself, the true realm of freedom, which, however, can blossom forth only with this realm of necessity as its basis.

Marx's 'realm of freedom', which receives few other mentions and no further detailing, grounds Bloch's futures by refusing to describe what it might look like or how it might be recognised. It begins where something else ceases. On the other hand, Marx specifies, in the next sentence, that shortening the working day is the necessary first step, and in the cited passage it is clear that the social regulation of work, rather than its exploitation by capital, is the first political goal. We have no idea what freedom might be like, but we are obligated to make such first moves towards it.

Today, precisely those 'first steps' seem so impossible to take. One reason is the sheer force of wealth and power promoting the idea that no change is possible. A specific technique, allied with the neo-populist tendency to seek out enemies, is to blame activists for creating unnecessary anxiety. Increasingly draconian laws on protest, for example, evidence a state response to both the material and psychic threats posed by climate activists, targeting both the actions themselves and the activists' sheer existence. A second reason, with far more widespread effects, is to shift the blame from the industries that produce pollution – plastic bags, fertilisers, industrial meat production – onto consumers. The most extreme and most researched offenders in this activity are fossil fuel companies. The process began, at least in its contemporary form, in 2000. As American journalist Michael Kaufmann explains, 'British Petroleum, the second largest non-state-owned oil company in the world ... hired the public relations professionals Ogilvy & Mather to promote the slant that climate change is not the fault of an oil giant, but that of individuals'. This PR round generated the prize-winning campaign that popularised the phrase 'carbon footprint'. The five major oil companies spent more than three and a half billion dollars on advertising between 1986 and 2020. In a particularly egregious case of hypocrisy, Exxon spent millions on climate research but millions more on paid advertorials in *The New York Times* denying climate change and blaming consumers. Even the most influential media events, like the much garlanded *An Inconvenient Truth*, with Al Gore's famous PowerPoint presentation, can scarcely hope for the kinds of reach, repletion, and impact that this scale of advertising spending, backed up with access to and influence over politicians and political parties, can have on setting agendas, stifling contrary opinions, and promoting an overwhelming sense of guilt that, as individual consumers, nothing we do or can do seems to make a difference.

This eco-economic disaffection of consumers is matched with a series of more directly political modes of disempowerment. An old joke – 'how can you tell when a politician is lying? Their lips move' – meets a deep distrust of journalism, a distrust largely borne out by the immorality and triviality of celebrity-watching and much crime reporting as much as by the readiness to accept advertorial spend, kowtow to advertisers, and seek, like fossil fuel or any other major industry, the succour and support of governments. A growing belief that all politicians are corrupt not only protects those caught *in flagrante* but stains all members of the profession, down to the most downtrodden of public servants. 'It doesn't matter who you vote for, the government gets in,' as another old gag has it – now a truism for millions of disaffected citizens. Most distressing of all is the economic, political, and increasingly cultural turn away from the obligation of hospitality in the case of migrants. In a culture of victim-blaming that now extends from victims of sexual and domestic violence to migrants, the most powerless are credited with the most heinous assaults on the immobile conservative values espoused by the new Right. The 272 million people or 3.5 percent of the global population living in countries other than those of their birth – by 2019 figures which do not even include those 'internally displaced' by war, famine, and environmental collapse – are among the most powerless, despite being blamed for a range of ills over which they have no control.

These relatively limited cases – of consumers in the wealthy parts of the world, of migrants and other victims of abuse and discrimination, and the large but still discretely problematic section of the citizenry that has given up on politics – can account for a substantial part of the social generation of apathy. We do not want to continue the process of blaming the innocent by pursuing these relatively specific instances, but to ask why apathy is an available stance to everyone. Some people are apathetic all the time, but all people are apathetic some of the time. We want therefore to identify a formation in the contemporary conjuncture that will help explain why, alongside the 'resources of hope', there are also, everywhere, resources, if not of despair, at least of disaffection. We offer two simultaneous accounts of the sources of apathy, the first political, the second economic.

Slow Death

Is apathy an anaesthetic? Concluding an essay on 'slow death' – 'the physical wearing out of a population and the deterioration of people in that population' – the American author Lauren Berlant writes that, while some find activist routes out of the condition,

> for most, the overwhelming present is less well symbolised by energising images of sustainable life, less guaranteed than ever by the glorious promise of bodily longevity and social security, than it is expressed in regimes of exhausted

practical sovereignty, lateral agency, and, sometimes, counterabsorption in episodic refreshment, for example, in sex, or spacing out, or food that is not for thought.

Where 'practical sovereignty' is, loosely, the lived experience of being ruled, 'lateral agency' refers to 'an activity of maintenance, not making; fantasy, without grandiosity; sentience, without full intentionality'. Berlant's essay might be read as a response to an earlier and far less precise meditation on modes of existence among 'the silent majority' by the French philosopher Jean Baudrillard. In the comedown after the ecstasy of 1968, he wrote about:

> the refusal of socialisation which comes *from the mass*; from an innumerable, unnamable and anonymous group, whose strength comes from its very destructuration and inertia. Thus, in the case of the media, traditional resistance consists of reinterpreting messages according to the group's own code and for its own ends. The masses, on the contrary, accept everything and redirect everything *en bloc* into the spectacular, without requiring any other code, without requiring any meaning, ultimately without resistance, but making everything slide into an indeterminate sphere which is not even that of nonsense, but that of overall manipulation / fascination.

Berlant and Baudrillard describe similar phenomena: Berlant's 'spacing out' describes what Baudrillard calls 'making everything slide into an indeterminate sphere' of meaningless fascination. But Berlant advances on Baudrillard by insisting that Left/Green utopians and, we might add, all who believe in the final justice of the Last Days, cannot afford to cede public access to resistance or sovereignty, however misleading they may be philosophically, or attenuated socially and economically. This is not silent passivity but an active refusal of advertising's promises of perfect bodies in perfect homes in perpetuity, where working-class pleasures (junk food, booze, recreational sex) are at once forms of consumption that accord with the disciplines of contemporary capitalism, but consumed wrongly. 'Nothing so aggravates an earnest person,' American writer Herman Melville writes in *Bartleby, The Scrivener*, 'as a passive resistance' – or, we might add, the aggravation brought by 'bad taste,' 'unhealthy' and 'immoderate' consumption within the reign of the commodity form and exchange. Capital asserts the responsibility of each individual consumer for their own health and well-being. Over-consumption, by ignoring the expectation that consumers will not consume so much that they cannot also work, is the only resistance available to an emotionally and physically drained population, and which sees no alternative – no new social link that could mobilise for change – to the cycle of labour and consumption.

No Thanks

Kant, in his *Critique of Judgement*, admires 'LANGUID' affects – based, as American author Rei Terada points out, on dumb, feminine sympathy – while also preferring 'interesting sadness' over 'insipid sadness.' Terada notes the odd conclusion in the *Critique*, where Kant writes: 'the absence of emotion (*apatheia, phlegma in significatu bono*), when found in a mood that adheres emphatically and insistently to its principles, cannot only be sublime but most admirably so.' This sublime, for Kant, is the degree zero of emotion – no pathos, anxiety or sympathy are on offer, only an a-pathos, or loss of the symbolic. Yet emotion pervades our relation with the world, making this affectlessness a sublime mirage. Terada ultimately suggests apatheia can be considered two-sided – one facing out (which we cannot experience in Kantian terms), one facing in. Inwardly, this suggests not the lack of emotional relation to oneself but a looping paradox: 'the feeling of the failure of feeling,' a situation of being 'without affects' that is itself a feeling, apathy is pathetic, 'feeling nothing is feeling nothing'.

Berlant also describes an experience of 'coasting' in the chronic crises of our contemporary moment: 'under a regime of crisis ordinariness, life feels truncated – more like doggy paddling than swimming out to the magnificent horizon.' These are lateral states that don't quite opt out and don't quite raise hell, but also don't quite accede to hyperconsumptive demands, or strive for the horizon, or the impossible, apathetic Kantian sublime. These states stand in a troubling relationship to presumed models of agency, activity, participation – and crisis. The apathetic ostensibly disengage, at least from some of the more lucrative circuits of capital accumulation today. Recently, the English political economist, William Davies has further developed the work we cited earlier, arguing we live in a reaction economy for which 'engagement' is the headline concept of public participation. For Davies, the spread of smart scrollable devices since 2008 has generated an economy of reaction in which individuals are not viewed as autonomous agents with reason and interests, but as junction boxes in a complex network — tasked with endlessly sending, receiving, and processing information in real time. Individual reactions are one more piece of information that can be used to search for counter-reactions – and so it goes, along a reaction chain that encourages 'viral' content to elicit emotions or moods, then their counter-reactions and on until a new chunk of reactable content enters global orbit.

What are the likely politics of a world chained to the pinging nervous systems of platformed users? Digitally tracked 'emotions,' or at least their behavioural footprint, appear in the marketing and political technics of sentiment analysis and affective computing, forever scraping usage data from platforms, apps, and surveilled public space. These analytics aspire to find clusters of those who feel similarly, clumping them together for targeting as audiences for whatever needs a market — be it Spotify podcasts, nationalist politicians, or probiotic dog food. Davies, taking this argument about reaction with his earlier work on nervous states and neoliberalism, thus suggests that this emphasis on reactions may be symptomatic of a broader cultural shift away from a modern liberal idea of personal freedom (autonomy) towards a naturalistic (neoliberal) idea of impulse, for which affect is the visceral kernel. For Davies, anger and laughter have developed important political and critical functions in the digital public sphere, as they allow individuals to express frustration with political and economic systems that are seen as unfair. If these online spaces are both 'sad by design,' as Dutch visual artist Geert Lovink suggests in a recent book, and sites of 'digital lethargy,' as poet and digital media scholar Tung-Hui Hu argues, the user's 'expression' of sadness or frustration is simply routed back through the same circuits and chains. Here, all of culture should aspire to the signalling and ordering of the market, with 'spontaneous' reactions boosting certain items and 'downvoting' others.

Where do the apathetic stand in such a cultural set-up? Are the apathetic — taken in the strict definition of those without emotion or passion — virtually dead, invisible in the reaction economy, junction boxes to nowhere? If emotions are the currency and the apathetic become misers, subtracting their strong affects from circulation, do they even exist in this economy? And if emotions are the source of so much cultural and economic value, is it any wonder that a reaction formation appears in the form of an emotional withdrawal, a Bartlebian posture of simply preferring not to engage?

Engines of Apathy

This cultural and political account of the sources of apathy (which, incidentally, ought to be distinguished from nihilism) can, we believe, be given strength through a different understanding of how time is experienced in states of apathy: empty; unmoving as much as it is immovable. This takes us on a detour through the theological aspirations of contemporary economics. When Adorno noted that the 1755 Lisbon earthquake 'sufficed to cure Voltaire of the theodicy of Leibnitz', he pointed towards the end of a certain kind of hope grounded in the vindication of God's mistreatment of humanity. Bereft of a guarantee that everything would end well in the Last Days, there remained only the indescribable future Ernst Bloch had proposed in his conversations with Adorno. We are confronted with a blunt choice. The principle of Bloch's apothegm remains: we hope for a future when the profit motive is not the sole arbiter of value, without having to picture what Marx's 'realm of freedom' should look like – honouring a *Bildverbot*, or ban on images, that Adorno explored. But faced with an apocalypse, and denied a God to usher in a posthumous paradise, a principle of hope intrinsically tied to deferral may need a supplement. It requires a reversal of Bloch's rule: Hope would not be hope if it could not be realised.

A principle of hope (to recall the title of Bloch's major work) that can work in the twenty-first century requires, then, not only a refusal to repeat the present endlessly, but also a kind of faith that there will be a future. For reasons explored, among others, by literary theorist Fredric Jameson, identifying our period of history by secularism is internally inconsistent, and in any case fails the test of elementary observation: a vast proportion of the world's population avow a faith. We do not, therefore, propose to blame secularism for the rise of apathy. The immense inertia of the oil and other industries and the political forces that support them are far stronger candidates as core engines of apathy.

Economic Theodicy

We turn to economics, equally, for the widespread principle that no future other than the present can emerge. Joseph Vogl goes back to the seventeenth century mathematician and philosopher Gottfied Wilhelm Leibniz's theodicy – namely, the faith that even the worst events form part of God's plan – to propose that the theological doctrine has been replaced by an economic one. The ungainly term Vogl coins for this is oikodicy, putting 'oikonomia,' or managing the economic household, where 'theologia' once stood. Vogl thereby describes 'a liberal or capitalist oikodicy, a theodicy of the economic universe: the inner consistency of an economic doctrine that – rightly or wrongly, for good or ill – views contradictions, adverse effects, and breakdowns in the system as eminently compatible with its sound institutional arrangement'. The *nomos* (law) of the *oikos* (household) demands knowledge, conduct, measures, and techniques.

As with its theological forbear, oikodicy holds a particularly rigid relation with time, its own variant on the problem of predestination. Vogl observes that since mid-century, the equivalent problem concerns the market in futures, effectively bets on the likely future price of a commodity. Initially a matter of planning investment in a product that will take some measurable time to reach a buyer – how much to spend on planting next year's barley, for example – by the mid-twentieth century, futures markets were auctioning contracts between suppliers and investors ready to take the risk that their products would have a value over the amount they invested in the auction. The risk and rewards depended on successfully guessing what the future price would be, given there was no way to foretell them. The major challenge for economic thought, then, was 'to find a formula that makes the transition from present futures' (the price paid at auction in the present for the right to sell on in the future) 'to future presents' (the moment in the future when the contract comes up and the product is to be sold, not for an imagined or planned price but for a definite sum). Such a formula makes this transition 'both predictable and likely, transforming what lies in the future and therefore differs from the present into something that resembles the present'.

The miracle duly appeared in the form of the Black-Scholes formula, which provides a mathematical equation for hedging bets on future prices, implying there can only be one correct price. The 'oikodicial' aspect of this is then that present expectations and future actualities can be reduced to a single number. Since Black-Scholes, according to Vogl, 'the commercial routines of financial markets are based on the premise that future expectations can be translated into expected futures and that, in the long run, homogeneity between the future present and the present future is more or less guaranteed to prevail'. This apparently arcane cog in the machinery of financial markets, today often buried invisibly in the algorithms underpinning high-frequency, computerised trading systems, has important implications for our theme.

Unlike the individual traders playing it, the Market, capitalised to indicate its unity, its mystery, and its pseudo-divine control, 'knows' the future. Individuals can bet successfully, or lose their shirts, but the Market comes right. Even though, from a different perspective, the Market's existence depends absolutely on each and every trade, which as well as shifting money from A to B, establishes the fact that a Market must exist for the trade to occur, the Market continues to exist, now and in the future, indifferent to any difference between temporal points and indeed ensuring that no difference can emerge. Crucially, the power of this projection of the present into the future, this equivalence of now and the future we hope for, destroys any possibility that the unknown and unrealised future of Bloch's formulation can ever come about. There is no future other than the indefinite extension of the present.

The chaos of collapsing derivatives markets in the global financial crisis of 2007-2008 (which continues in the 'cost of living crisis' of 2023), does not disprove this thesis. As the Lebanese economist Elie Ayache writes, 'traders don't use derivatives to trade the underlying; they use derivatives to make volatility tradable'. The new finance market not only turns disasters into profits – it actively seeks out unpredictable trends and events ('volatility') as sites where the greatest differences between prices are likely to occur. The sad truth is that many traders made 'a killing' from the market collapse. Now that everyone can afford computers capable of risk management, the most advanced computer trading systems rely on their capacity to seek out and seize upon instabilities at speeds faster than their competitors. As the

American anthropologist Arjun Appadurai says, risk 'is simply immeasurable by any quantitative means. This amounts to saying that, in regard to such trades, risk and uncertainty have no practical difference'. Now that risk is a tradable commodity in its own right, any uncertainty about the future, any possibility of its being different, is already calculable in terms set in the present. Even the unknown, reduced to a calculus, has become tradable in forms that never change. There is no future.

Life and Systems Under Erasure

It is then not only that there are causal factors pushing many sectors of the population towards exhaustion, disaffection, alienation, and apathy, but that the one thing that might motivate them, the mere possibility of a condition other than the one we all occupy, has been erased. In the Market perspective, even if we strung up the last capitalist in the entrails of the last oligarch, the system would still prevail, and the planet still spin inexorably towards extinction. There are certainly causal factors arriving from the past to drive people towards apathy, but there is also this blank wall where not even the greed of corporate CEOs is to blame, anger is of no avail, and there is no point wasting energy on a nervous breakdown.

A second technical problem concerns scale. The success of predictive models can be measured by the match between predictions and later measurements, and by the wide credibility of models such as those predicting global climate change, evidenced by their take-up in the logistics, recruitment, and training of emergency services. Even the circumscribed, indefinite future that Bloch appealed to, appears today to evaporate in the face of predictive computing and its orientation towards catastrophe.

Earth systems science presumes that the planet operates like a cybernetic system. Even if this is the case, and even granted the assimilation of complexity into system modelling, the predictive system operates at the planetary scale and pulls back from predicting local events like fires and floods. A local forest fire is strictly unpredictable, to use the vocabulary of systems science, because of the excessive number of variables operating at local scales. Even if the planetary system no longer operates in equilibrium, it evolves in harmony and as a whole; but local events can rapidly become chaotic, for example through spot fires or arson (itself often a symptom of disaffection). The Market as a whole may operate predictably through Kondratieff cycles and evolve through foreseeable trajectories of technological innovation and new financial instruments, but local catastrophes on the scale of the FTX cryptocurrency collapse are strictly unpredictable. Earthquakes and acts of greed are equally unpredictable, even though the former is external to any system and the latter internal.

Emergency services must plan on the basis that local events may be even worse, even sooner. The wealthy plan their survival on the basis that certain locales will offer better chances of living on. The triumph of predictive modelling for risk management – that is, for controlling the future – has now extended to the point that contingent and even random events can be built into predictions. The arrival of unforeseen events can be planned for using advanced computational techniques, and as above, chance occurrences are occasions for profit.

Systems thinking depends on massive data sets – already an issue of scale operating at levels that preclude local access – and on cybernetic models geared, as the word's etymology recalls, towards governing and management. Though systems theory long since gave up on the equilibrium model in favour of turbulence, it remains pledged to subordinating the unforeseen to the regularity and goal-orientation of modelling, which is to say to abstraction, the only way of thinking about very large numbers. There is a similar tendency in ecocritical thinking and in social and political theory more generally. Vogl for example suggests critique should move in the opposite direction from *ressentiment*, advancing from tangible and concrete instances to the conditions of their production: *ressentiment* can only localise abstract processes in particular figures or sites of disgust, envy, and hate. Critique's task is, for him, to advance towards generalisable conditions, causes, and trends in order to conduct analysis and interpretation. We are grateful to the Italian activist and publisher Alessandro Ludovico, for a hard-earned response to this characterisation: it might be good for critique to work from local to universal, but the local is the privileged place where activism counts. Just as now is the only moment for action, here is the only place to act.

There remain two aspects of the scale problem that need further work, critical and practical. The first is the real displacement – physical and spiritual – experienced by migrants, especially those forced to migrate by famine, war, and climate change, whose own place is no longer viable and whose adopted place is not theirs or refuses to accept their actions. A more metaphorical displacement is a common enough experience, especially in big cities. A sense that not only the future but the here-and-now evades our abilities to act for change is another feature of apathetic disaffection. The second problem is that the local is open to action to the degree that it is exceptional when compared to whatever abstract generalisation or statistical averaging is required to make a model work at scale. The exceptional is however exactly where contemporary finance and information capital looks for profit. Worse still, in a phrase the Italian philosopher Giorgio Agamben draws from the Nazi legalist Carl Schmitt, 'sovereign is he who decides the exception'. The implication is that every exception is exceptional only because it is in some way permitted or actively constructed in the process of rule. This creates a further paradox or closed loop, addressed by American anthropologists Erica Robles-Anderson and Arjun Appadurai when they discuss the need 'to think about the unthinkable, whose brutalised form is the exception and whose routine form is the future itself.' All too often, to be exceptional is to be marked for punishment, while the potential exceptions of the future become matters for routine management. So, the challenge for apathy is not just that problems are too big: it is that when addressed at scales that do allow for action, action becomes either exploitable or punishable or both.

One social problem for the success of predictive modelling is that it can abolish hope, contributing to apathy. Doomscrolling, a resonant description of screen-based 'leisure time' today, links our scrollable devices to unremitting bleakness of current news and predictions – suggesting a certain numb coasting. Why bother, when either the world climate is on track for Armageddon or there can be no future distinct from the present. We face a gamble reminiscent of the French philosopher Blaise Pascal's wager: either God exists, or He doesn't. If you bet that He does, you have a 50 percent chance of salvation. If you gamble that He doesn't, your chance of salvation is nil. We know if we gamble on continuing the same trajectory we are on now, within fifty years the planet will be uninhabitable, or so depleted that inhabiting it will bring no joy whatever. So, the smart bet is the one that looks riskiest: change.

Alienare

It may be that the distinction between two words, both translated in Marx's *Economic and Philosophical Manuscripts* of 1844 as 'alienation' can help understand the stakes in Pascal's wager. American philosopher Amy E Wendling tells us to distinguish Hegel's term *Entäusserung* (alienation, but with a shading from Luther's translation of the biblical term *kenoisis* used to describe the 'self-emptying' or 'renunciation' Christ undertook in becoming human) from Marx's term *Entfremdung* (estrangement). Both words occur in Marx's writing, as in this passage from the section on alienated labour in the 1844 *Manuscripts*:

> labour's realisation is its objectification. In the conditions dealt with by political economy, this realisation of labour appears as loss of reality for the workers; objectification as loss of the object and object-bondage, appropriation as estrangement [*Entfremdung*], as alienation [*Entäusserung*].

Wendling's point is that the immense influence of these pages on estranged (*entfremdet*) labour, translated as 'alienated labour', has shaped a discourse on alienation that misses the redemptory potential locked up in the older, Lutheran *Entäusserung*.

The significance for our discussion of apathy arises not from Marx's initial description of capitalist production processes but from his observation of one of its consequences. When capital 'realises' labour, it forces it to confront not only the tools that discipline it but the objects it produces as objects, even foreign (*fremd*) entities, that confront the human worker only as property of the boss. 'The estrangement of the object of labour merely summarises the estrangement, the alienation in the activity of labour itself,' writes Marx. Estrangement places the worker over and against both the tools and the products of labour, not just as objects but as enemies. The very act of production in capitalism (where a worker is constrained to work for someone else) produces alienation. The worker then becomes estranged from every reality that has become property of the boss, and as a result from everything that, for the young Marx, made humans human, leaving only the 'animal functions' of 'eating, drinking and procreating'. This retreat into basic bodily pleasures – Berlant's slow death – this lack of engagement in creative work or cultural and political engagement is what we have been calling apathy. Wendling argues that because such interpretations of the *Manuscripts* have the Hegelian concept of alienation as a passage through the lowly towards an overcoming of it (*Aufhebung*), they fail to observe the positive prospect of apathy as a passive reaction to hyperactive capitalism that nonetheless contains the germs of a new beginning. The wager here is that apathy is a form of reclusion, withdrawal or, per Berlant, lateral agency. The opposite of apathy today is no longer fanaticism or enthusiasm but the dogged insistence on the responsibility to act rather than not-act.

If Neumann suggests alienated withdrawal from politics precedes authoritarian power, what are the dangers of mass powerlessness and inaction? In 1937, the German psychoanalyst Erich Fromm wrote 'On the Feeling of Powerlessness', grappling with the two-sided nature of the 'bourgeois character'. On the one side, the bourgeois character is always at work in its 'environment, consciously shaping and changing it', while on the other, this character feels alienated from its own creations. Capturing this deadlock, Fromm writes:

> in light of the tremendous possibilities for human happiness and security achieved through industrial development, historians may … ponder the question as to how the great majority reconciled themselves to inaction, and to passively watching the haphazard and helpless coming and going of crises and subsequent short periods of prosperity as if it was the work of unfathomable forces of fate.

How different do the citizens of the wealthy West – bourgeois characters with declining real incomes – feel today? Alienation is undoubtedly rife today. In this work derived from his therapeutic experiences, Fromm suggests powerlessness is manifold and, much like Marx's 'alienation', is experienced regarding people, things, oneself, and situations, with varying levels of intensity and awareness. Yet he also notes that people may rationalise and form reactions to this feeling, leading to rage, defiance, anxiety, and passivity. His essay, originally published in 1937 in the wake of Hitler's rise to power, ends with a portentous comment that 'the helplessness of the individual is the basic theme of authoritarian philosophy'.

THE SEVEN

Gwen Adshead

In reflecting on the nature of evil, I find two different kinds of lens particularly helpful. First, to view evil through concepts of mental disorder, as commonly used in Anglophone European psychiatry. Second, as viewed through a traditional account of harmful thought patterns in Christianity, colloquially known as 'The seven deadly sins'. I am a therapist who works with violence perpetrators in prisons and secure hospitals, so I have spent many hours talking to people who are sometimes described as 'evil'. What I want to explore here is how the concept of the seven deadly sins (here abbreviated as The Seven) might fit with contemporary psychiatric ideas about evil.

My starting premise is that evil is not a 'thing' or an external force in the world, but a psychosocial problem that begins with an individual state of mind. This is a state of mind which every single person can be in, just as every person has the capacity to be in fruitful and beneficent states of mind. I think it is also noteworthy that evil is a performative word in the sense that those who use it are making a powerful statement for a social audience. When people use this word, they are not only saying something about the state of mind of the perpetrator and their intentions, they are also making a kind of totalising comment about the perpetrator as a whole, and where the perpetrator stands in relationship to the communities they come from.

This totalising aspect is reflected in the assumption and attitude that humans who once do evil are now and forever perpetually in that state of mind: 'once evil, always evil' seems to be the message, as though a human could not be 'somewhat' evil or only 'evil' at a certain time. In terms of relationships with communities of other humans, the use of the word 'evil' often denotes someone who is now excluded from those communities by reason of their choices and actions. Humans who do horrible things to others are often described as 'inhuman', and then attract news media titles involving the word 'beast', and this kind of language conveys a sense that this offender has now lost their status as a human being and is also deprived of ordinary social rights or duties.

Defining Evil

I suggest that for someone (or their actions) to be designated as 'evil', a number of key features must be present. First, what has happened or what this person has done must have affected other people in ways that caused those victims *excessive* suffering, harm, damage, and denigration; that goes beyond the 'very bad' or disgusting. Even severe injury is not enough: for example, criminal judges at sentencing do not typically or always identify all perpetrators of bodily assaults as 'evil', although this language is open to them. This exceptionalism of evil is what gives it the degree of social power and significance noted above.

Second, an 'evil' act must be planned and intentional: there is no such thing as 'accidental' evil. This is to distinguish it from acts of violence which are impulsively driven by high levels of painful emotions, such as fear, pain or distress. Relatedly, this intentional aspect of 'evil' makes it a uniquely human feature: natural disasters that cause massive suffering and death are not evil because they are not intended, and animals who cause suffering to humans are not identified as 'evil' because they lack intention. This stance is potentially confusing however because of the labelling of humans who cause evil as 'animals' (or 'beasts', *vide supra*); however, the use of the word 'animal' in this context is really denoting a change in social status as a human, and the loss of associated rights, as opposed to actually identifying the perpetrator as an animal who damages without intention.

Third, the perpetrator of evil must intend to prolong any suffering caused and actively seek to extend and exacerbate it. What is 'evil' about this process is the sustained and intentional dehumanisation of the victims combined with exploitation and denigration of their vulnerability. In an evil state of mind, the perpetrator wants to communicate to the victim an experience of being worthless, powerless and helpless; that the perpetrator has full control and they have none, and *because of that lack of agency*, the victims deserve their suffering. It is clear from accounts of the Nazi policy of persecution that this kind of dehumanisation of the victims was also key to Nazi policies of extermination and also became a justification for killing them. The English historian Michael Burleigh shows how the psychosocial elements of the 'Final Solution', set out in 1941, were actually rehearsed in an earlier Nazi policy of killing people who were deemed mentally unfit to be 'worthy of life'. Denigration of human dependence or need and exploitation of vulnerability are therefore key features of the evil state of mind, and potentially maintain that state of mind, whether at the level of the individual or the group.

Finally, and relatedly, evil is associated with a state of mind in which victims are reduced to things and objects to be owned. It is this factor that makes slavery and slave owners perpetrators of evil, whether they actively treated slaves badly or not on a day-to-day basis. The idea of reducing a person to 'thing-ness' is significant because it adds another level of dehumanisation. In psychological terms treating a person as a 'thing' also encourages people to assume that they can treat 'their' things in any way they wish. But as the English scholar and Christian writer C.S. Lewis suggested in his 1942 book *The Screwtape Letters*, there are moral objections to this idea: possession of anything does not automatically confer a right to maim or destroy it, especially if that might cause harm. An 'evil' interpretation of the word 'mine' supports a relationship of abuse, defilement, and fracturing suffused with cruelty and hostility.

The evil state of mind may be associated with a brief experience of triumph and excitement. However, in general, this is short-lived and so for some individuals and groups, the evil state of mind may become addictive so that perpetrators may actively seek that 'high' they felt before. It is important to note the absence of pleasure or joy here; rather there is craving and compulsion which are both psychological features of addiction. Addiction and the evil state of mind also have in common that they involve preoccupation with possession and agency; addicts are often preoccupied with getting and possessing the drug they crave, which may be why it is not unusual for people to commit acts of evil while heavily addicted to substances.

Psychiatry and Legal Responses to Extreme Violence

Traditionally, the evil state of mind is not one that is experienced by the perpetrator as uncomfortable or disturbing. It is unusual for someone to visit a doctor to say, 'I feel evil today; can you help me?'. It can sometimes happen that individuals actively seek help because they are worried by thoughts and fantasies they consider evil, and actively seek *not* to act on them. The legal process traditionally also seeks to distinguish evil states of mind from mentally disordered states of mind; which is why many psychiatrists are often asked to evaluate defendants charged with unusually dreadful violence. In the US, forensic psychiatrist Michael Welner has attempted to assist the courts by devising a Depravity Scale or Standard, which include many of the features described above. Its value lies in helping judges distinguish evil from states of mind that should be assessed by a psychiatrist, which is a complex task and not always obvious.

A recent example demonstrates the complexity and limited role of psychiatry in distinguishing evil from mental disorder. A man in England has recently been convicted of murdering his wife and daughter. The defendant represented himself at the trial and pleaded not guilty to murder; he argued that his life was ended when his wife told him she was leaving him for another man. He told the court that it was 'logical' for him to kill his wife and their twelve-year-old daughter, who was, in any event, his 'property' to do with as he liked. He was psychiatrically examined but the psychiatrists did not make any kind of diagnosis of mental disorder. Despite the fact that what he did was highly unusual as well as dreadful, neither its rarity nor its horror makes it evidence of mental disorder. This is the kind of case in which a judge passing sentence might use the word 'evil', although many might wonder if this man could truly be said to be mentally 'well'.

The relationship between law and psychiatry is closely related to evidence about the relationship between mental illness and violence. It took hundreds of years, and relatively recent empirical study, to finally establish that most people with severe mental illness pose no risk of harm to anybody but themselves. However, in the nineteenth century, lawyers in Europe and the US began to explore the extent to which mental illness might affect criminal responsibility for violence to others. Laws emerged all over the US and Europe which articulated the Aristotelian idea that a person could not be responsible for something that they were compelled to do. If mental illness could, as it were, 'compel' someone to act, that person might lack the capacity to form a harmful intention which truly reflected their ordinary agency.

Psychiatrists began to appear as experts in murder trials in the late nineteenth century to explain to juries how symptoms of mental disorders might 'compel' a person to kill, thereby mitigating their criminal responsibility and reducing the degree to which they were objects of public/legal condemnation. If successfully argued, the law allowed for someone to be found 'not guilty by reason of insanity', and therefore innocent of any crime; although laws were also passed to ensure that they could be detained indefinitely to prevent harm to others.

Later laws recognised that there might be a spectrum of criminal responsibility for violent actions, including homicide, and that mental illness might 'impair' responsibility rather than abolish it. Many countries, including the UK and some US states and European countries recognise a sliding scale of criminal responsibility which allows for a variety of judicial responses at sentencing. For example, in England and Wales, the court may find that an offender had 'diminished responsibility' at the time of a homicide, but might still be sufficiently blameworthy to be sent to prison for an extended period. Alternatively, the accused might be so obviously unwell at the time of the offence that it would be more just to send them to a secure psychiatric hospital for treatment than to send them to prison.

Research in the 1990s provided evidence for a more nuanced understanding of the relationship between disordered mental states and violence. As described above, not everyone who commits an act of violence is in an evil state of mind: for example, many people who kill have never been violent before, and often kill in a highly emotional state of mind, which is a function of the relationship between them and the victim. They do not plan to kill or extend the victim's suffering and are often highly remorseful thereafter. These people may be said to be distressed and disturbed but not mentally disordered, and they are not typically deemed to be 'evil'.

If a person is found to be mentally ill at the time of their offence, this mitigates their responsibility and blameworthiness; such that they would not usually be seen as in an 'evil' state of mind. To put it in colloquial English, most people who get sent to secure psychiatric hospitals are deemed 'mad and/or sad', but they are rarely 'bad'. Studies of childhood trauma in violent perpetrators have shown that there is a real, albeit complex, relationship between childhood victimisation and later violence.

Studies in both the US and the UK have found very high levels of childhood adversity in prisoners who have committed severely violent crime; in the UK study, only 20 percent of prisoners had not experienced childhood adversity, and in the US study, no prisoners had escaped such trauma.

There are some *symptoms* of mental illness that do increase the risk of violence; especially disturbance of reality testing due to intoxication (due to a range of substances), and other symptoms associated with intoxication such as high levels of agitation, hyper arousal, and paranoia. 80 percent of perpetrators of violence are intoxicated at the material time, and concurrent paranoia (whether from mental illness or drug use or both) only increases the risk. Essentially, any kind of situation which distorts or disorganises an individual's capacity to perceive and test social reality, and which causes excessive levels of fear, is a situation where the risk of violence is high.

However, strange and terrible ways of killing people or causing suffering may not necessarily indicate a disordered state of mind nor general risk of violence to others. In another recent news report, an elderly man confessed that during WWII, he was a member of a resistance group in Europe, who murdered a group of German POWs. They made these helpless vulnerable men dig their own graves before they killed them. This would seem, on the face of it, to be an act of evil; planned, intended, not driven by passions, and exploiting the vulnerability of the victims. Nevertheless, there is no suggestion that the resistance fighters were mentally ill, and there might be some resistance in some minds to calling their act 'evil', given the social context.

Psychopathy and Evil

There is one psychological disorder which has often been linked with 'evil' states of mind, namely 'psychopathy'. This term emerged in the early twentieth century to describe people who did not seem to care about breaking social rules or causing distress to others. The first account of psychopathy however did not include any descriptions of serious violence or physical cruelty. Rather, 'psychopaths' in this study, conducted by the American psychologist Hervey Cleckley, were people who did not 'see' or recognise other people's distress, and if they did show concern, it was short-lived and shallow. Deception and general social unreliability were also noteworthy features of these people; but Cleckley did not use the word 'evil' to describe his subjects. He argued that they must have brain dysfunction which led to them lacking an emotional capacity for awareness of others' feelings that is crucial to social relationships.

The Canadian psychologist, Robert Hare applied Cleckley's concepts of psychopathy to prisoners actually convicted of crimes involving serious violence and cruelty to others. He developed a 'checklist' of features of psychopathy. He found that about a third of prisoners serving time for violence scored highly on this checklist. The higher their score, the more likely they were to have been extremely violent; and some later studies suggested that high scores on the checklist were associated with increased risk of violence in the future. Unlike Cleckley's account, previous criminality and violence is a key feature of Hare's account of psychopathy, which is now widely used in the assessments of violence perpetrators. But even Hare's account of psychopathy is not a measure of evil in any sense; not least because it is possible to commit an offence that looks 'evil' and not score highly on the checklist.

The study of psychopathy is an active one, and there are continuing debates about its nature and definition. That there are such debates indicates that the concept of evil may have different psychological and social constructions which are used in different ways in different contexts. There has been a long-standing concern that in relation to individual acts of violence, psychopathy is a concept which risks circular argument, i.e. the violence indicates psychopathy, which is then used to explain the violence. This is exemplified in a recent case in the English criminal courts. A woman tormented and killed a five-year-old boy who was the son of her then partner; the father and son had moved in with her and her children during the pandemic. She had not known the child long at the time of the killing. While she was abusing him brutally, she was caring for her own children (aged six and four), in an ordinary way. She claimed that he was 'naughty' and she was 'disciplining' him. Only two years earlier, she had made a serious suicide attempt, and there was professional concern about her mental state because she was the mother of two small children. But nothing about her story or presentation *before* the killing would have led anyone to label her as either psychopathic or 'evil': it is only *after* her offence that the label is of psychopathy or evil is invoked to explain the killing which gave rise to the use of those terms in the first place.

Most clinicians working in prisons or secure psychiatric settings do not have much use for the concept of 'evil', even when some of the features described above are present. This is because there are usually too many other variables to consider, such as histories of mental distress, addiction histories, poverty, social stress, and unresolved trauma. In time past, the concept of 'evil' was more likely to be applied to social and political atrocities such as the Nazi policies of extermination of different groups of people and similar subsequent genocides in Cambodia and Russia. All the mental health professionals who assessed the Nuremberg defendants found that they were essentially mentally well, albeit they also used the concept of 'psychopathy' to explain their crimes.

The Seven Deadly Sins

In the Christian tradition, the Desert Fathers Evagrius Ponticus and his disciple John Cassian developed an account of nine different kinds of disturbing thought pattern which could damage the ordinary human appetites and emotions. The Evagrian account of nine kinds of harmful thought became in time the 'Seven Deadly Sins' attributed to Pope Gregory in 590, who later dropped both 'despair' and 'boasting' from the original list.

Attention to the 'deadly sins' formed part of catholic confessional practice and tradition, but only the Catholic tradition still encourages discussion and reflection on them. The Seven are deemed 'deadly' because of their effect on an individual's relationships with other people and with God, who is ultimate goodness. People who regularly engage in this kind of thinking become cut off from other humans as well as from God in a way that deemed to lead to spiritual and psychological 'death' in terms of an absence of liveliness, pleasure, enjoyment of others, and creativity. A further reflection on the deadly sins reveals possible connections between Pope Gregory's account of the Seven, and more recent research into the psychological traits and states of mind that make cruelty and violence possible.

Pride

Traditionally pride and avarice have been seen as the deadliest of the Seven; chiefly because of their effects on relationships with other people. In this sense, the word 'pride' is distinct from having self-respect and enjoyment of one's identity in a way which encourages the growth of community bonds as well as personal achievements. Humans are group animals insofar as we share 98 percent of our DNA with other social primates; so, it is essential that humans can maintain both an individual personal identity and a relational identity within a group. To do this successfully, persons have to be able to flexibly manage a kind of figure-ground dynamic in which individuals can step up and assert their own values and beliefs as important but can also step back to be let others' views and values be respected for the good of the group as a whole and be part of consensus building within that group in a cooperative manner. Key to managing this figure-ground dynamic of competition and cooperation is the capacity to mentalise other minds; to be able to understand that others have minds like one's own, and can form ideas and intentions, even if they are hard to 'read'.

C.S. Lewis argues for pride being the deadliest of the Seven, because it leads to serious distortion and misunderstanding of oneself in relation to other people and to goodness. Lewis observes that 'if one is looking down on others all the time, then it is impossible to look up towards God'. We could expand further on Lewis's view, by noting that if you only admire yourself, and cannot admire other people, then it is impossible to change or develop your personality across the life span of relationships with others. But human beings have to live in different kinds of relational groups across the life span, so some degree of interpersonal flexibility is essential to both individual and relational wellbeing, and good mental and physical health.

Pride is thus deadly because it encourages a kind of complacency about disconnection from others, so the individual becomes further mistaken about their social situation and social capital with others. Looking down on others is also bound to encourage states of mind in which one denigrates others which further exacerbates a sense of separation. In the context of evil states of mind, pride is therefore deadly because it encourages a false sense of superiority of self and inferiority of others, which can lead to a kind of sense of entitlement that facilitates dehumanisation and denigration of others deemed to be inferior or unworthy. Psychologically 'pride' in this context resembles the psychological concept of 'narcissism'. This is a complex concept in psychology because it includes a broad spectrum of psychological experience; from a normal developmental phase of self-preoccupation and self-belief at one end to extremes of pathological narcissism at the other. Some degree of self-belief and confidence in the face of adversity may well be useful in some situations; but a grandiose assumption of superiority and disdain for others is not.

Pathological narcissism is often found in offenders who score highly on Hare's psychopathy checklist, and it may be a risk factor for the kinds of violence we call evil, because it enables denigration and contempt for vulnerability. The link between pathological narcissism and psychopathy may be mediated by the way such individuals reason morally about how ethical dilemmas are resolved. They may favour crude consequentialist reasoning, whereby the ends justify the means, and they may favour rights-based discourse in terms of personal entitlement, as opposed to duties-based discourse which is essentially relational.

Narcissism is also a complex concept because although grandiosity is its most obvious manifestation, most psychological research in this area suggests that grandiosity may oscillate with extreme sensitivity to shame, especially in relation to loss of status. American psychiatrist James Gilligan has argued that shame is a potent driver for violence in men whose sense of self is fragile. For many people who appear narcissistically grandiose, their pride is a defence against an intense sense of shame, which could lead to violent action, whether against the self or others. Those who seem to have a narcissistic aspect to their personality may also be at increased risk of suicide if they lose someone or something they value, or if they feel belittled in some way. An exquisite sensitivity to social status and to how one 'appears' in the social domain is a notable aspect of narcissistic personality disorder and mirrors the 'deadly' aspect of pride discussed above.

In summary, pride as a deadly sin has much in common with pathological narcissism, which is often found in individuals who have acted cruelly to others, or talk enthusiastically of doing so. Although some degree of narcissism is probably found in everyone, it is a trait that may wax and wane in strength depending on other events and relationships in our lives; and may cause problems thereby. In the pathologically narcissistic state of mind, only the self exists, and everyone else is hardly real.

Avarice

Avarice, reflecting human greed, also reflects a kind of excessive attachment to objects, possessions, and money. There is something in the concept of avarice which involves both a sense of deprivation and a grasping attitude to the possession of things that one desires, so that they must be grabbed and held onto often in coercive ways. Although most of the writings on avarice have focused on the desire and grabbing for money, and the things that money can buy, it is also possible to have an avaricious approach to other people which then sees other people as property or possessions or as things to be exploited and used.

Such an attitude of possession and seeing others only as potentially useful or exploitable clearly has something in common with both the deadly sin of pride and the concept of evil. Again, we see the absence of relational identity and the dominance of individual desires for objects to the exclusion of other values. If you are in a state of mind in which you see people simply as your property to be done with as you choose, then there is a good chance that you will be happy to treat other people badly. Avarice is a state of mind described by Oscar Wilde as one in which a person 'knows the price of everything, but the value of nothing'.

One of the earliest warnings against this state of mind is found in Buddhist teaching that excessive desire or grasping after things or people can cause great suffering. It is therefore beneficial to practice or cultivate a capacity to notice and then let go of such desires, because they hinder the capacity for compassion and loving kindness towards others. Many writers on addiction have linked the recovery from addiction with the Buddhist teaching on letting go of the kind of grasping state of mind that is characteristic of avarice; and other faith traditions have also warned against the dangers of avarice in terms of individual suffering.

In psychological terms, the state of avarice resembles accounts of compulsive thoughts and behaviours which can impair social relating and both physical and mental health. The concept of addiction can be applied to a variety of human appetites that get out of control: whether it is excessive food intake, compulsive starvation, hoarding, or use of pornography. A contemporary psychological approach to avarice would argue that it is a defence against feelings of scarcity and emptiness. Avaricious behaviours help the individual maintain a sense of psychological security. It is a kind of self-deception that all is well.

Historically, avarice has been a powerful driver for crimes involving theft and fraud, and alone, it is a state of mind that is not inevitably linked with violence. Yet the concept of avarice has much in common with pride in that others can be exploited or used for what they have. For many violence perpetrators, their wants and wishes are the only thing that matter. It is hard to tell when normal desire or longing becomes a kind of compulsion that forms the basis of a self-justificatory narrative for violence. This is beautifully told by JRR Tolkien in the story of Gollum and his 'precious'. The wanting of something can become a distorted belief that it should be mine, is really mine, and that I must do what I need to ensure my possession of it. Human greed is rigid in its addictive quality, and as we have seen above, addictions and substance misuse are a common feature of severe and disturbing violence to others.

Lust

Lust is the deadly sin which is normally discussed in the concept of excessive or aberrant sexual desires. However, lust arguably has much in common with avarice and pride insofar as the lustful state of mind sees others' bodies as a means to an end; whether carnal or psychological. Traditionally, lust is seen as a state of mind which does not reflect a healthy desire for the other, and their pleasure; but instead is a preoccupation with possession of another person's body, and/or the satiation of an appetite (much like avarice).

Optimal sexual relationships are other related. Tender and creative, they are a form of communication in which the body is the speaker. In contrast, in a state of lust, the individual is saying 'I want this and I want this now, and I do not care what you think about it'. Lust is a *carnal* state of mind; it is the opposite of a mentalising or relational state of mind, and therefore it is a mental state which increases the risk that other people will be used 'carnally' – treated like meat. Here is Shakespeare on this very point (emphasis added):

> Thou rascal beadle, hold thy bloody hand!
> Why dost thou lash that whore? Strip thine own back,
> Thou hotly lust'st *to use her* in that kind
> For which though whippst her'

King Lear, IV, vi

We may note also that Shakespeare is also drawing our attention to the excitement that the punisher has in causing suffering to another and how that excitement is lust-like in its carnal exploitation of a person's vulnerable body. The distinction between sexual and carnal is most obvious in relation to the offence of rape. Although classified as a 'sexual' offence, victims do not have a *sexual* experience but a *violent* experience; and many perpetrators are actually unable to perform sexually during the act.

In psychological terms, some therapists conceive of lust in terms of 'sex addiction', although 'sex' in terms of Eros and sensuality is absent from the lustful state of mind. What lust has in common with addiction is the compulsion to satisfy one's own desires, whatever the cost, and the *absence* of a relational state of mind. Lust and avarice have obvious commonalities. These are found most obviously in the pornography industry which has vastly expanded since the development of the Internet. The pornography industry is based on the production of carnal images of people being used, shamed, and denigrated on a regular basis. Typically, the people who are being used and denigrated carnally are vulnerable people such as children.

In a fascinating essay, American writer David Foster Wallace describes attending a convention about pornographic media, where he noted how shaming and degrading others is central to pornography and the enjoyment of those who use it. Pornography exists to satisfy the lustful state of mind, in which there is rarely any pleasure associated with mutuality. Rather, the excitement comes from exploitation of others; and the dirtier and more shameful, the more likely the thrill. This product is being made to satisfy the lusts of millions of people worldwide. It is a massive industry which hides behind the idea that 'lust' is a normal manifestation of desire for humans – especially men.

Gluttony

Gluttony has traditionally been associated with excessive intake of food; and has a particular significance in this twenty-first century when so many people are now pathologically overweight, and when obesity has a direct relationship with poverty and risk of long-term ill-health, both physically and mentally. Like the other deadly sins, gluttony is a disturbance not only of appetite but of focus and attention. It can be characterised as an excessive attentiveness towards getting the right kind of food, the most fashionable food, or exactly the right amount of food. Gluttony also has something in common with lust insofar as a person can treat their body as an object of abuse to satiate an appetite.

The point about gluttony is its preoccupation with food or drink and associated addictive qualities, rather than a concern about eating food itself. Again, Lewis makes this point in his example of a woman who sends her food back in restaurants repeatedly or stresses other people out with her demands for her food to be perfect or just as she likes it. The individual who says that they can 'only eat in five-star restaurants' is exhibiting a kind of gluttony, even if they only eat a very small amount. In psychological terms, anorexia nervosa is a form of gluttony, even though it involves self-deprivation of food.

Gluttony, therefore, has something in common with pride in that it is a focus on the specialness of individual wishes and desires to the exclusion of other concerns, and is also a kind of avarice in the sense of grasping after food. Gluttony is also clearly related to addiction and loss of control over appetites; an alcoholic is a 'glutton' for alcohol as is any kind of drug addict.

One of the burdens of addiction is the constant preoccupation with the getting or not getting one's substance of choice. It is intriguing that many prisoners often suffer from degrees of eating disorder, whether obesity or anorexia; this is particularly noticeable in female prisoners, whereas male prisoners may spend a lot of time building up their bodies in the gym. Psychologically, food (like money) can stand for care and comfort that was not offered to a needy child by adults, so that in adulthood those same children attempt to control any psychological pain by excessive use of food. Disturbances of appetite are common when people are sad, anxious, angry, or fearful; and gluttony may well be best understood as a defence against a fear of loss of control.

Envy

Envy is one of the most complex of human emotions. Although often associated with jealousy, envy is different in important ways. Both have in common an attachment to something or someone of value, and an anxiety or fear of loss or deprivation of the valued person or object. Both are relational emotions, but jealousy involves a fear of loss of attachment, and an anxiety about sharing with others; it is not uncommon for new fathers to be jealous of their babies, or older siblings to be jealous of sharing parental attachments. Even old friends can be jealous of new attachments, especially in the teenage years. Jealousy can be dangerous (especially if pathological as in Shakespeare's *Othello*) but it can usually be managed by most people and it tends to recede with time.

Envy is also relational, but the relationship is generally one of status and achievement, especially in groups. The envious person is anxious about comparing, not sharing; especially comparing how they are perceived and ranked in relation to others. In an envious state of mind, you perceive that someone inferior to you has been admired or given something that you should have, *and they should not*. Competition is key to the envious state of mind – especially successful competition that confirms the individual's sense of being special and recognised as such.

The idea of pleasure in someone else's success is impossible in the envious state of mind.

The envious person not only resents that someone else has done well or been applauded, they seek to spoil that person's pleasure in their success and even destroy it completely. In the envious state of mind, there are rigid conceptions of success and failure, whereby someone else's success is a kind of insult to oneself. This envy can be a powerful source of hostile resentment; especially if there is some real conflict in the relationships between the envious and the envied.

Psychologically, envy has much in common with narcissism as described above in relation to pride, and therefore it is also a state of mind in which feelings of shame and deprivation are strong. It is a moot point whether envy is always destructive, but the risk of cruelty is undoubtedly increased in individuals with pathological levels of narcissism in their personality make up. It is not unusual for envy to drive people to speak spitefully of others' success or achievements, but really malignant forms of envy can lead people to act destructively, including fatal violence. In the homicide case described above, the man who killed his family appears to have taken the view that if he couldn't have the life he wanted on his terms, then neither should they. Such a world view is thankfully rare, but terrible when enacted.

It is arguable that envy, avarice, and pride are overlapping states of mind, which relate in some sense to our identities as group animals who must share, compare, and conflict at times. They reflect what happens if personal, individual identity excludes any sense of social identity; as if there is only 'I' not 'we'. Such a state of mind can respond with ferocious hostility in response to any sense of rejection, grievance, or exclusion and can lead to fatal violence towards self as well as others.

Sloth

Although sloth is named as one of the Seven, there may be something lost in translation. In the original sense as described by Pope Gregory, sloth here is not merely laziness or sleepiness or acting slowly. The original word was '*acedia*', which is more like 'boredom' with an element of passive hostility and indifference. In this state of mind, a person can't be bothered to engage with others or issues or even life itself. They may claim that such stuff is pointless and futile. Sloth in this sense also includes a tendency to passive hostility towards others' enjoyment and flippancy about attempts to do good or create beauty.

As we have seen, the deadly sins do not sit neatly in separate categories, and sloth may be a manifestation of envy or pride. Although sloth does not have an obvious parallel with any psychiatric disorder, lack of engagement with the social world can foster a sense of self whereby others do not seem real, which in turn fosters envy and pride. It may be that 'despair' was dropped from the original list of nine deadly sins, because it is an aspect of 'sloth'; and despair can indeed be deadly, for example in the minds of those who are depressed or in pain. It may be that the 'deadliness' of sloth lies in its capacity to drain joy and liveliness out of human experience, and so allow other evil states of mind to proliferate. It is also the case that opiate and alcohol addictions result in the kind of sloth that leads to despair and increased risk of suicide.

Anger

Anger is an emotion that humans share with many other mammals, especially group animals, and it is also a state of mind which has long been recognised as being dangerous. Pre-classical, classical, and Judeo-Christian texts warn of the dangers of unregulated anger, especially of being angry with the wrong person at the wrong time and in the wrong way. Anger's obvious 'deadliness' lies in its potential to be acted out on another person, causing massive harm.

Contemporary psychological accounts of anger note that it can be a response to pain (whether physical or psychological), and that it can also be a response to fear, especially fear of loss of something or someone. Anger is a common emotion in response to bereavement and to hearing that one has a life-threatening illness. Arguably, this kind of defensive anger is not what was identified as 'deadly'. Rather, anger becomes deadly when it becomes focussed on another person as an object of hatred or resentment. Therefore, anger may be most risky when it is combined with other deadly states of mind, like envy, pride, and avarice.

Psychologically speaking, anger is perhaps less a deadly state of mind but an emotional energy that needs to be understood, managed, reflected on, and attended to with compassion. It may be the only one of the Seven to have a healthy aspect in certain circumstances, and it may also be the only one that need not take over and dominate the identity, making other relationships impossible. It is relevant here to note that it is possible to teach people to understand and manage their anger better, using psychological programmes which are proved to be effective. It is also noteworthy, in terms of mental health, that many people turn their anger inwards towards themselves in the form of hostile self-criticism. This process may be a significant risk factor for a range of mood problems and also psychosomatic disorders.

Conclusion

The Seven Deadly Sins have much in common with those states of mind and personality dysfunctions which are also associated with the commission of violence and cruelty. Rather than seeing the Seven as something that people may or may not do, it makes more sense to see them as states of mind which afflict everyone, and which therefore make evil possible for everyone. Pride, envy, avarice, and anger easily come together to form a state of mind where only the individual matters, and where others are merely means to an end or an object to be used. In this state of mind, people may also denigrate neediness and vulnerability, and have contempt for anything that looks like tenderness or compassion. Whether at the level of the group or the individual, this is the kind of mental state we can accurately describe as 'evil'.

I wonder if the public fascination with true crime and 'evil' persists because people are aware that anyone of us in the right circumstances could be in an evil state of mind. I perceive a tension here between attempts to explain evil as mental 'sickness' or damage; and a mythology that there are 'monsters' out there who are very scary but also rather exciting, because they are essentially normal. Many discussions of psychopathy show this tension, even in academic journals, which may describe both real people and imaginary people, such as James Bond or Sherlock Holmes. There is even a study which suggests that many famous people in history score highly on a measure of psychopathy including leaders, prime ministers, and military heroes.

The Seven provide us with a useful way of thinking about how and why people let themselves be cruel to others. The fact that they are ancient and/or couched in old-fashioned language does not make them untrue or irrelevant and, in fact, makes it more likely that they are phenomenologically accurate. Such accuracy is essential when formulating risky states of mind, and can ensure that some aspects of risk are not overlooked. It also gives us a deeper way to think about disorders of personality and identity; and how therapy could help change minds for the better.

Perhaps what is most notable about the Seven deadly sins is what they have to say about the relational mind; and how crucial it is for social health and community well-being that individuals have healthy relationships with other people. It is said that there is no health without mental health, but attention to the Seven provides evidence that there can be no individual mental health without an equally healthy social self. We ignore our identity as social animals at our peril, especially when the evils of avarice, pride, and envy can be more deadly at the level of the social than any individual. Humans do terrible things to each other in evil states of mind, but they may do even more deadly things to the planet and to human communities.

GRINDING MILLS OF EVIL

Zaina Erhaim

The ninth of June, 2023, and I'm in London. Ten urgent notifications hit my WhatsApp. A friend, a father of a three-year-old girl, shares the breaking news – 'Four Toddlers Stabbed in a Playground in France.' The headline is quickly followed by anxious consecutive messages: 'Can you believe this? Toddlers?', 'Among them is a kid younger than my daughter!', 'This is the ultimate evil. May he suffer for the rest of his life for this!', 'Oh, he is Syrian too! God damn it!', 'And an asylum seeker!'

I wrote back: 'God only knows what drove him to this evil action. He might have seen his kids slaughtered in Houla, or they might have suffocated to death on sarin gas in the Ghouta. They could also have drowned and turned blue while holding his hand on their way to Europe.'

I appeared to shock my friend, as he kept typing and deleting. Then he ended our conversation by writing, 'We live in an evil world.'

It turned out that the attacker, Abdalmasih Hanon, thirty-one years old, hadn't witnessed any of the events I cited. He had in fact worked for the regime which perpetrated the Houla and Ghouta massacres. He also has a child of the same age as those he attacked, and in the last ten years he had applied for asylum in four countries. His role had shifted from armed oppressor to homeless refugee, and then apparently to child murderer. Was Abdalmasih Hanon the only evildoer in this story? But first, what is meant by 'evil'?

For the political philosopher Hannah Arendt, radical evil involves making human beings superfluous as human beings. This is accomplished when human beings are made into living corpses who lack any spontaneity or freedom. According to Arendt, a distinctive feature of radical evil is that it isn't done for humanly understandable motives such as self-interest, but merely to reinforce totalitarian control. So is totalitarianism the source of evil? Thirty-two years ago I was taught that totalitarianism was the righteous norm while everything else was wrong and evil.

*

Idlib city, northern Syria, September 1991. It was my first day at school. I wore my beige uniform with the Communist-inspired scarf and hat. For the first grade, the triangle scarf is orange, the same as the hat, and bears the symbol of the Ba'ath Vanguards Organisation, the children's section of the Arab Socialist Ba'ath Party which has dominated Syria since March 1963. The orange set is used until we reach the fourth grade when it's replaced by a dark blue one that has a white line on the side. The line becomes green in the fifth grade and red in the sixth before we reach secondary school and change into a full military khaki suit and hat.

But let's return to my first day as a *tale'a* (a young Ba'athi girl of the Vanguard). I was automatically enrolled in the organisation as soon as I entered the school door. The Ba'ath Vanguards Organisation was established in Syria in 1974 by decree of the Regional Command of the Arab Socialist Ba'ath Party — Syria Region, we were told. The daily indoctrination ritual in the school yard started with us standing in straight lines. When a student in front of me deviated from his line, a teacher hit him on his back with a wooden stick. After that I was always careful to keep to my place in the line.

Before singing the national anthem, we had fixed slogans to chant. The student leading the ceremony was 'standing still like a pen' like a good young *tali'e*. He started the chant:

Troop Attention! Rest! Attention!

With each order we had to stamp our right foot on the ground. Then he ordered us to raise our right hand toward the right shoulder of the student ahead of us. We called it '*taraduf*', and it looked very much like the Nazi salute.

One Arab Nation…

We responded in one collective voice:

Bearing an eternal message!

Our goals...

Unity, liberty, and socialism!

Our pledge...

To confront imperialism and Zionism and crush their criminal
tool, the criminal Muslim Brotherhood gang!

I don't remember the rest of the day, but I recall coming back home
proud of becoming a member of the Ba'ath Vanguards. As our teachers
had asked us to practise the slogans at home with our parents, I did,
because I was a good *tale'a*, and when I reached the last sentence about the
Muslim Brotherhood, my mother's face turned yellow, she turned her
face away and took a deep breath to suppress her bodily reaction. I felt her
fear of me, and I felt powerful without understanding why. I also kept my
tale'a hat on until bedtime.

It took my mother thirteen years to tell me that over ten members of her
family had been killed, imprisoned, or disappeared during 'the Brotherhood
Events' as we called them. I was preparing to travel to Damascus to study
journalism, and she only told me this because she wanted to warn me that
her surname, Said Essa, might bring me trouble there. She also told me that
not all these relatives had been evil, that some were in fact intelligent
engineers and doctors who had been 'brainwashed by evil to stand against
the government and harm our homeland with their actions.'

I only found out the full truth when the Revolution started in Syria in
March 2011. Then my mother finally stopped fearing me, and I became
trustworthy enough for her to share her story.

Before that, our relationship was built on fear. I was scared of her,
because where I come from this is what children are supposed to feel
toward their parents, and she was scared of me, because I could have her
arrested by the security forces if I offered any unsolicited information
about her at school.

I vividly remember the one and only time she slapped my face. I was in the fourth grade, wearing my dark blue with green line scarf and hat, and I told her, 'I am going to tell the teacher that my father doesn't like Hafez al-Assad.' She lost her temper, shouting contradictory statements: 'He does love him, we all do! You'll be an orphan if you tell anyone this! You seem to be hallucinating! Do you have a fever?'

At school I learnt to praise the *mukhabarat* (secret police) attitude. Informers were always celebrated. If you prepared a list of names of classmates who spoke badly about the teacher, ate during the class, left early or didn't wear their full uniform, you'd be awarded the position of *arref as-saf* (the leader of the class), and if your report was comprehensive enough to cover the other classes as well you would be *arref al-madraseh* (the leader of the whole school) who was usually the student who led the morning ceremony. Added to this network of behaviour monitors there were the Disciplinary Committees which consisted of militaristic and power-hungry students. The committees didn't only monitor students but also the class leaders and the school staff, as they reported directly to the Ba'ath branch during their regular meetings attended by different security forces' representatives.

I learnt that we must obey orders without question. This was the military law I had to pledge to while wearing my full school-military uniform in secondary and high school. During those years, I didn't see anything wrong in forcing my hijab-wearing best friend, Thanaa, to take her headscarf off during the morning ceremony and the military classes. The most I was capable of was sitting in front of her so she could hide behind me when the male teacher entered the room. I also bragged about being able to assemble and disassemble a Kalashnikov quickly, and I enjoyed the shooting trips we were taken on twice a year, not only for the shooting but because we used to sing on the way and had lots of fun stuffed in a truck that was usually employed for transporting cattle.

My aunt Maha was an English teacher before she emigrated to Canada. She told me that twenty years ago, when we were all still living in Idlib only a few meters away from each other, she considered breaking traditions and dishonouring family to be the definition of evil, but that now she thinks that the education system she was once part of is evil epitomised. 'It was all based on fear. As kids, we were dragged crying to school because it was a scary establishment for us, in which we were punished and threatened. Then when I was a teacher, I applied the same methods. I used to beat my students with sticks, and I terrified them.' These days my aunt doesn't only seem remorseful, she is also in shock that she could have done such a thing. 'It's pure thoughtlessness, I was just following the current,' she says. This absentmindedness which is planted and cultivated in totalitarian systems is emphasised in Arendt's 'Eichmann in Jerusalem,' in which she argues that 'desk murderers' such as Eichmann were not motivated by demonic or monstrous urges. Instead, 'it was sheer thoughtlessness that predisposed [Eichmann] to become one of the greatest criminals of that period.'

*

At home, evil was encapsulated in the figure of Satan, who caused any mistake we made. 'Damn Satan,' we would say when we hurt a loved one, broke a glass or thought of something *haram* like love or sex. In his book 'The Problem of the Human being', Egyptian thinker Zakaria Ibrahim writes: 'humans invented Satan to hold him responsible for all the disharmony, bickering, turmoil, conflict and strife in their world.' Ibrahim believes that it's easiest for humans to blame Satan for evil, 'while all the evidence proves that humans themselves are the devil. They spread division and strife, make war prevail over peace, and excel in creating torture and pain.'

In order to connect the two sources of evil – Satan and those Ba'athism declared to be the enemies of our nation – I concluded that the USA was Satan.

On the afternoon of 9/11, al-Jazeera was playing on our TV as usual, but muted. I was speaking on the telephone with my first boyfriend, Fares, who was eight years older than me, so twenty three years old. In the middle of our conversation, the flashing red news bar on the screen grabbed my attention, and I read the breaking news to him: 'Two planes struck the Twin Towers of the World Trade Center in New York.' Excitement overcame Fares, who shouted 'Allahu Akbar!' I didn't understand why he was celebrating. He was a moderate, fashion-conscious, and handsome Muslim man who loved football as well as me, one of the few teenage girls in the city who were challenging social pressures to wear the hijab.

In response to my confusion, he said, 'after all that they've done to the Muslims, we are finally terrorising the evil US.' I too had learnt in Nationalism class that the US was evil, but what did those shocked civilians on the screen have to do with it?

When the US invaded Iraq two years later, we were no longer together, so I watched the toppling of Saddam Hussein's statues on my own at home. Something inside me was pleased at the sight, because we had learnt at school that Saddam had betrayed the values of the Ba'ath party, that he was a tyrant who invaded other countries for personal glory. Our passports at that time stated that we Syrians could 'travel to all the countries of the world except Iraq.' But I was still confused. If one evil force toppled another, with whom should the good young Ba'athist stand?

Next day at school I received the answer. We stood with the Iraqis, following the logic of the Arabic proverb: 'I stand with my brother against my cousin, and with my cousin against the stranger.' The switch from being pleased that an evil tyrant had been toppled turned smoothly and immediately into anger against the western forces crossing the Atlantic to invade our lands.

On the second evening of the invasion, I was sitting in the bedroom of my best friend Thanaa. We were frustrated that, as girls, we couldn't join the many boys and men who had started to travel towards Baghdad, which had suddenly became accessible. It was the first time I had ever heard that someone was going to Iraq from Syria, and the list of the boys joining the *mujahideen* grew longer and longer. Every day we would hear a story similar to Hussam's: Hussam was going to his exams in the medical faculty. Then, as far as his family and girlfriend knew, he disappeared into thin air for a couple of days. Eventually he called them from Iraq to announce that he had joined the *mujahideen*. (Later on, many reports confirmed that the Syrian intelligence agencies were deeply involved in facilitating and providing cover for the terrorist pipeline that helped build up al-Qaeda in Iraq, which later became ISIS.)

That week the teacher told us we would be rallying against the war. We considered this to be great news. It meant we could escape classes for a whole day, walk the streets of the city with our girlfriends, and take advantage of the unique opportunity to walk closer to our crushes in the boys' schools without fear of being caught and punished.

As an unveiled girl with light skin and green eyes, I was asked to stand in the front lines of the demonstration. 'We want the world to see that we have good looking Baathi girls,' *al-muwajiha* told me once. *Al-muwajiha* is literally translated into 'an educational lead' but for us she was the mean woman (usually a woman) who always held a long wooden stick, and who was ready to hit you with it at any moment. Often she would stud the stick with nails so as to cause deeper wounds. She had a high-pitched loud voice and evil eyes. In those days, the sentence 'I will take you to the *muwajiha*' was enough to drop your heart into your legs. The *muwajiha* was usually a good friend of the military coach, which makes lots of sense. They were the most evil people in the school.

*

That day, in front of the state media camera, the *muwajiha* was nice to me. She gave me a big picture of Hafez al-Assad to raise and asked me to shout so loud that my voice would reach America. Although the slogans I was chanting meant nothing to me, it was liberating to hear my voice loud in the street. Loud female voices were acceptable to the regime so long as they were saluting the president, but they were not compatible with the patriarchal rules of my conservative community.

According to my society, I was walking hand in hand with Satan in the maze of social evil, rejecting traditions, social norms, and misogynist rules. *Aieb* (fault) and *haram* (forbidden) were the words most commonly used. Our lives were marionettes suspended from these two words. Everything was determined by them – what we wore, the colour of our outfits, how tight they were, the style and colour of our hair, the pitch of our voices, the way we walked, talked, looked, ate, loved, expressed ourselves, and behaved in public and privately. The eating of ice cream in public, for example, was reason enough to shame a girl. 'How could you get your tongue out and lick your cone in public!' they would say. Sitting in a park alone or with other girls, laughing in the street, speaking with a unrelated male in a public space, practising sport – all these and more would expose you to criticism. As I turned fifteen and reached puberty, evil for me took the shape of the sentence: 'No, because you are a woman.' This phrase forbid me from doing anything but studying and hanging out with my girlfriends at home.

I posed the question 'What is evil to you?' on the family WhatsApp group, which includes my mother, Maha, and another four aunts. All six used to be teachers in Idlib, and today all six are refugees spread across the world. My mother, who lives in southern Turkey, was the first to respond. 'It's marriage,' she wrote. 'The suppressive social system including the extended family.' My aunt Rihab, who lives in Egypt, added, 'Restrictions, being under constant surveillance, not just by the *mukhabarat*, but by people evaluating your honour against their closed-minded system. Evil is not being to express my dreams even to my friend for fear of being judged, and having to ask permission for every movement I make from the men of my family.' 'Don't forget the social stigma of being divorced, which boxes you in a coffin and disgraces you if you refuse to die,' my aunt Ghada, who lives in France, continued.

Syrian women are forced to be puppets and robots in their everyday lives, or in Hannah Arendt's words in *The Origins of Totalitarianism*, the 'living dead who are strangers from themselves,' and the Syrian state's laws enforce this social misogyny which seems to have left the deepest pain in the memory of my family's women. In her gender analysis of the Syrian Personal Status Laws, laywer Daad Mousa writes, 'The personal status laws of the religious authorities – of all religions and sects – discriminate and promote violence against women by subjecting them to the rule and jurisdiction of men, thus bringing forth legislation that has deprived Syrian women of all their rights.'

Sometimes just thinking felt like a challenge to the totalitarian regime we lived under. Why would we think? We were told that our government did that on our behalf. Hence all those who tried to think beyond the brainwashing surrounding us, to connect with other communities, or to break the small bubbles we were forced to live within, lived in fear of informers. The informer could be anyone – a sibling, a neighbor or a boyfriend. 'Walls have ears' was the alarming conclusion ending any conversation that might lead to trouble.

Fear is surely the most common and persistent evil. It began with fear of school, where I was beaten whenever I made any mistake, and continued through the fear of being sexually harassed on the way to school, through anxiety for my reputation, to fear of asking questions about life, God, politics, traditions, and so on. My grandmother used to say, 'we live our days in the palm of a demon.' Rejecting the sexual advances of an influential man could result in you and your family disappearing without trace in one of the many security branches. All it would take is for this influential harasser to write a report accusing you of hating the president, harming the state, or having connections with a foreigner or a member of the Muslim Brotherhood, and you would be gone.

The Syrian novelist Samar Yazbek believes that we Syrians have lived in a 'panopticon prison' for decades. The panopticon prison was first conceptualised by the English philosopher and social theorist Jeremy Bentham in the eighteenth century. It's a circular prison with cells arranged around a central well from which prisoners can be constantly observed. 'I believe the Assad family regime has torn all the connections which could have formed a unified national identity under their rule,' she told me in an interview 'We were besieged in separate cells,' she added, 'and we suffered the mere illusion that we were seeing each other, under the supervision of a mafia-like dictatorship acting within a monstrous international system. As soon as we discovered that we could be free to say and do what we wanted, the non-national identities exploded inside and outside, and we moved into a digital version of the Panopticon.'

Between the two stages that Yazbek highlights there was 2011, a year like no other in our collective memory. Many texts describe this year as 'breaking the republic of silence', as a 'revolution', or as part of the 'Arab Spring'. For me, it was simply the year in which we defeated two big evils in our lives – fear and hate.

How to describe the love that explodes in your heart and grows faster than a magic beanstalk when someone you don't know takes a bullet from the security forces on your behalf? How did he take this split-second decision in the heat of the demonstration? Why did he decide my life was worth more than his? How to describe the love that pushed women activists to attack with their bare hands the armed security forces detaining protestors at Aleppo University, claiming that those detained were their fiancés, brothers, or fathers when they didn't actually know them at all?

A friend studying dentistry was detained in Aleppo's National Security branch in early 2011. When he was released he told us that three women had gone to the branch separately to ask for him, each claiming to be his fiancée. Each knew that she might be put in prison for doing so, and none of them was actually related to him. However, the *mukhabarat* officer was impressed with this womaniser who had three loving fiancées ready to risk arrest on his behalf, and he decided to set him free.

In and around the demonstrations, love spread like rain drops on the desert. It sparkled in the eyes of masked faces. Its stream swept around me in the streets. I had never felt as secure as a woman. The men I had always feared as potential harassers had finally become trustworthy. They loved me without knowing who I was, just for demonstrating beside them, and I loved them back.

When regime forces killed peaceful protestors they committed a despicable crime, but for me, the ugliest evil they perpetrated was to deform that wave of love in 2011 into sheer hate. They achieved this by using the same old methods – torture, terror, blackmail, by spreading suspicion and loneliness and by provoking desperation, helplessness and anger.

In the final demonstration I attended, someone chanted, 'Our leader for ever is our Prophet Muhammad.' The chant was new but it sounded very familiar, copying even in its Arabic rhythm the slogan we had grown up repeating – 'Forever, forever, oh Hafez Al Assad'. It was a cue for all the evils to reveal themselves again, but this time wearing different masks. Soon many people became indifferent to violence, not only the violence committed by their group against the regime but even the violence committed against opponents of the regime. That's why Yazbek describes evil in the Syrian context as 'an immortal multi-headed monster – whenever you cut off one of its heads, another grows, and it doesn't die.'

We replaced *'sayedi'* ('my master', a term by which we used to humbly address any *mukhabarat* member) with *'sheikhi'* (my sheikh). Instead of the state, military, or Palestine security branches, we now feared the Ahrar al-Sham *sharia* courts, the Jabhat al-Nusra prisons, the ISIS checkpoints, and so on. All of these practised the same old evil but against different people and using different justifications. Those who questioned or challenged their rule were declared *'khawarij'* (those who had left Islam). Each battalion had its own *'sharie'* (religious authority) alongside the military leader, and most of them ran their own *sharia* courts and prisons. If any jihadists had doubts concerning the evil actions required of them (like kidnapping a media activist or executing a fellow Muslim), they would be told 'this is a *fatwa* (religious judgment)', which killed any dissent. Such jihadists were walking examples of the banality of evil Hannah Arendt wrote about.

Abdo was one of them. When I met him in the Idlib suburbs in early 2012, he was seventeen years old and a member of the Tawheed group. He refused to be called an FSA rebel. 'The Free Syrian Army!' he would say. 'Those secular thieves! I am a *mujahid*!' During our first three meetings we argued about his misogyny and sectarianism. He wanted to wipe the Shia and Alawites off the Syrian map. Soon the inhabitants of Fu'ah became his main enemy.

Fu'ah is a small Shia town surrounded by Sunni towns in Idlib province. At the beginning of the uprising its men were armed by the regime in order to suppress their Sunni neighbours. This resulted in unprecedented and constantly escalating sectarian conflict between the towns. Fu'ah ended up besieged by the jihadists, and eventually those left in the town were evacuated south to Damascus in the 2018 Four Towns Agreement brokered by Iran and Turkey. Their houses were given to those who had been forcibly displaced by the regime and who had travelled in the opposite direction, from southern Syria to the north.

Abdo refused to admit that his hate for Fu'ah resulted from his older brother's murder. His brother had been driving near the town in 2011 when he was shot dead. 'I hate them because they are the regime and they live only to wipe us out. It's either them or us,' he argued.

The fourth time we met, I had just been released after being kidnapped by a Fu'ah-based militia. I had to wait at Abdo's father's farm until I found a taxi that would take me to the border. I was sitting on the sofa when he came in with a blanket and a *labneh* sandwich. He threw the blanket over me, saying, 'it's cold. You left Fu'ah in good health. I don't want your family to blame me for your sickness. And eat this – you look like a ghost!' I greatly appreciated the gesture. The fifth time we met was at my mother's house in Antakya in southern Turkey. I woke up to find him drinking coffee with her while listening to Fairooz. He was killed in battle a couple of months later.

As the war worsened, these human connections became weaker. By the end of 2014, when fighting erupted between ISIS and other Islamist groups, life in rebel-held areas became too chaotic to make sense of.

*

2015. I was sitting at my desk in Saif al-Dawla in eastern Aleppo. I tried to type, writing some unrelated sentences, then deleting them.

Another try: *Today, the sixth of January 2015, the Abu Amara Battalions, considered until now a moderate rebel group, threw a gay man from the roof of al-Bayan hospital, the highest building in eastern Aleppo's al-Sha'ar neighbourhood, applying the supposed sharia rule. His body smashed in front of the audience which had gathered to witness the punishment. But he wasn't dead, so someone shot him.*

I wasn't there, but the noise of the victim's head striking the street still shook my ground. I felt sick and dizzy, but I feared expressing my feelings even to my close secular comrades, for many reasons. I feared someone might inform one of the Islamic 'authorities' of my support for the LGBTQ+ community, which would – in the best case – force me to leave the rebel-held areas. As it was impossible for me to enter the regime-areas, that meant leaving Syria altogether. I also feared that my comrades would mock me for being oversensitive – people were dying every day, so why did I feel particularly upset about this victim?

Exactly a year before this religiously-justified murder, in January 2014, when the Islamic State started kidnapping media activists in northern Syria, the Abu Amara battalions had offered the activists protection in their base. War taught me that fighting evil once is no guarantee that you won't fight on its behalf at a later time.

Another example: Abu al-Hasanein, once a leader in Jaish al-Mujahideen (a coalition of Islamist groups formed to fight both the Syrian regime and ISIS), protected me by stopping the advance of Assadist forces which would arrest me because I reported their abuses. He also risked death daily as he fought ISIS, which would have kidnapped me simply for being a journalist. For a while he stood between me and death, yet Abu al-Hasanein still thought I should be killed for condemning the killing of *Charlie Hebdo*'s staff.

It took me years and many extremely emotional experiences to deconstruct the Manichaeism installed in me for thirty years, defining what and who was good or evil. According to Neville Buch, 'Manichaeism teaches an elaborate dualistic cosmology describing the struggle between a good, spiritual world of light, and an evil, material world of darkness.' Before leaving my desk in Saif al-Dawla on that sad day in 2015 (mortars were being fired near the window), I wrote that 'evil is like energy in its physics definition: it can neither be created nor destroyed; rather, it can only be transformed from one form to another.'

*

Samar Yazbek told me, 'Violence begets violence, hate brings hate. So my only way to dismantle evil is to put myself in the shoes of those doing evil. No matter how much the evil they produce is aimed at me, I still view it in its context.' She calls this contextualisation 'combing Medusa's hair.'

My kidnapping experience in al-Fu'ah forced me to put myself in 'the other's shoes'. I was saved by Hussein, the leader of a militia working for the Military Security forces. This militia clashed with another militia loyal to the State Security, which was trying to abduct me. When the State Security's militia surrounded us in Fu'ah's bakery and started shooting, I saw Samir for the first time. He was short and unremarkable, with a poker face and a very low IQ, making him the perfect loyal soldier. He mentioned Assad's name in every other sentence to prove his loyalty and to silence any dissent. Assad's name there was like a *fatwa* on the Islamist side – just as non-negotiable.

Samir wanted to hand me over to the regime in Damascus, but Hussein told him, 'you know they will eat her alive! She is from our region. We can't do this to our women.' Samir didn't deny that I would be tortured to death by his bosses, but responded instead, 'Bashar al-Assad's shoe is on my head! If he says she is not a traitor working for the international conspiracy against our homeland, I will carry her around on my shoulders, but now she is here without permission and she must be handed over.'

When I was finally released, I told my family that if evil had a face, it would have been Samir's. Now as I write this, however, I feel Samir and the young men in his militia were victims of the banality of evil, just like my young friend Abdo.

It was Abdo's turn to observe the road between al-Fu'ah and Idlib when I was in a car rushing toward my second chance at life. 'I saw a white car passing at 8.30 pm. I tried to activate the bomb I'd planted earlier on the road, but we had forgotten to charge it.' He told me that later, when he realised I'd been in the car, he hit his forehand with his palm, thanking God that he hadn't killed me. 'I thought they were thugs,' he added. 'They were,' I responded. 'They were pro-regime fighters, but one of them decided to risk his life to save me, and the others risked theirs for him.'

I had sat in the back seat next to a fighter who pointed his rifle toward what I learnt later was Abdo's group. An exchange of fire followed. It felt more like a 'hi, we are here' kind of firing than a serious clash, but as I lowered myself in the seat, taking the emergency flight position, I prayed from the bottom of my heart that if this was going to turn into a battle, it would be me who died first. I didn't want to witness the death of either the rebels fighting on my side (against the regime) or the pro-regime men who were then literally on my side.

All my ideas of sides, of evil and good, of us and them and right and wrong, were destroyed that night. My new understanding of the world provoked new enmities and new enemies, and some of the fiercest were my previous comrades. Those who dreamt of democracy were defeated by various forms of evil. This produced hatred in their hearts, which they sometimes direct at each other.

For over four years I haven't worked on any project related to Syria. When I started working on other countries in the SWANA region, I discovered that my ex-comrades' evil had distorted my mirror. On a trip to Baghdad, where I felt loved and appreciated by my colleagues, I was surprised! So am I not evil for being who I am? For staying independent, feminist, objective, and 'seeing evil through its perpetrators' pain' as Yazbek describes it.

Yazbek says, 'as women, we are expected to play the role of the weak victim. If you manage to have your voice heard and receive international recognition, you turn into a moving target in our Arab world.' She argues that intellectual methods are the only way to fight the smear campaigns of which she has been a target. But preserving your intellect under attack is difficult, just as it is difficult to survive in Syria, a country which, in Yazbek's words, is 'the perfect theatre for the international representation of all kinds of evil.'

By the end of our discussion, I noticed that I too have developed the habit of combing Medusa's hair. That's what made me want to put Abdalmasih Hanon's crime in France into a context. Does this mean I am a step closer to dismantling evil? Maybe. One source of evil is thereby neutralised. Many more remain.

CRIMEAN TATARS

Lutfiye Zudiyeva

> *Father, speak of that day,*
> *This is vital and crucial to me.*
> *Don't spare me, don't have pity on me,*
> *Again go away from your home,*
> *Lose your relatives in the train cars anew,*
> *Again count those who are left alive.*
> *I want to get to know everything*
> *To be able to pass it on to your heirs.*

From a poem by Lilâ Bucurova

Today, I was in Bakhchysarai again. I skimmed through my father's historical books. He used to bring them home and always asked me to look at them closely. I was ten when I first touched them. They lay in the cabinet under the TV set where they periodically caught my eye when I cleaned the house with my mother, and needed to shift them. Then I did not really want to read them as there was too much pain in them. I also saw how my father's eyes sparkled with tears when he opened them.

At the age of fifteen, I read my father's entire library. However, I was able to genuinely comprehend everything written in his books only after 2014, when events from the past began to come to life.

I would very much like my contemporaries not to write such books. However, we live in some kind of terrible historical spiral in which my small Muslim nation has been trapped for centuries.

*

My father always dreamed of living in his parents' house. When in 1988 he returned to Crimea from Uzbekistan, where his mother had been deported in 1944, however, he found that other people were living in the family home in the village of Tav-Badrak. He did not seek their eviction, and would hardly have been able to, but he often brought us to look at the house.

Dad bought a house in another village, where we lived for many years. Later, after my marriage, he moved to Bakhchysarai, the former capital of the Crimean Khanate, and settled in its old town. He bought an old Crimean Tatar house opposite Khan Saray, the former residence of the Crimean Khans. This is the political centre of our people, redolent of four hundred years of history.

Shukri Seytumerov, a historian and a close friend of my father, lives a few blocks from my parents' house. He told me the Khan Saray, 'has been a witness to important events. For two and a half centuries until 1783 the palace served as the centre of the political, religious, and cultural life of the Crimean Khanate. The historical as well as political significance of this architectural monument is undoubted. The Khan's Palace remains a significant symbol of the statehood of the Crimean Tatars. Each ruler of the Crimean Khanate lived with his family in the palace only for the period of his reign.'

Unfortunately, a significant part of this heritage has been destroyed. For a start, the original appearance of the Khan Saray has long been lost. First the palace was burned by the troops of Field Marshal Burkhard Christoph von Münnich in 1736, when priceless archives of books and state manuscripts were also destroyed. After that, the palace was rebuilt several times, but after the final conquest of the Crimean Khanate by the Russian Empire in 1783, the palace was turned into a place for the entertainment of the Russian authorities. Russian emperors and members of their families used it as a temporary residence. At the beginning of the twentieth century, it was used as a museum of Crimean Tatar history and ethnography. In 1934-1941, it was turned into a centre for ideological Marxist-Leninist propaganda on the supposed achievements of the Soviet state and the Soviet way of life. During this period, the palace suffered the greatest damage of all.

Following the deportation of the Crimean Tatars in 1944, the palace was used as a propaganda tool against them. Exhibitions on 'the fight against

Turkish-Tatar aggression' were shown in its halls. 'To give an analysis of the Crimean Khanate as a parasitic state,' 'To wind down the ethnographic department,' and 'To revise the museum exhibitions within the framework of Crimea having been a Russian land for a long time' are just a few reports from a declassified archive of the Communist officials. And today, still under the guise of restoration, the remnants of the Khan Saray's authenticity are being destroyed by the contemporary Russian occupation authorities. Builder-contractors brought from Russia are changing roofs, drawing over Muslim wall paintings, and erasing the last traces of our history. No one can stop it.

Due to this vandalism, the main mosque, which once received hundreds of people for Jummah — Friday — prayer, is closed. For several years now, my father has not been able to pray there but travels to another part of the city instead.

'Khan Saray,' says Shukri Seytumerov with regret, 'has gone through all historical stages — from the once formidable centre of the Crimean Khanate, which covered vast territories at various periods of its existence, from Moldova to the Kuban and the North Caucasus, including the northern Black Sea region, and spreading its influence in Eastern Europe, to an insignificant building in the possession of Russian emperors.'

*

The first documented appearance of Islam on the territory of Crimea came with the Seljuk Turks' defeat of the Kipchaks (or Polovtsians) in 1221. The Seljuks built the first mosque in Crimea at Sudak, on the territory of the modern Genoese fortress. After that, and throughout the thirteenth and fourteenth centuries, Islam became politically, culturally, and socially dominant on the peninsula. Most of our predecessors became Sunnis, followers of the Hanafi school like most of the Turkic peoples from Central Asia to Anatolia.

Later the Crimean Khanate became an outpost of the Ottoman state in Eastern Europe, effectively defending its northern borders and blocking neighbouring states from seizing the Black Sea coast. The Russian Empire, meanwhile, constantly strove to reach the shores of the Black Sea. To this end, Russian diplomats repeatedly attempted to persuade the rulers of the

Crimean Khanate to declare independence from the Ottomans. When, in 1770, Russian Count Pyotr Panin, speaking on his government's behalf, suggested that the Crimean Khan secede, Qaplan Giray Khan replied, 'We are completely satisfied with the Ottoman Porte, and we enjoy prosperity … In this intention of yours, there is nothing except for idle talk and recklessness.'

But the Ottoman empire was weakening, while Russian power was steadily rising. The Russian-Turkish war of 1768 to 1774 ended in disaster for the Crimean Tatars. In 1772, with Russian troops present in the Crimea, a gathering of *beys*, *murzas*, and Nogai *seraskers* in Karasubazar was forced to sign a treatise proclaiming the independence of the Crimean Khanate from the Ottomans and 'alliance, friendship and trust between Crimea and Russia.' In 1774, the Ottoman Porte in turn was coerced into concluding the Treaty of Küçük Kaynarca, which recognised both the 'independence' of the Crimean Khanate and Russia's right to station troops at Kerch, Yeni-Kale, Kinburn fortress on the mouth of the Dnipro, and Azov on the mouth of the Don.

The pretence of independence was finally abandoned in 1783 when Russian Empress Catherine II signed the 'Manifesto on the accession of the Crimean peninsula, Taman Island and the Kuban region to the Russian Empire.' Russian troops were then stationed throughout Crimea and a new imperial governing system was forcibly established.

Because the Crimean Tatars did not support the new regime, the machinery of Tsarist imperialist repression was launched against them. Protests and any other manifestations of dissent were severely suppressed. Religious figures were persecuted, Qurans were burned, and *haj* and *umra* pilgrimages were banned. After a law of 1836, only religious figures loyal to the Russian regime could be appointed to spiritual positions. Russian police checked all mullahs, imams, and muezzins for political reliability. Those who did not obey were subject to removal from office. Any Crimean who had been educated abroad, even in a secular institution, could not become a mullah. And Russian governors would veto the muftis elected by the Crimean Tatar community, while promoting their own candidates, sometimes including criminals.

Soon a campaign was launched to seize the written heritage of the Crimean Tatars, or according to government documents collected in

Arslan Krichinsky's 'Essays on Russian Politics in the Outskirts', 'books and manuscripts that are harmful to them and the general peace of mind ... those that do not conform to the laws and rules of prudence.' These were texts which, in the opinion of the Russian governor of the time, would 'only damage the honour of the Russian Tatars who are loyal subjects of our father, the sovereign.' The Russians confiscated Arabic-language manuscripts from the clergy as well as from family homes. Later they burnt the books, by order of the Minister of the Interior. And so a resource of enormous historical and cultural significance was destroyed.

In the following years, as a result of the colonial presence and various Russification policies, a significant proportion of the Crimean Tatars emigrated to adjacent Muslim lands. In the words of orientalist Mikhail Yakubovich, 'Unlike the case of other Muslim peoples from the imperial hinterland (the banks of the Volga or the north of Kazakhstan), Crimea was located on the border with Turkey and the Balkans, and the Crimean Tatars themselves preferred to leave rather than integrate into the community of prisoners of the 'prison of peoples'.'

The Russian government facilitated the emigration of Crimean Muslims in every possible way. Shukri Seytumerov quotes a document from the government archives (from the Complete Collection of Laws of the Russian Empire, Edition One, Volume 21), which states, 'It is not appropriate to object to the open or secret exodus of the Crimean Tatars. On the contrary, this voluntary emigration should be regarded as a beneficial action, calculated on the liberation of the territory of the peninsula.'

The emigration occurred in three main waves, the peaks of which were in 1874, 1883, and 1901-1902, and led to the formation of Crimean Tatar diasporas in Turkey, Bulgaria, and Romania. According to the 1792-1793 census, the Crimean Tatar population decreased from 500,000 to 75,000 in just twenty years of Russian rule. Tens of thousands of Muslims were killed by Russian imperial soldiers, and the remaining hundreds of thousands, not wanting to submit to tyranny, left their lands en masse for Muslim Turkey and the Balkans. Those who remained in Crimea at the end of the eighteenth century sought to survive, to raise children, and to restore their numbers.'

*

The next phase in the oppression of our people followed the Russian Empire's reinvention as the Soviet Union. After cracking down on religious figures, the new dictatorship set to work on the secular intelligentsia. On 17 April 1938, dozens of people were shot dead. The goal of the purge was to eradicate the active, passionate, thinking stratum of the Crimean Tatar people so as to eliminate any potential alternative to non-Communist leadership. Scientists, politicians, writers, and teachers considered objectionable by the authorities were among the victims.

Muslims were persecuted under the Soviet regime. The Crimean Tatars were forbidden from studying the Arabic alphabet, and thus were prevented from understanding the texts of the Qur'an. At the same time, mosques, mektebs, and madrasahs were closed and destroyed.

During these years, my great-grandfather Ismail Osman was dispossessed and exiled from Crimea to the Urals. He was born in the village of Tav Badraq in the Bakhchysarai region where he raised horses and sheep. According to the 1897 census, there had been 575 people in the village, of which 532 were Crimean Tatars. The vast majority of the inhabitants of the village professed Islam.

In the Urals, he and his wife were forced to cut wood. Their daughter, my grandmother Lilya Osmanova (born in 1930), who at the time of her exile to the Urals was about three years old, fell from the second floor in a special settlement while her parents were doing compulsory logging work. She remained disabled for the rest of her life as a result of medical neglect.

In 1938, the family managed to return home to Crimea and began to restore their household. With the outbreak of war with Nazi Germany in 1941, Ismail Osman used his property to provide for the partisans of the Soviet army, even though he had previously been dispossessed by the regime.

The war catalysed the bloodiest episode in the long history of the persecution of the Crimean Tatars. On 10 May 1944, the Secret Police chief Lavrentiy Beria sent Joseph Stalin a draft decision on the deportation of the entire population of Crimean Tatars. A day later, Stalin signed Decree No. 5859 'On the Crimean Tatars.' The Crimean Tatars were accused of treason and collaboration with the Germans.

According to official data, 183,155 Crimean Tatars were deported from Crimea on 18 May 1944. Most were transported in cattle cars. In the first year and a half after this date, 46 percent of those deported died. This incomprehensibly high number, and the totality of the crime committed against the whole population, surely justifies the charge of genocide.

My father's grandparents, Osman and Fera, along with their six children, were deported to special settlements in the Tashkent region of Uzbekistan. The family were given only fifteen minutes to gather their belongings – just enough time to pack a Quran, a little food, and a few clothes for the children. They travelled in a train carriage full of corpses. When they arrived in Uzbekistan, Osman and Feru were very sick and could not work. Lilya, my father's mother, used to tell us how in the early days of their exile they were constantly hungry.

Many other Muslim peoples in the Soviet Union – Karachais, Chechens, Meskhetian Turks, Balkars, Ingushes, and others – were forcibly deported. Muslim religious and cultural values interfered with the Soviet regime's demand for faith in the leader and the party rather than in God. Muslims' collective spirit and mutual devotion irritated and frightened the authorities, so Stalin pursued a tough anti-religious policy.

My father remembers the incomprehension felt by the deportees: 'They didn't understand why they were treated like this. They couldn't come to terms with it, and they raised their children with the hope of returning to Crimea. They continued to secretly read prayers and to fast in the month of Ramadan.'

The older children in the family started working early to support their younger siblings. But the young ones still died — two from dysentery and two more for reasons unknown to us. The eldest daughter, Emine, worked sorting apples, and after work hours she went to the railway line and collected grain, beets, and carrots that had fallen from the train carriages. At home, everyone was waiting for her return, because she brought food for the whole family.

A few years later, grandmother Lilya was moved again, this time to a special settlement in which barracks surrounded bast-fibre factories. Here flax was immersed in special containers with water and soaked. It was then beaten, and threads for tarpaulins and ropes were made. It was very hard work in inhuman conditions. The Soviet regime took all the 'undesirables' to such special settlements. My father's parents were actually born in these settlement colonies. Until 1957, they did not even have passports of citizens of the USSR, but only the status of special settlers. Other Crimean Tatars were forced to work in mines.

When I interview historian Elvira Kemal, he told me about the cold-blooded and calculated nature of these genocidal crimes. 'If we look at the deportation of the Crimean Tatars in 1944, and then the decades of forcible retention of the entire people away from their homeland ... as well as the creation of ideological, legal, administrative, organizational, material, and simply gangster obstacles to their return and restoration to their inalienable natural rights, not as a stand-alone episode but rather in the entire historical context of the centuries-old systematic policy of genocide pursued by different states, regimes, and political forces, then there is no mystery in this. The goal was the total appropriation of Crimea at the cost of destroying its autochthonous population, both physically and morally.'

*

In March 1953, Joseph Stalin died. A year later, Moscow decided to transfer Crimea to Ukraine as a result of – according to the draft decree of the Presidium of the Supreme Soviet of the USSR – 'the territorial attraction of the Crimean region to the Ukrainian SSR, the common economy and close economic and cultural ties between the Crimean region and the Ukrainian SSR.'

From that moment, the deportees began to return to Crimea, first individually and then collectively. My father joined the struggle for the right to live in his own home, attending mass rallies, organizing pickets, and printing leaflets. My grandmother Lilya was able to return in 1988. Of the family of eight, only she returned. All the others died in exile. Then in the uncertainty following the fall of the Soviet Union in 1991, entire villages and large families returned to Crimea. The return of the Crimean Tatars has rightly become a central event in our recent history. It became possible thanks to our joint efforts. This rebirth after many years of wandering has resulted in a stormy search for national and religious self-identity.

Crimean Tatars found it difficult to re-establish themselves but they worked hard to restore what had been lost. Schools teaching the Crimean

Tatar language began to appear. New mosques were built where religious literature was freely available. Muslim organizations carried out their activities and were not banned. Young people left to study Islam in Muslim countries. The political consciousness of the people began to develop; various parties and organizations freely operated.

*

In 2014, Russia invaded Crimea once again, and Crimean Tatars protested peacefully against the new occupation. Their opposition to Russian imperialism was heightened by their history and genetic memory. Having twice been pushed to the verge of extinction by Russian regimes – both Tsarist and Soviet – Crimean Tatars suffer from a collective trauma. This means that the majority of Crimean Tatars will not accept, or even enter into dialogue with, the usurping Russian authorities.

The authorities, in turn, have applied mass repression against the Crimean Tatar people. In the Kremlin, despite declarations concerning the rehabilitation of repressed peoples, there is still no admission of the scale of the long-term persecution of Muslim peoples under Russian rule. On the contrary, there is a continuation of the colonial policy of the Tsarist and Soviet eras. Searches of private homes and mosques, intimidation, administrative fines, arrests, and physical attacks against Crimean Tatars have become commonplace.

Since 2014, more than 120 Crimean Tatars have been arrested under various articles of the Criminal Code of the Russian Federation. The charges have almost always been politically motivated. Islamic literature has been confiscated from mosques, and imams have been removed from their positions. Thousands of people have fled the peninsula to avoid prison. Speaking in court, Emir-Usein Kuku, one of the imprisoned Muslims of Crimea, connected these contemporary horrors to those perpetrated in the eighteenth century: 'Apparently, it was necessary to fulfil the goal set by Catherine II — that is, the cleansing of Crimea from the Crimean Tatars and other 'unreliable' Muslims, who, under the Ukrainian authorities, had fortified themselves in threatening proximity to Sevastopol, the main base of Russia's Black Sea Fleet. And now if someone dares to raise their voice in defence of those who are unjustly accused and oppressed, they immediately fall under the gun of the FSB secret police.'

It is difficult not to draw these historical parallels. Practically every family of current political prisoners remembers its relatives deported and repressed by the previous Russian regime. The only difference is that at that time the Crimean Tatars were persecuted by the Soviet NKVD rather than the FSB, and were accused of 'counter-revolutionary agitation.'

After his arrest, the political prisoner Lenur Khalilov told me in a letter from prison: 'Now, every Muslim in Crimea faces a choice – either cooperation with the FSB, or his religious choice. If he opts for the second, pressure naturally awaits him. This is not a new practice either. My grandfather graduated from a madrasah and was an imam.' (Lenur's grandfather was an imam in Alushta, a small town by the sea.) 'From the age of twenty, he worked in the village of Ai-Serez. Before his expulsion, he taught the basics of religion and the Crimean Tatar language. After the deportation, he ended up in the Urals. On the second day of his exile, the commandants went from house to house making lists of people's professions. My grandfather's relatives told him they would give him a tool for sharpening saws and would tell the officers he was a saw sharpener, and not an imam. But when my grandfather was summoned he was unable to lie. He admitted that he was an imam, and after that he never returned. Many years later, we learned that he had been imprisoned for eight years. He ended up in the Yaroslavl region.'

By inventing a non-existent terrorist threat and initiating criminal cases against Crimean Muslims for supposed acts of terrorism, Russia is trying to convince international powers that its presence in Crimea is justified. The myth of Islamic terrorism is once again being manipulated in Russia to divert the public's attention from the Russian state's crimes against civilians in Ukraine and elsewhere.

In Bakhchysarai alone, where my father now lives, sixty Crimean Tatar children saw their fathers taken away on trumped-up charges as a result of four waves of mass detention. In Crimea as a whole, there are currently 210 children of political prisoners. Seytumer, the son of my father's friend Shukri Seytumerov, has also been imprisoned since 2020, along with his brother and uncle. Speaking in court, he addressed the audience with the following words: 'Because of Russia's rule over our people, the Crimean

Tatar diaspora in Turkey numbers millions, and only several hundred thousand remain in their homeland in Crimea. However, even this small number of Crimean Tatars in Crimea does not allow any rest to the Russian leadership. Once again, Crimean Tatars, because of their loyalty to their life principles and their unshakable position, are being slandered and intimidated. Therefore, we no longer believe any false promises. We, Crimean Tatars, have our religion — Islam, our traditions and principles of life, according to which we wish to live peacefully and happily in Crimea, on the land that was given to us by Allah. We demand only our right to life, but even this is considered a luxury or a crime in Crimea today.'

Seytumer's great-grandfather, teacher and imam Murtaza Mustafa, was arrested in February 1938, and was sentenced to death by the NKVD troika of the Crimean Autonomous Soviet Socialist Republic. He was kept in the Ekaterininska prison in Simferopol, until the sentence was carried out on 4 April 1938. As my father unfolds a prayer mat, he laments the fate of this family: 'Their great-grandfather was shot, their grandmother was deported, their parents were not allowed into Crimea for a long time, and now he is under arrest. There are thousands of such stories in our nation. It's an endless spiral of evil.'

Despite all these troubles, my father believes that the Almighty will not abandon us. As we talk, I am brewing his favourite brand of coffee in our kitchen. We both feel very happy because we are in our own home. We might not be safe but we are on our land. And this fills us with strength.

ENCOUNTERING THE SHADOW

Jeremy Henzell-Thomas

Al-Masih ad-Dajjal, the 'false Messiah' in Islamic eschatology, corresponding to the 'Anti-Christ' in Christianity, is a false Prophet and impostor who, according to tradition, will seek to impersonate Jesus shortly before he returns to earth in the 'last days' at the end of time. In his *Concise Encyclopaedia of Islam*, Cyril Glassé states that according to a hadith, *al-Masih ad-Dajjal* will be the last and greatest of a number of dajjals in history. Glassé also points out that some traditional commentators changed the word *masih* ('Messiah') to *masikh,* meaning 'deformed', giving the term *ad-Dajjal al-Masikh* ('the deformed deceiver'). 'This play on words is done by the addition of a single dot over the last Arabic letter, *ha',* changing it to *kha',* to symbolise how easy it is to deform truth into falsehood. The nature of the *dajjal* is precisely the deformation of truth into its exact opposite, and a complete inversion, or parody, of spirituality.'

The primary meaning of the root word *djl,* according to E.W. Lane's Arabic-English Lexicon, is 'to cover or conceal the truth with falsehood', to beguile, enchant, gild, varnish, adorn with false lustre, or, in very graphic, concrete terms, 'to smear a mangy or scabby camel with tar' so as to make it more attractive to a prospective buyer. Lane explains that the root also has the connotation of adulterating the truth through mixing things up and confusing or confounding them. Lane's analysis of the characteristics of *ad-Dajjal* might be summarised as follows: he will tell lies, he will arrogate to himself godship, he will traverse most of the regions of the earth, he will cover the earth with the multitude of his forces, he will manifest the contrary of what he conceives or conceals, treasures will follow him wherever he goes, he will defile the ground, and he will have one eye. The depiction of the Dajjal with 'one eye' is striking, given the Greek myth of the Cyclops, a one-eyed, man-eating giant, defeated by the hero Odysseus who blinds him by driving a stake into his eye, but the 'one eye' has greater significance as a symbol of evil in the disembodied flaming eye of Sauron in Tolkien's *The Lord of the Rings*. Sauron, the chief lieutenant of the Dark Lord Morgoth, and compared by some commentators to Balor of the Evil Eye in Irish mythology, rules the land of Mordor and has the ambition of ruling the whole of Middle Earth. He is also identified as the 'Necromancer' in Tolkien's earlier novel *The Hobbit*. Sauron's deceit is only too evident in his claim that he was acting not out of a lust for power but out of a sincere desire for peace, and that he longed to heal Middle Earth from the wounds it had suffered during the long, bitter war against Morgoth. While Tolkien denied that absolute evil could exist, he stated that Sauron came as near as possible to a wholly evil will.

It is worth noting that various commentators maintain that the characteristics of the Dajjal can be discerned in current world events, and to adherents of the anti-globalisation movement they could be identified as sounding uncannily like the forces of globalisation 'traversing most of the regions of the earth.' They might interpret his single eye as monocultural imposition, the homogenisation of diversity and pluralism, the misappropriation of Divine Unity, as well as the exponential proliferation of CCTV and satellite surveillance with the prospect of unlimited expansion through artificial intelligence (AI) applications. 'Arrogating to himself godship' might be associated with two of the self-aggrandising slogans adopted by the US after 9/11 in its 'war on terror', namely, 'infinite justice' and 'full spectrum dominance' ('covering the earth with the multitude of his forces'), enforced by the economic power of unregulated corporations ('treasures will follow him wherever he goes').

It goes without saying that the single eye of the Dajjal could also be associated in equal measure with the forces of monolithic religious fundamentalism which would seek to impose its own one-eyed, one-dimensional theocratic tyranny on the world. The parallels I have drawn between some of the characteristics of the Dajjal and the post-9/11 militarism of the US are not intended to ally myself with any ideologically motivated 'anti-Americanism' and could equally well be applied (without identifying myself as 'anti-British') to the colonial ambitions of historical British imperialism or, indeed to any brand of colonialism seeking to gain power and wealth through the subjugation or exploitation of weaker nations. Just as Sauron misleadingly claimed to be intent on healing Middle Earth instead of exercising his lust for power, so imperial ambitions have always been framed as virtuous, often as a means of bringing 'order' or 'civilisation' to benighted regions of the world. Let us never forget that the tendency of the Dajjal to exalt one's own motives is in every one of us.

'In the darkest Middle Ages,' C.G. Jung once said, 'they spoke of the devil; today we call it a neurosis.' Jung claimed that he often saw the devil in his consulting room in his patients' states of 'possession', the conscious mind having been overwhelmed by the grotesque and sinister side of the unconscious. He saw the devil's handiwork in delusions, division and fragmentation, confusion, chaos, and worldliness, as well as the entrenched rigidity that resists opening to change or new possibilities.

The 'grotesque and sinister side of the unconscious' can be equated with the 'shadow' archetype in Jungian analytical psychology. Also known as the 'repressed id', the shadow is the self's 'blind spot', the repository of those aspects of the personality that are hidden, repressed and rejected because they do not reflect the 'ego ideal', the inner image of oneself as the person one would ideally like to be. When we fail to recognise our shadow side, insisting for example that we could not possibly be sexist, racist, bigoted, hypocritical, coercive, or violent (amongst many other vices), we open ourselves to the self-righteousness that Jung claimed was one of the chief avenues for the 'devil' to enter the human psyche. And, of course, the Dajjal is adept at deceiving oneself in protecting one's 'ego ideal' in the same was as deceiving others. The acknowledgement of the shadow, by which we bring into the light of conscious awareness, is one of the prerequisites of personal integration, or, in Jungian terms, 'individuation', by which the true Self is united with the ego.

A common way to disown our own shadow is to project it, to see it as residing in 'the other', where it can be vilified. This is the phenomenon of 'demonisation'. In his State of the Union address in January 2002, less than five months after the 9/11 attacks, President George W Bush coined the phrase the 'axis of evil' to refer to Iraq, Iran, and North Korea, echoing President Ronald Reagan's speech delivered to the National Association of Evangelicals on 8 March 1983 at the height of Cold War and Soviet-Afghan War, in which he referred to the Soviet Union as an 'evil empire' and as 'the focus of evil in the modern world'.

Demonisation of other nation states or political ideologies is of course a common feature of nationalism, in no way confined to the US! In an article for the European Council on Foreign Relations, Maria Lipman reports that in Russia 'the West is routinely portrayed as evil incarnate, and an aggressive mix of facts and fantasy fills the media, the internet, and the daily discourse.' She relates that 'in his public speeches in late 2013, Putin sounded like a preacher: he harshly criticised the 'Euroatlantic' countries for their decadence and immorality. He said they had abandoned their roots and their Christian values and equated belief in God with belief in Satan.' One 'clever propaganda trick' she added, has been 'to enhance the image of the evil West by merging together the social conservative and the anti-Western posture. In this way, the West and Westernisers, gay people, liberals, contemporary artists and their fans, those who did not treat the Russian Orthodox Church with due respect, and those who dared to doubt Russia's unblemished historical record were all presented as one indivisible evil.'

In the same way, the common Orientalist narrative denying modernity to non-Western cultures often uses derogatory terms such as 'dark', 'barbaric' and 'savage', and also attaches negative connotations to essentially neutral terms such as 'medieval'. As Norman Cigar has revealed in his study of how Serbian Orientalists justified genocide against the Muslims of the Balkans, the Serbs differentiated and isolated Bosnian Muslims by creating a caricature, 'a straw-man Islam and Muslim stereotype' and 'setting and emphasising cultural markers' which focused on Islam and the Muslims as reflections of the 'darkness of the past', inimical to modernity, alien, culturally and morally inferior, threatening, and perversely exotic.

Orientalist bias has been perpetrated in similar vein, with various scaremongering stereotypes at different times, perhaps most perniciously in the scathing racism of Sinophobia (or Chinaphobia) which had developed during the high imperialism of the mid- and late-nineteenth century. The 'yellow peril' was vividly embodied in the caricature of Fu Manchu, the Chinese master criminal of exotic malignance, hatred of the white race, and lust for world domination. This character, a classic example of demonisation, was depicted in a series of films in the late 1970s by Christopher Lee, famous for his depiction of Dracula in the Hammer horror films *The Brides of Fu Manchu* (1966), *The Vengeance of Fu Manchu* (1967), and *The Blood of Fu Manchu* (1968). Pitted against the Chinese supervillain are Nayland Smith of Scotland Yard and Dr Petrie, who personify the epitome of stolid, wholesome and upstanding Britishness in the face of inscrutable deviousness, ingenious cruelty, and ruthless megalomania.

It would be mistaken, of course, to attribute all instances of derogation or harsh criticism to the wholesale projection of the 'shadow' since they may well contain elements of truth to a greater or lesser extent. In the case of demonisation, what the shadow does is to amplify negative judgements by creating a demonic caricature of the 'other' through the use of loaded language, the emotive, hyperbolic rhetoric exploiting words and phrases that are either strongly condemnatory or self-righteous.

In his important development of a psycholinguistic approach to Critical Discourse Analysis (CDA), Teun van Dijk, Professor of Linguistics at the University of Amsterdam, identified the language of self-glorification, superiority, derogation, and demonisation amongst a considerable body of discursive structures, strategies, moves, and ploys employed to promote the exclusion, marginalisation, and, ultimately, persecution and even genocide of the 'other'. He pointedly remarked that to inflict such suffering was 'only one step from an assertion of national or cultural pride.' I referred to his work in some detail in a lecture I gave on the 'Language of Islamophobia' at the *Exploring Islamophobia* conference at the University of Westminster School of Law in London just two weeks after 9/11 and in the face of widespread fulminations against 'Islamic terrorism' in the national press in the UK. I pointed out that behind such prejudices lurked the demonisation of what is perceived to be a dark and dangerous manifestation of the 'other', the singling out of the most extreme position which can be imagined as somehow representative of the totality of Islam, as if there is one absolutely monolithic, cohesive and uniform Muslim mindset, a kind of immutable, undifferentiated abstraction. Sadly, this fantasy about a monolithic and aggressive Islam persists to this day and is not merely the outcome of ignorance. It goes deeper than that. It is quite simply a psychological phenomenon, a pathological state. The very vehemence of the language with its absurdly simplified polarisation of reality into competing and mutually exclusive positions is itself symptomatic of deeply unconscious projections. That is what is so intractable about this pathology. The people who think like this are deeply unconscious of their own psychic processes, or, even more dangerously, they are people who are intentionally exploiting this tendency in the human being to dichotomise, to split reality into polar opposites, to see only black or white, and hence to foster division and confrontation. And, of course, this demonising pathology is not restricted to Islamophobes, as I have already pointed out in referring to Sinophobia and 'Westophobia'. To these we might add the general term 'xenophobia', the irrational fear or hatred of people perceived as alien or foreign, a phobia escalating alarmingly in our times as a reaction to large numbers of refugees, migrants, and asylum seekers.

Taking a leaf from Jung's self-revelatory *Memories, Dreams and Reflections,* I would like to relate one of the 'dreams of my life', a dream of thirty years ago which has carried a guiding message about my own shadow ever since.

In the dream, I was in Wells Cathedral, the earliest Gothic cathedral in England dating from the twelfth century. At the time I was living in Glastonbury, not far from Wells, and used to visit the cathedral occasionally. Having moved to Wells last year, the cathedral is now within walking distance, and my visits have become more frequent. Near to the High Altar stands the cope chest, a wooden chest used for storing the vestments of the clergy. In the dream I was standing next to the cope chest, although it was not in its normal position on the right side of the cathedral but was now on the left side where it was very dark. I knew that a beautiful young princess had been locked up in the chest by a dwarf, who I sensed was 'sinister', even malefic. The word 'sinister' comes from a Latin word meaning 'on the left side', the position of the cope chest in the dream, although the earliest uses of the word in English dating from the fourteenth century pertain to some measure of evil, foreboding, or malevolence. I knew that my purpose was to liberate the princess from her internment, so I approached the chest and opened it to reveal the princess lying inside in a shimmering white dress. She had been gagged so as to silence her, so I removed the gag, and lifted her out of the chest, kissing her chastely on her cheek. She ran to meet the King and the Queen who were walking up the central aisle of the cathedral, and as she did so, the cathedral was flooded with light.

Reflecting on this dream over many years, I have a strong sense that the sinister dwarf is a personification of an aspect of my own 'shadow'. I could not see him in the dream, for he operated in the dark on the left (sinister) side. I knew in the dream that his name was Malik, and this was the clue that enabled me to understand what he represented and what I was intent on keeping repressed in the unconscious. In Arabic, *malik* is the owner or king, the master and ruler. In one of my assignments as a teacher overseas in the early 1980s, Mr Malik was a fellow teacher (master) who was very dictatorial and would brook no laziness, lack of attention, disobedience, or 'bad attitude' from his pupils. I wondered if my own shadow included an authoritarian 'schoolmaster'.

At the time of the dream of the princess in the cope chest I was indeed a Director of Studies and schoolmaster teaching English to able students at an independent school. During one of my lessons, I noticed one of the students, a gifted artist, sketching something instead of taking notes, and on examining the sketch I was highly amused to discover that it was a cartoon, a parody of Judge Dredd, the draconian enforcement officer and eraser of miscreants, played by the hugely macho Sylvester Stallone in the science fiction movie of 1995. However, instead of depicting Judge Dredd holding an automatic weapon, the caricature depicted me brandishing a huge pencil sharpened to a fine point, with the hilarious caption 'FREEZE! Judge Henzell. English is the Law.' I duly 'confiscated' the sketch and framed it, and to this day it stands on my desk as a reminder not to be excessively rigorous, judgmental, critical, dogmatic, or pedantic. It is typical of the shadow that I was really not conscious of such traits in myself, having always seen myself as a very liberal-minded teacher, even to the extent of offering a gold star (award of merit) to any student who could provide convincing evidence for disagreeing with me.

It is only too clear that any repressed tendency to lecture, preach, or pontificate was also contained in the 'rulership' aspect of Malik in supressing the feminine, so aptly symbolised by the shadowy confinement and silencing of the youthful princess in an antique wooden chest storing the heavy and uniquely patriarchal clerical vestments used in the rituals of formal religion. The cope chest actually dates from 1120 before the construction of the Gothic cathedral, so it is a relic from the original Saxon church on the site. What is more, the opening of the 'chest' of course symbolises the opening of the heart, just as the removal of the gag symbolises the liberation of the feminine 'voice'. In short, this 'shadow' aspect represented by the dwarf Malik seemed to me to be the rule-bound, patriarchal (and historically misogynistic) aspect of formal religiosity.

While I am certainly open to acknowledging the judgmental and critical aspect of the shadowy schoolmaster in my own psyche, I am less comfortable in admitting to any hidden patriarchal and misogynistic traits associated with formal religiosity. My 'ego-ideal', my inner image of how I like to see myself, has always been the passionate non-conformist, iconoclast, and reformer, resident in my DNA at least since my French Protestant (Huguenot) ancestors were persecuted by the Catholics, driving them into exile to England at the end of the sixteenth century. I was always the arch-rebel at school, dismissive of those rules which I judged to be outmoded or senseless. I have also always seen myself as a champion of the feminine.

In view of all this, I incline to the position that there is not only a personal shadow, but also an ancestral and collective shadow deep in the unconscious in the same way that psychiatry recognises the existence of ancestral and collective trauma on the individual psyche. The horrific persecution of women by the patriarchy in the name of religion is a matter of history, and there has long been a crying need to release the princess from the cope chest and let her speak. Whether or not any unseen patriarchal trait is buried in my own personal shadow (and if so I need to bring it into the light of consciousness) I am convinced that it is prominent in the collective shadow, although the advent of feminism has done much to erode some of its manifestations.

On a grander scale, in the broader sweep of history, the liberation of the princess is akin to the process of paradigmatic change, what Jean Gebser has described as the periodic evolutionary advances in the structure of human consciousness. The antique chest is the old paradigm, an obsolete structure of consciousness.

In the epilogue to his remarkable book, *The Passion of the Western Mind*, Richard Tarnas affirms his belief that the resolution of the crisis caused by the over-valuation of the masculine in Western culture is already emerging in various movements which reflect an epochal shift in the contemporary psyche, a fulfilment of the longing for a reunion with the feminine, a reconciliation between the two great polarities, a union of opposites. This can be seen in the 'tremendous emergence of the feminine in our culture... the widespread opening up to feminine values by both men and women...in the increasing sense of unity with the planet and all forms of nature on it, in the increasing awareness of the ecological and the growing reaction against political and corporate policies supporting the domination and exploitation of the environment, in the growing embrace of the human community, in the accelerating collapse of long-standing and ideological barriers separating the world's peoples, in the deepening recognition of the value and necessity of partnership, pluralism, and the interplay of many perspectives.'

I would add the important caveat that we are now at a point of maximum intensification of those negative aspects of masculine consciousness, as they redouble their efforts to forestall the impending paradigm shift. Alongside the increasing awareness of the ecological is a potentially catastrophic acceleration in the assault on bio-diversity and in climate change; alongside the growing dissolution of ideological barriers separating the world's peoples we have the pernicious doctrine of the Clash of Civilisations which threatens to engulf the world in catastrophic conflict; alongside the deepening recognition of the value and necessity of partnership, pluralism, and the interplay of many perspectives, we have the resurgence of dangerously divisive forms of unilateralism, isolationism, nationalism, patriotism, militarism, supremacist ideology, triumphalism, and other forms of narrow identity politics. In all of this we can see the common thread of an autonomous solipsism which has reached the stage where it has assumed a pathological character, a kind of malignant egophrenia.

In envisioning the new emergent paradigm as the union of opposites in the integration of the masculine and feminine archetypes, Tarnas confirms the conclusion of Jean Gebser whose wide-ranging study of human endeavour convinced him that humanity is at the stage of transition from the 'Mental' to the 'Integral' structure of consciousness which is not fixated on dualistically opposed categories, one-sided perspectives, and the like. And it is precisely the union of opposites that occurs at the climax of my dream of the cope chest. Released from the chest, as light floods the cathedral, the princess runs to meet the King and the Queen (masculine and feminine rulers) walking up the central aisle between the left and right sides. This is the *coniunctio oppositorum* which Jung regarded as the completion of the Great Work of alchemy.

Reflecting on the path that spontaneously opened up in writing this essay, it seems appropriate that it started with the single eye of the Dajjal, unveiled the 'shadow' and the problem of 'demonisation', and concluded with the enlightenment of the union of opposites and the promise of a new mode of integral human consciousness. Let us keep striving to articulate and usher in the new paradigm!

ARTS AND LETTERS

REMEMBERING STALIN

Boyd Tonkin

> *He rolls the executions on his tongue like berries.*
> *He wishes he could hug them like big friends from home.*

Osip Mandelstam, 'The Stalin Epigram',
translated by WS Merwin and Clarence Brown

Bushy moustache to the fore, rainbow-hued decorations strewn across a broad, uniformed chest below, the kindly face of political evil beams out from a finely woven Tajik carpet, its borders friskily adorned with equestrian motifs. Another lavishly stitched carpet, from Azerbaijan, depicts the people's hero fraternally united with a local leader. The hall crammed with official and private gifts to Josef Vissarionovich Dzhugashvili, aka Soso, aka Soselo, aka Koba, aka Stalin, confirms how far the cult of the Great Helmsman spread during the decades of his power. Lovingly crafted tributes from the Middle East and Asia abound: an Iranian rug; a bas-relief portrait carved into a cedar of Lebanon; a comradely greeting microscopically engraved in Delhi onto a single grain of rice.

As for the crowds that throng the Stalin Museum in Gori on a fine spring day, they prove that the fascination the Soviet dictator exerts on posterity remains undimmed. People from Africa, the Middle East, and many parts of Asia join visitors from Europe and the Americas. Georgia unrolls its welcome mat in many different directions: even, still, to Russia. Anti-Putin refugees mingle in cafés and hotels with the usual tourists who have been coming to the southern land of wine, scenery, and sunshine – their very own Tuscany or Provence, to both the Tsarist and Soviet empires – for more than two hundred years. The United Nations crowd milling through the Stalin Museum suggests as well that the astonishing ascent of a poor kid from a colonial backwater to dominion over half the world may still echo around the global South. With no English-language tour due soon, I tag along with a coachload of Israelis. Their Hebrew-speaking guide considerately adds an English commentary as well.

As many travellers have reported, the Stalin Museum – located in the autocrat's birthplace – ranks as one of the more surreal destinations on any tourist itinerary. Opened in 1957, four years after Stalin's death but also after Khrushchev had denounced his predecessor's crimes, it adorns the city – an hour's drive west of the Georgian capital Tbilisi – where Dzhugashvili aka Stalin was born, a drunken cobbler's son, in 1878. A handsome neo-classical edifice, more Italian than 'Soviet' in its architectural style, the museum sits in a lush landscaped park. Preserved in the grounds, the Dzhugashvili family shack now sits canopied by a sort of Greek temple: a humble shrine next to the vast basilica of the museum itself. On the main building's other side stands the sea-green private railway carriage that accommodated the leader on his long train journeys around the Soviet Union and beyond. Green, wooded hills rise beyond the city under an already-fierce spring sun. As Simon Sebag Montefiore's biography of Stalin's early years points out, Gori (along with much of Georgia) 'resembles Sicily more than Siberia'. East of the Black Sea, west of the Caspian, the city lies closer to Baghdad than St Petersburg.

Inside the museum, over two grandiose floors, well-lit halls gather photographs, documents, relics, and memorabilia to trace the life and afterlife of the Bolshevik revolutionary who rose to exercise supreme power across the world's largest state for a quarter-century and, after the Second World War, redrew the map of the modern world. I visited Gori in May 2022, weeks after Stalin's latter-day cheerleader Vladimir Putin had invaded the nation whose inhabitants the Georgian often treated as his curse or nemesis: Ukraine.

Read travellers' tales about Gori and its Stalin pilgrims and you might assume that the museum represents not just an anomaly but an atrocity: a secular cathedral uncritically dedicated to the worship of a mass-murdering tyrant. You can, for sure, buy various kitsch souvenirs in the gift shop – with ironic intent or otherwise. Still, the overall experience makes the head spin rather than the flesh creep. Captions now uneasily blend the hagiographical tone of the original displays with amendments that nod to the dark side of the Stalinist decades. Downstairs, slightly tucked away, a newer exhibit recreates an interrogation room of the NKVD secret police and recalls the persecution of Georgia's political and cultural leaders in the 1930s by their tyrannical compatriot. Other visitors have told of guides who bizarrely spout the Communist Party line c.1950. But I went round with an astute and well-informed history student. She argued that the museum's value rests chiefly in its aspic conservation of the Stalinist mindset. In other words, it becomes a meta-museum: the curated record of an outlook and an ideology.

In this light, a thorough overhaul – as some Georgian politicians have demanded – to reflect the whole truth about the Gulag, the Great Terror, and the deportations would serve little purpose. In Tbilisi itself, an evocative if strident 'Museum of Soviet Occupation' already covers the history of Georgia between the brief independence of its first post-Tsarist republic (1918-1921) and the collapse of the USSR in 1991. Historical memory needs to address not only facts but feelings and beliefs. At a time when Putin's Russia has sought to redeem Stalin in the service of its own expansionist, 'Great Russian' ambitions, Gori's spectacular reminder of the cult and its allure has a time-defying appeal.

'Retain and explain,' runs the mantra of many Western curators confronted with calls to topple monuments to slavers or conquerors. Retaining and explaining in Gori would require not just tougher captions but a separate installation, devoted to the victims of Stalinism, of equal size and scope. Berlin's exemplary 'Topography of Terror' about the Third Reich might serve as a model. Nothing like that will happen soon. For now, seekers after the truth about the past can merely hope for guides as enlightened as mine as they stroll through these lofty light-filled galleries towards the inner sanctum where the dictator's death-mask rests.

How many lives did that serene face, that brain behind it, prematurely end? In the Cold War era when fervently anti-Communist (often ex-Communist) historians such as Robert Conquest did the calculations, popular estimates settled around 15 to 20 million. In *The Gulag Archipelago* and other works, Aleksandr Solzhenitsyn raised the total for the Soviet period as a whole to 60 million. Now, the most scrupulous researchers into Stalin's policy and legacy – such as Timothy Snyder – attribute six to nine million excess deaths, by torture, execution, massacre, famine, disease, deportation, and forced labour to his regime's account. Even-handedly, Snyder scores the civilian, non-battlefield victims of Stalin and

Hitler together in the eastern European 'bloodlands' they fought over at around 14 million.

Both in everyday journalism, and in sober works of scholarship, you will find Stalin routinely described as one of the most evil men who ever lived. If, in the absence of a scientific measure for the corrupted soul, we reckon according to the number of innocent human lives he took, there's little reason to dispute that claim. Young Soso, or Koba – poet, insurrectionist, and sometime bank-robber (a heist undertaken to raise Bolshevik funds in 1907) – may have embraced a take-no-prisoners brand of Marxist materialism from an early age. He started out, however, in a trade that dealt in notions of evil every day, as a Tbilisi seminarian preparing for the Orthodox ministry from 1894 to 1899. Stalin was, in the Irish phrase, a 'spoiled priest'.

Addressing his earlier schooldays, Sebag Montefiore sketches a pious lad 'so devout that he hardly missed a mass'. In Stalin's later displays of hard-headed indifference to others' suffering ('no man, no problem', he notoriously said) you glimpse a personality in furious flight from the code he once pledged to uphold. A fine choral singer and gifted fledgling poet, the cobbler's boy gained high grades (scripture among them) before, in the later 1890s, a new-found faith in revolution lured him from the church.

Stalin was never a moral illiterate or an unreflecting thug. Among the forbidden novels he read and annotated at the seminary was Dostoevsky's lacerating drama of revolutionary struggle and the cost of utopian dreams, The Possessed. After he had shed Orthodox Christianity, Stalin maintained a keen interest in and respect for literature that explored the inner life of values and ideals. To do evil, not merely to inflict harm, you must know what it is. Stalin did.

Yet here I am, under a benign springtime sun, tagging along with the queuers who pay their 15 Georgian lari (about £4.50) to support the shrine to this world-ranking monster. This particular devil can still arouse a kind of sympathy. Or, if not sympathy, then an awestruck curiosity about how humdrum, even genial 'Uncle Joe' (as the British and American publics learned to call him during the wartime alliance), could have left such a giant footprint on our times. Even the millions who loathe him with a personal animus – descendants of individual victims or of populations targeted by his crimes against humanity – still want to know why.

Whichever mind-boggling statistic of his death-toll finds favour, the singularity of Gori – or of other commemorations such as a planned 'Stalin Centre' in the Nizhny Novgorod region of Russia – lies in its very existence. Though Nazism and Maoism may still flourish, overtly or disguised, a well-appointed institution to honour the memory of Hitler or Mao remains, for the moment, unthinkable. Dzhugashvili-Stalin is the only wholesale slaughterer among the alpha despots of the twentieth century who has kept his grip on both sentimental and strategic disciples. No other 'evil' dictator from the totalitarian epoch can still convince – even charm. The sentimentalists recall the 'Great Patriotic War' that crushed Hitler's own genocidal system (after two years of close Nazi-Soviet collaboration) or the blood-stained achievements of the Soviet dash for industrial development. The strategists stand in awe of the extraordinary land grab that made great swathes of central-eastern Europe a Soviet fief and, just as significantly, consolidated Moscow's hold on middle Asia.

The victor over Nazism and the peerless empire-builder fuse in Putin's own decade-long rapprochement with Stalin's memory: a process well advanced when he deplored the 'excessive demonisation' of the dictator to filmmaker Oliver Stone in 2017, and near-complete when his forces entered Ukraine in February 2022. In 2023, a commentator for the Russian state press agency voiced mainstream Kremlin opinion in maintaining that criticism of Stalin is 'not just anti-Soviet but is also Russophobic, aimed at dividing and defeating Russia'. Stalin rehabilitated Ivan the Terrible as a mighty patriotic warrior; Putin and his allies do the same for the architect of purges, famines, and massacres. At the same time, historians and human-rights groups who have painted a more complete portrait of the Stalin era face harassment and, recently, outright bans. A Moscow court outlawed Memorial International, the leading resource for documentary evidence of Soviet repression, in December 2021 – just weeks before the Ukraine war began.

In the West, meanwhile, the nostalgic loyalties of diehard Stalinist 'tankies' stir indulgent derision of a gentleness that unrepentant neo-Nazis would never be allowed. Martin Amis's freewheeling study of Stalin's life and myth, *Koba the Dread*, makes much of the laughter that old Stalinists, but never old Hitlerites, provoke: 'And what kind of laughter is it? It is, of course, the laughter of universal fondness for that old, old idea about the perfect society'. In the eyes of later utopians, Stalin's annihilating evil wins, if not a free pass, then a reduced sentence, because it once wore the mask of good. Faith in a glorious future clothed – and for some, still clothes – ugly acts in beautiful raiment. Solzhenitsyn, in the course of his own tormented interrogations of the Stalinist myth, lays the blame on 'ideology – that is what gives evil-doing its long-sought justification and gives the evil-doer the necessary steadfastness and determination.'

For Bolsheviks in the Soviet period, and their supporters abroad, memories of the revolutionary quest for hope and joy still clung to the man whose absolute power had buried their dreams under a mountain of corpses. Even a Gulag survivor such as Eugenia Ginzburg, in her great memoir *Into the Whirlwind*, refuses to break with the Bolshevik good that, for her, underlay the Stalinist evil that had engulfed the USSR. 'What interesting lives we had led,' she writes of her radical youth, 'and how wonderfully everything had begun!'

In this reading, a lingering tenderness for utopian ideology dilutes revulsion against the calamities Stalin unleashed. The high ideals and good intentions of the Bolshevik revolution form one aspect of the mitigating circumstances that have allowed a celebratory Stalin Museum – but not a Hitler museum – to thrive within a democratic state in 2023. Another is what might be called the argument from rationality. In contrast to the deranged barbarism of the Nazis, it runs, Stalin and his cohorts worked according to a plan – indeed, they mapped the Soviet present and future as an unfolding vista of Five-Year Plans. They drew inspiration from the philosophical heritage of the European Enlightenment, as Kant and Hegel yielded to Marx, Lenin, and the Soviet Union's master-thinker, Stalin himself.

Terry Eagleton's book *On Evil*, for instance, in no sense exonerates Stalin's tyranny. But he distinguishes, as many have, between the Nazis' racialised savagery and Marxist-Leninist planned catastrophe. Stalin and Mao 'massacred for a reason,' Eagleton asserts, and 'for what they saw as honourable ends'. That hardly ensures that they did so in a reasonable way. Stalin's record reveals many episodes of wanton destructiveness as crazily self-harming as anything in Hitler's dossier: from the war on 'kulaks' in Ukraine and elsewhere that devastated food production, and the mass execution of Red Army officers prior to the Second World War, to the deportation of loyal (often Muslim) national minorities to Siberia when the war effort needed them most.

The military purge of 1937, when Stalin well understood Hitler's long-term aggressive aims towards the Soviet Union, eliminated around 90 percent of senior officers. Just before the German invasion of June 1941 (Operation Barbarossa), Stalin's denial of reality had seen him ignore eighty-four warnings of an impending attack and, a week previously, officially dismiss rumours of imminent war as 'clumsy fabrications'. Timothy Snyder finds in the state-enforced starvation of Ukrainian peasants in 1932–1933, which killed over three million, not a cunning plan but 'a position of pure malice'. The anti-Darwinian genetic voodoo peddled by Trofim Lysenko, which Stalin zealously backed for two decades, damaged crop yields at times of desperate dearth. If the residue of utopian idealism cannot save Stalin from the taint of evil, neither will the claims of logic, reason, and progress.

A linked source of attraction may draw the sort of visitors to a Stalin shrine who would never countenance a trip to some neo-Fascist or neo-colonialist monument. It has become a commonplace to note that the chief killer despots of the totalitarian age had strong artistic and intellectual interests. If Hitler's watercolours won few accolades, both Mao and Stalin managed to pen decent verse in a fairly conservative style. The young Dzhugashvili had his Georgian poems printed in leading anthologies long before 'Stalin' saw the light of day. 'To the Moon', typical in its romantic and rhapsodic lyricism, tells us:

'Know for certain that once
Struck down to the ground, an oppressed man
Strives again to reach the pure mountain,
When exalted by hope'

(translation by Donald Rayfield)

As a rebel seminarian he devoured French fiction (Victor Hugo above all) and remained a devoted bookworm – and marginal annotator – all his life. Geoffrey Roberts's study of *Stalin's Library* calculates that his book collection comprised up to 25,000 items, spread around his Kremlin quarters and dachas outside Moscow. In the 1920s, he ordered around 500 new titles a year. And, of course, every aspirant Soviet author sent him a complimentary copy of their works.

This voracious consumer of print – not just politics and economics but history and literature in various genres – had serious and eclectic tastes. Already general secretary of the CPSU, Stalin bothered to find the time to take philosophy tutorials, with an emphasis on Hegelian dialectics, from 1925 to 1928. That did no good for his teacher: Jan Sten, shot during the Terror. In literature, despite his backing for the straitjacket of 'Socialist Realism', Stalin could also speak up for artistic diversity and deplore crude propaganda books. 'You have to let people express themselves,' he once argued; writers should shun party-line fairy-tales. Take Chekhov, who 'has no heroes but rather grey people'.

Notoriously, Stalin toyed with and tormented not second-rate hacks but the finest Russian authors of his time: Osip Mandelstam, Boris Pasternak, Anna Akhmatova, Mikhail Bulgakov, Isaac Babel. He lured the renowned Maxim Gorky back to the Soviet Union from Italian exile and, tragically, confined his talent and integrity in a gilded cage of privilege and compromise. In 1934, after Mandelstam's arrest, Stalin famously phoned the detained poet's friend, Pasternak. 'Why haven't the writers' organisations come to me?' Stalin asked. 'If I were a poet and my friend had fallen into disgrace, I would climb the walls to help him.' Stalin then turned literary critic to enquire, 'But is he or is he not a master?' Pasternak, distraught, replied 'That's not the point!' Stalin hung up. Later, he did not quite murder Mandelstam but let exile, jail, and sickness despatch him. With Pasternak, he relented and told his henchmen during the Great Terror: 'Leave that cloud-dweller in peace.'

A cultivated butcher deserves no more or less mercy than a boorish philistine. But Stalin the reader, critic, and even creator has an enduring power to intrigue, even seduce, people who would recoil from an unlettered thug. He could even display a winning sort of ironic self-awareness. Editing the official *Short Biography* of himself in 1946, he bridled at its unctuous hero-worship: 'What are people supposed to do? Get down on their knees and pray to me?' Effectively, they had to do just that.

Any visitor to modern Georgia will spot another valuable asset in the portfolio of Stalin memories. Whatever the harm, the damage, the pain, or – if we choose the term – the evil that he orchestrated, Stalin looms in hindsight as an outsider of giant stature. He surged from the margins to seize the centre. Dzhugashvili spoke Russian as a second language. He never lost a thick Georgian accent and to the end (the British-American historian Robert Conquest reports) made mistakes with Russian grammar. His Georgian identity, grounds for suspicion among Tsarists and Bolsheviks alike, became a lasting source of pride. He loved Georgian poetry and wine all his life. As an apprentice revolutionary, he modelled his cheek and swagger on the mountain bandits who plagued the unruly fringes of the Tsarist empire. Indeed, some of those bandits turned Bolsheviks under Stalin's command.

The pre-revolutionary Tbilisi Stalin knew harboured not only Georgians and Russians but Armenians, Jews, Azeris, Iranians, and other Muslims – both local and incomers from elsewhere in the empire. Stalin's father reputedly spoke not only Georgian and Russian but Turkish and Armenian too. Georgia's own Muslim minorities included the Laz people of the Black Sea coast: among the forebears of Türkiye's President Erdogan. Russia incorporated parts of Georgia into its empire in 1801 as the Tsars pushed into areas of the Caucasus ruled by khanates with Ottoman or Persian ties; the takeover was complete within a decade. Today, in Tbilisi, the main synagogue, the elegant Tsarist-era mosque and Ottoman-style hammams cluster near the old cathedral under the Narikala fortress, built and re-built by Georgians, Persians, and Umayyads. In the usual nineteenth-century imperial vein, however, Stalin's schooling in Gori exposed him to routine disparagement of Georgian language and culture as backward, provincial, and in sore need of Russian rescue.

He would become the ultimate colonial boy made good: a shrewd operator who could play the rough hick from the backwoods when required, and did so when it suited him. Stalin could turn on the exotic, 'ethnic' manner to cajole or to convince, and to wrap chosen guests in what Sebag Montefiore calls 'an irresistible embrace of folksy intimacy'. His biographer usefully reminds us that, in pre-dictatorial days, 'the foundation of Stalin's power over the party was not fear; it was charm' – a distinctively Georgian charm.

By choice, Stalin never became wholly 'Russian'. Indeed, after the October Revolution in 1917, Lenin stamped his lieutenant with an ethnic brand by making him Commissar of Nationalities. Not that his official responsibility for non-Russians guaranteed any of them – even Georgians – an easy ride. Stalin spearheaded the suppression of the pluralistic, independent Georgia that flourished between 1918 and 1921, when Soviet forces quenched its autonomy. Notably, he also ousted the Tatar Muslim theorist and militant Mirsaid Sultan-Galiev, who worked to combine Islam and Bolshevism across an anti-imperialist, pan-Asian front.

When the Great Terror of 1937–1938 struck Stalin's homeland, it did so with an intimately vengeful force. Around 30,000 Georgians suffered repression at the time; half of them died. In Tbilisi, the handsome Writers' House of Georgia – built as the town mansion of a cognac magnate, and later the headquarters of the Soviet-era literary union – now hosts a moving 'museum of repressed writers'. It documents the imprisonment, ruin, exile, and murder that Stalin, through his fellow-Georgian terror chief Lavrenti Beria, visited on the intelligentsia of his beloved birthplace. Paolo Iashvili, a charismatic symbolist poet, committed suicide in this very building in 1937 after persecution had driven him to despair. The popular Georgian writer Mikheil Dzhavakhishvili was beaten to death on Beria's orders. In all, around 25 percent of Tbilisi members of the writers' union were executed.

So Stalin never left his own folk in peace; quite the opposite. His and Beria's origins only sharpened the edge of oppression in their own backyard. Yet Stalin remains incomparably the most famous Georgian who has ever lived. On his home turf, a grudging recognition that the murdering bastard was *our* bastard persists in some places. In a nation divided by clashing attitudes to their mighty Russian neighbour, views of Stalin tend to track wider assessments of the Soviet era and its aftermath.

Since independence in 1991, Georgian governments have understandably fumbled the hot potato of the dictator's legacy. Parties which urge distance from Russia, and closeness to the European Union, deprecate his memory. The Georgian Dream movement, currently in power, has proved more willing to indulge Stalin-friendly nostalgists. Disputes flare over the preservation of existing busts and statues or the erection of new ones – even over the ubiquitous sale of miniature effigies in souvenir shops. In Tbilisi, you can still visit the private collection of Stalin memorabilia built up by its late creator, Ushangi Davitashvili.

The political scientist Beka Chedia, who has studied the image of Stalin in contemporary Georgia, cites a 2012 poll showing that almost 45 percent of respondents expressed a 'positive attitude' to the dictator. Most of those would be older people, many with memories of the Second World War. Their numbers will have fallen year by year. Putin's accelerating neo-Stalinism, allied to Georgian outrage at the invasion of Ukraine, may make the dictator feel less like a cherished native son in his homeland. (In Russia, by 2021, 56 percent of those polled deemed Stalin a 'great leader'.)

Meanwhile, historical investigators in Georgia such as the Soviet Past Research Laboratory, or SovLab, work to locate and study the sites of Stalinist terror. I took a walk with a SovLab-produced map around the picturesque Sololaki neighbourhood of Tbilisi. Here chic bars and restaurants sit mind-bendingly near (or even within) mansions that once hosted torture chambers and execution cells. Despite these labours of remembrance, the occasional Stalin monument does still arise, with one unveiled in a village near Gori in 2022. A former Georgian Dream minister comments that 'although Stalin could not tolerate democracy, democracy must tolerate Stalin.' Georgia's reckoning with the evils of the past remains – as in other countries – strictly a minority pursuit. For many citizens, myths, and pieties endure.

If Stalin's deeds and policies do not count as 'evil', it would be hard to attach any meaning to the word. Even Terry Eagleton, still vestigially attached to a Marxist vision of future bliss, puts him firmly 'beyond the moral pale'. However, Stalin's own mental equipment gave him an exit from the court of judgment – not on the grounds of moral innocence, but of personal irrelevance. In keeping with his doctrines, he disavowed the 'cult of personality' even as he fostered and embodied it. He liked to present himself merely as the modest vector of historical inevitability. Stalin once upbraided his adopted son Artyom Sergeyev, who had made too much of his family connections. 'You're not Stalin,' the autocrat scolded. 'I'm not Stalin. Stalin is Soviet power.'

But did 'Soviet power' rather than one aberrant individual consign all those millions to suffering and death? Pose the question and you blunder into the fogs of 'counterfactual' history, with its speculations about alternative outcomes of the succession battles before and after Lenin's death in 1924. We do know for certain that Stalin, along with many others, ascribed evil to history and its relentless advance rather than to the malevolence of a perverse private will. Not only Marxism makes this exculpatory move. Susan Neiman's profound study of *Evil in Modern Thought* shows how, with the Enlightenment, the idea of theodicy – the justification of human sorrow and pain by reference to a divine plan – migrated from religious to secular thought.

Providence came down to earth as progress, which human agency might advance or retard but which would happen anyway. Hegel, Marx, and a variety of radical or liberal ideologists came to believe that (in Neiman's words) 'If history is the history of progress, it would contain its own cure'. In her classic memoir *Hope Against Hope*, Nadezhda Mandelstam remembers the 'determinist theory' that rendered any attention to 'real life' irrelevant: 'Why undermine the system and sow unnecessary doubt if history was in any case speeding us to the appointed destination?' From the starvation and deportation of Ukrainian peasants labelled 'kulaks' to the ethnic cleansing of long-settled Muslim populations such as Crimean Tatars, Chechens, and Meskhetian Turks, Stalin's historical determinism liked to punish not only rivals and enemies but entire populations as laggards on the march of progress.

As Snyder makes clear, Stalin's twisted logic dressed up the outcomes of his will, his choice, his policy, as the objective proof of irresistible trends. The massacre of opponents or the 'terror-famines' in Kazakhstan and Ukraine 'could be presented as the verdict of history'. Consider his career and you may pause before judging an argument or cause as being on the wrong – or the right – side of history. The Gulag or the Ukrainian 'Holodomor', political strategy posing as historical fatality, may lie at the end of that road.

Start to think about evil – in its moral, political or metaphysical guise – and you will soon find that it blends into the disputed territory of free will and human agency. Stalin, the inflexible exponent of the iron laws of history, nonetheless bent those laws towards his will throughout his career. And never more so than in the wake of the cataclysmic shock of Operation Barbarossa in 1941. Reports describe a dumbstruck, immobilised leader who could scarcely speak or eat. Nine days after the German invasion, he mumbled 'Fine' when Molotov and other ministers arrived – to arrest or shoot him, he apparently thought – and told him that the country should resist, and he must front the fightback. For a while, Stalin really did act, or fail to act, as the powerless plaything of insuperable forces. Then he recovered his will and began to lead the struggle that, for good or evil, would shape the post-1945 world.

So the grotesque idolatry still evident – if now contested – in Gori's Stalin Museum has at least a foothold in reality. Stalin made a historical difference to his era and ours, as solid, massive and unignorable as the monuments to him that still rise in Georgia and Russia (a new memorial in Volograd, formerly Stalingrad, was inaugurated in February 2023). Charitably, you may judge the cosmopolitan crowd of visitors who tramp up the museum staircase and chuckle over the branded knick-knacks in the shop – as I did – not as disciples of political evil but of human will and choice.

In his less deterministic moods, Stalin the student of history saluted the decisive freedom of pivotal individuals. When he took issue with an over-theoretical Soviet textbook, he insisted about the great Tsars that 'Peter was Peter, Catherine was Catherine. They rested on certain classes, expressed their moods and interests, but they acted, they were historical figures'. 'Historical' in that they made history, for better or worse, not merely channelled it. As did Stalin himself. However gigantic, his evil stemmed not from a divinity, a demon, or a cog in history's wheel. It has the human face that smiles out from that gaudy Tajik carpet.

CAESAR AND MAZEN PAINTINGS

Marc Nelson

I create drawings, paintings, prints, and sculpture that respond to literature, history, and human rights issues, both past and present. My interest in depicting the victims of war and persecution began as a child, when I discovered my grandfather's collection of World War One photography. These stark images of brutality and industrialised destruction shattered any boyhood illusions of war as a heroic game.

I am drawn to photography's ability to both suspend time and suggest movement, and I seek a way to use art to create works that are both static and fluid. In the last several years I have focused on responding to contemporary images, shared on social media, of civilians affected by the conflict in Syria. Unlike the Holocaust, whose horrors were revealed to the wider world after the camps were liberated, photos and videos of the civilians murdered by the Syrian regime are being shared in real-time, for everyone to see. I feel that there is an inherent ephemerality to media shared on Twitter and Instagram, and I attempt to reflect on these quickly scrolled-by images through the time-consuming act of drawing and painting. Often, my work has abstracted the photographic source image enough so that it can bypass social media's graphic content filters, and be shared freely on the Internet as well as in publications, exhibitions, and documentary films.

Many of my paintings and monotypes depict the 'Caesar Photos'. These are digital images of thousands of corpses secretly captured by a Syrian military photographer known only by the codename Caesar. These photos, taken between 2011 and 2013, document the death by torture of over 11,000 Syrian civilians. In August 2013, Caesar risked his life to smuggle these images out of Syria via a thumb drive hidden in his sock. As the digital photographs are extremely graphic, I have focused on using 'analog' charcoal and pigment as a way to both emotionally process the disturbing material, and allow a wider audience to bear witness to these war crimes.

Alongside these Caesar paintings/prints, I draw weekly images of one of the 100,000 disappeared Syrian civilians - my friend, Mazen al-Hamada. Mazen was arrested by the Assad regime in 2012 for attempting to smuggle baby formula to a besieged suburb of Damascus. He was tortured for a year and a half before being released in September 2013. After his release, Mazen was given asylum in the Netherlands, and spent the next seven years tirelessly recounting his nightmarish experiences in government detention, and advocating for his fellow detainees. Mazen and I became friends in 2017 after we were introduced by documentary filmmaker Sara Afshar. In 2020, Mazen lost his refugee status in the Netherlands, and was lured back to Syria with the promise of releasing more detainees. He was arrested at Damascus airport on 23 February 2020, and has not been heard from since. Immediately after being notified of Mazen's disappearance, I took screenshots of his social media photos before they were erased by the Syrian government. Every week or so I make a drawing based on the screenshots, and share it on social media. Along with the drawing, I include a written memory of Mazen, and the number of days he has been missing in an effort to keep my friend's story alive.

All Caesar images are oil, charcoal, ink, acrylic on canvas or paper. The Mazen sketches are digital drawings printed on watercolour paper.

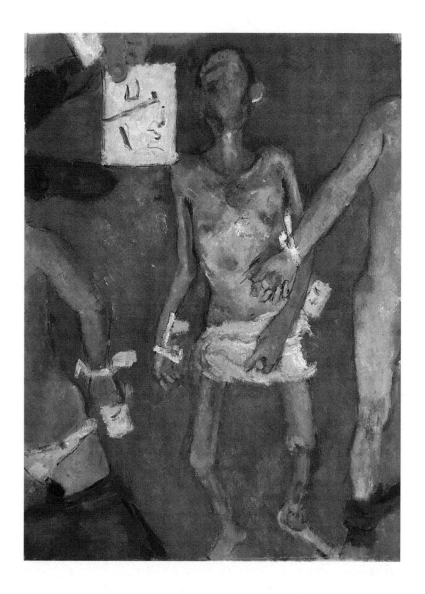

THE TRAGIC DEATH OF ANTHONY BOURDAIN

Tam Hussein

God had blessed Nizam with a pair of hands that made everything taste delightful. Whatever Nizam touched tasted wonderful. He could make a boring lentil soup, *Ades* which the Indians and Turks had stolen from Naqshistan, and turn it into something quite extraordinary. He could make a simple *sandeech,* which the English had stolen, and transform it into something that men outside of Shahrepour would travel for. Sometimes women, unaccompanied by their husbands would turn up too. Nizam cared for nothing but that. He made sure to scour the Google reviews daily to check that none of his customers complained about his food. He would take it as a point of honour that the plate was empty when his customers left. If it was not and a simple crust was left, he would inquire as to why the crust was still on the plate.

As all the restaurants and chefs in Shahrepour sneered, Nizam was not a chef. He did not have the training in Paris, Istanbul or Dubai, like they did. He wasn't a Michelin star chef. He'd never even been out of the city. He used too much of everything, too much butter, too much cheese, too much onion, too much dill. He was nothing, just an Instagrammer and influencer who got lucky.

Nizam was proud that he wasn't a chef. He refused to use the Persian term for the word too. He was a *Babursi* and challenged each and every one of the chefs to come and eat in his restaurant. Sometimes, he would stand in front of their restaurants in his traditional Naqshi clothes, remove the white cooking cloth which he always had on his rounded shoulders, and throw it down on the floor as a challenge. In the olden days this was usually a challenge a warrior made to another – an invitation to duel. But none of the chefs or their proprietors would take him up on the invitation. They said that his restaurant was too small, a rectangle of a box with six tables, and his kitchen was his domain, not theirs. So, he would say, let me cook in your shop. Still they would not take him up on his offer.

He knew they would not; one bite and they would be enchanted. When CNN's Anthony Bourdain visited Naqsh where did he go? Did he go to their cheap imitation restaurants that served foreign food like La Pomodoro, Fook Yue Chinese restaurant, Bung Hole Irish bar or Phat Phuc Thai noodle bar and finally la maison il-Cráp. No, Bourdain came to his restaurant named after his grandfather, *Babursi Herpes*. When Bourdain said this tasted like Persian food, Nizam corrected him. Can you imagine! Correcting the American celebrity chef Anthony Bourdain! Yes, he did. The Mongols stole the *samsa* which became the humble samosa consumed by all of the subcontinent. The Persians stole their food and it became part of their culture.

Of course, no one in Naqsh saw the episode, because, last minute, Nizam had asked Bourdain to pull it. He was already inundated by people coming to the restaurant, he didn't want foreign tourists to come to his restaurant as well.

This was probably why fortune had smiled on him. To think that he had been nothing, just showing the wonders of Naqshi cooking on Instagram. He cooked simply, with purity and excellence. He cared for nothing else and took pictures, sometimes he would put his own spin on them, but not enough to be considered heretical and that would be it. He never put pictures of himself, just the food. He wanted the person to enjoy the food, not the one who made it. Sometimes, a substandard dish became good once the diner realised who had made it. This was against the principles of Naqshi cooking – in Naqshi cooking the author had to be invisible and the focus must be on the food. This is why his restaurant was so plain and dirty – the focus had to be the food not the hygiene, just like the worshipper must focus on God. Everything else was tantamount to polytheism. But he made sure to emphasise that this was Naqshi, not Persian, cooking. On one post he had said it with a picture of some food on his vigorous moustache: 'For too long,' he said, 'us Naqshis have passed off our food as Iranian. We were head Babursis in Istanbul, Shiraz and Isfahan and yet, everyone know of our food as Persian – enough of this!' Such calls to action gave him many thousands of followers and of course, detractors. He was either mocked for being the Babursi with the unnaturally white teeth and bristling mustachio who claimed to have recorded an episode with Bourdain, or hailed as the saviour of Naqshistan, allowing himself to be photographed with a mustachio and dress which smacked of impersonating the great Salvador Dalì. Nizam claimed to have met the American chef once, but insisted that he was never influenced by his way of cooking.

It must have been just after Nowruz when Behnam Gul came to visit. Nizam had sent his assistant and business partner, Hedayat, home and was closing up shop, arranging the sheep testicles tastefully on the glass counter and window, beaming with pride. He had required, in line with ancient Naqshi lore as told by Hedayat, that the sheep's oysters had to be prepubescent and obtained on the day they became full of vitality – full of spunky life! That was hard and required the farmer to go and have a squeeze to check if the eggs had ripened, as it were. And he had succeeded. What beautiful oysters! How delightful! Nizam was in a reverie. He was going to serve grilled testicles marinated in salt, pepper, olive oil and lemon juice; once grilled, add a bit of sumac, Naqhshi lemons, fresh bread and pickles! That would do! He was just picturing it, subconsciously grabbing his own as if to protect them, when he saw a well-dressed young man with long hair and an Assyrian-looking beard, coming out of a Mercedes Coupé with Shahr Jahan number plates. The man didn't appear to be lost but headed straight for his shop window and stared at him brashly. Nizam hid behind the lamb oysters pretending to arrange them; he did not want to entertain this arrogant man. But the man with the striking eyes tapped the window. Nizam stopped, looked at him and told him they were closed. The young man tapped the window and put his hands together as if he was pleading.

Nizam, seeing his contrition, opened the window.

'What can I do for you, sir?'

'Please *Agha*,' Behnam said, 'we've travelled all the way from the capital to eat.'

'I am sorry, we are closed. Come back tomorrow.' He did not like that effeminate drawl that those from the capital had. They always elongated the last vowel as if they were imitating those Iranians from Tehran. 'Come back tomorrow.'

'But *Agha*, I have to go back tonight. Please I will pay you money for your time.'

'I'm sorry, young man. It's not possible.'

'Sir, I cannot leave but eat your food. I saw your food on Instagram.

'I am sorry. Come earlier.' He huffed and returned to cleaning the surfaces.

'Look I will help you clean up, afterwards. Even if it's just a hamburger.'

'*Hamburger?*' that word incensed him, and the man had said it in an American accent too, 'Look city boy. I will have you know that I don't cook American food.'

'But what is that?' Behnam pointed to a picture where in between two buns was a brown piece of beef patty that looked not unlike a turd. 'Isn't that a hamburger?'

'My son, that's the father of the Hamburger, *hambakht!* These Americans, they steal everything from everyone, and then call it their own and say they invented it. When in reality, the hamburger comes from the Naqshis – some American geographers were mapping these parts of the world many years ago, came across the *hambakht* and next minute you know McDonalds calls it the hamburger. But then, what can you expect from the Americans.' He shook his head. 'This is why I refused CNN's Alain Bourdain to broadcast it, because he would steal the idea and put it in his restaurant and ruin mine. People will say I copied him, instead of the other way round. Theirs is a parasitic culture – ours my friend is one which creates!'

Behnam was amazed. 'To think that I had been eating a part of home for three years, thinking it quintessentially part of American culture! I can't believe it. No wonder it tasted so good.'

'Have you never had a *hambakht?*'

'No, never.'

'Really?'

Behnam nodded. Standing before Nizam was a man who had not tasted reality. Like a man content to be with a rubber doll thinking it a woman.

'Come in,' said Nizam looking out on the street. 'Baradar Jan doesn't like us over working. But in this case, He went to the controls for the electric shutters and turned the keys. The shutters with the benevolent picture of Baradar Jan came down.

That evening Nizam prepared Behman *Hambakht*. He fried the onions lovingly, and the mushrooms; brought out the paneer, which he melted and draped over the aged mince patty, giving it that turdy texture; added two slices of tomato – it had to be two. He served the *Hambakht* alongside *Aloo*, lovingly sliced potatoes cut in the shape of reed flutes.

'Why reed flutes?' said Behnam.

'Because it yearns to go back to the source; like the reed flute that wishes to return to its source, so too does the potato.'

Behnam didn't quite know what he meant by this reference to *Moulavi* Rumi but he accepted it, in any case. After gorging himself, he helped clean up the kitchen, getting his fine clothes dirty.

As he left, Behnam offered to pay the Babursi.

'I did not do it to be paid. I did it so you can know the truth, the reality as it really is.'

'Please, I insist.'

Nizam refused.

'Then at least, accept this gift.' Behman took his watch off and handed it to Nizam. The chef refused his offer at first, but then noticing that it was a Tissot, did not insist on refusing Behnam's offer and took it.

Nizam did not think much of this encounter. A month later, Baradar Jan came to Shahrepour to set up his Yurt to listen to the people. On the television, Baradar Jan always spoke of overzealous brothers with too much of the revolutionary zeal. 'Forgive them,' he would say, 'for too much of the blood of the Khan run in their veins! Too much.' In order to counteract them, he travelled to various parts of the country, set up his Yurt and received his fellow citizens. For Baradar was not a king, he was a citizen and insisted that he be referred to as such. In fact, this horse trader's son from the steppes would have no issue in going back to that life if necessary, and cutting open the veins of his sturdy steed, mixing the blood with mare's milk and drinking it. Fermented *Dood* was his favourite drink and he always prayed that God give it to him in paradise. In preparation for his arrival, the municipality poured perfume down the sewers, moved palm trees to line the presidential route and filled the street with flags and pictures of their favourite son.

Before a visit, it was said that sometimes Jan would travel in disguise to make sure that all was well amongst the people. Usually, prior to a visit many barren women in the city, were granted children by Baradar Jan's *barake* – known as the Khan's touch. This mystical touch, known in Europe as the king's touch, could cure many an ailment, including childlessness (even if one was a virgin). Other times, the news segment would report how Jan had fixed a wall that had been in a state of disrepair since the death of Garshasp IX. According to Jan, who had once been his Prime Minister, the king had taken a dip in the salt lake of Namakghah and had not come up. Jan cried for days, until the regency was thrust upon him. Another citizen spoke of Jan dropping round to an elderly couple, cooking for them, and granting their unmarried daughter a son, so that the elderly couple could be looked after by a man of the house, despite his infancy. Another soldier who had been at the front guarding Naqsh's borders for two years without respite, thanked Jan: his wife had been barren for two years and yet after a brief visit by the great leader, God had granted them a son. Such were the powers of the *Barake*. All such things were noted in Naqshi news, always in the last segment of news which was intended to lift and inspire the country's citizens to do better. After all, looking at the rapine and imperialism of the West, it seemed an apt way to end the news. Naqshis were not like *them*.

On the eve before the pegs of the Yurt were to be raised and Jan was to leave for the capital, Nizam found himself making some *Hambakht*. Hedayat, his assistant, was sharpening the knives in preparation for the next day, when he spotted three black Mercedes Maybachs pulling up to the shop. The windows were all tinted and the vehicles were escorted by police on motor cycles. Nizam was taken back by the distinguished cars. Soon the doors of the first Mercedes opened. Several burly men came piling out, wearing glasses despite the evening and head pieces. They immediately went into the restaurant without asking and threw out the last customer.

'Hey! Hey!' said Nizam grabbing a newly sharpened meat cleaver, 'you can't do that here. He's my customer, *haramzadeh!*'

But the security men did not listen and so Nizam lunged for one with the meat cleaver and would have struck him, had Behnam not stood in front of him.

'Stop! Stop! Babursi it's me Behnam!'

Nizam stopped in his stride. 'You better have a good explanation for throwing out my customer. He paid good money for that soup.'

'I apologise, sometimes security can be overzealous in their service to the nation. I told Jan about your food, and he wished to try it.'

'What do you mean? You told him about my food? Who are you?'

'At the moment, I am his Minister for Protocol.'

'What is that?'

'I make sure Citizen Jan's day is run according to plan and all his needs are catered for.'

'You?'

'Yes, I.'

'How? You are so young.'

'I am a trained hotelier.' Behnam smiled. 'Could you prepare a meal for him?'

'But I have not twizzled my mustachio and my beard is a mess for the seasoning.'

Behnam looked a bit puzzled. 'But why would you need that?'

'It is essential,' said Nizam, looking at Hedayat. 'A Naqshi Babursi must wear the traditional garments for a man such as this.'

'I am sure he will understand. He knows he's imposing.'

And so it came to pass that Nizam's repute went to places few Naqshis could imagine. For there sat Baradar Jan, complete in traditional robe, at his table, surrounded by nervous bodyguards looking through the shutters. Nizam blew his very spirit into the wings and drumsticks he lovingly brought out. He made a batter with breadcrumbs and used Naqshi chicken, not the ones that had been farmed, but those allowed to roam free on land that had Naqsi history ingrained. For these wings and eggs had a certain and quite distinct, 'flavoursome glow'. This was due to the USSR testing its nuclear arsenal that could obliterate half the world on that land. Once the wings and drumsticks were battered, adding a squirt of sheep oyster juice, he fried them in clarified butter and served the chicken on a plate alongside reed flute potatoes and pickled beetroot.

Baradar Jan, who had been watching the chef behind his dark glasses with curious wonder, did not touch the dish, and yet mysteriously said nothing. One of the burly security men was about to grab a chicken wing to taste, when Nizam slapped his hand away to the surprise of Baradar, and the mortification of Behnam as if his head had become separated from his neck.

'On my life,' said Nizam theatrically, 'he took a wing and ate it.' There was no poison in the food. 'To dishonour a guest is against our custom – to dishonour our leader is a disgrace.'

'Not leader,' said his Excellency. 'Citizen – first amongst equals.'

Nizam lowered his neck, bowing almost. Baradar was so touched by citizen Nizam's action that he touched him by the nape and with his little pinky gave him a subtle rub to show his delight. Behnam too, beamed at Nizam's act, which had initially horrified him. Then Nizam asked, 'May I?'

Baradar nodded and put his hat down to signal his permission to season. Behnam also nodded in reply, curious to know as to what this ritual would be. And so Nizam proceeded to pour the salt into his beard. Once the salt was in his beard he proceeded to rub his beard so the salt flakes fell on the battered chicken.

'This is what our Naqshi ancestors did to honour their guest since the time of Zoroaster.'

Neither Behnam and Baradar had ever heard of this custom. They assumed it must have been a disgusting tradition from Shahrepour and were reluctant to eat the chicken but moved by Nizam's patriotism, tucked in.

After the first wing, Baradar removed his robe to show his pleasure. In thus doing, he put all his medals on display. Nizam's eyes ran over them, he knew some from his days doing national service. Baradar had shown immense valour in administrative duties. He spotted a red and green medal which indicated that Baradar had stamped a thousand documents in one shift – no mean feat for mere mortals. It must have been when Nizam was lying wounded in hospital during the Naqshi-Uzbek war at the turn of the new millennium; a treacherous Armenian had sniped him from the back, and the bullet had taken out his left and right *animelles* resulting in an inability to bring forth any issue and his Begum was granted a divorce by the Kadi. Whenever he felt the phantom pains travelling down to his metal marbles, he remembered that it had been for a higher purpose: for king and country- that gave him temporary respite.

Baradar Jan stayed for several hours, so much so that Behnam became a little bit impatient. His Excellency was due to visit a barren virgin in the slums of Farhang, to help her family. But before Baradar left, he extended his oily hand and Nizam and Hedayat kissed it. His Excellency murmured something to Behnam, who stayed behind, and then the leader of Naqshistan was gone.

'Well?' Nizam looked at Behnam eagerly.

Behnam was silent for a moment, 'Baradar Jan did not like the food □ he loved it.'

Nizam shook Behnam's hand and went to Hedayat and hugged him affectionately.

'He loved it so much,' Behnam said coming closer, almost whispering, 'that he wants you to be his personal chef.'

'Personal chef?'

'Yes, you will have your very own kitchen and your own team of assistants.'

'What an honour!'

'Indeed!'

'Will you give me some time to discuss with my partner?'

'What is there to discuss? When Baradar says 'be' □ it is!'

'You see Hedayat is very attached to the business, I'm not sure he will leave for the capital.'

'But it's a great opportunity!'

'Yes, but he has his family here.'

'We will move them! What more could a man want? He will secure the family for generations!'

Nizam hesitated.

'If he doesn't want to come,' said Behnam, 'you come!'

Nizam shifted about uncomfortably. 'Without me, the business will cave in.'

'Don't worry, I will ask Mehrzad to run it for you.'

'Mehrzad, Baradar's nephew?'

'The one. I will personally make sure that he will run it. You know how every business he puts his hands to turns to gold. He's turned the ailing trains, telecommunications and roads into profitable businesses. By the time you are old, you will have more money than you can imagine.'

But Nizam still had some reservations, 'I am not sure he wants another Mehrzad Fast Food restaurant to open up in Shahrepour.'

'No, no, no, you keep it as it is. But Mehrzad will just bring it under his wing so it doesn't fail. He will make it more profitable. Don't worry.' But seeing the reservation on Nizam's face he said, 'Look, you discuss this with Hedayat and let me know. I am not asking you to decide in one day. Take a few days.' Behnam gave his card and left.

Nizam found Hedayat next morning, as usual with the kerosene lamp burning, a cup of tea by his side and cigarette in his mouth as he thriftily cut the parsley, dill, and coriander for the day. When Hedayat saw Nizam, he smiled so that his eyes smiled with him. He greeted him as he always did, 'Selaaam! Baba Jan'. He had that strange accent so typical of mountain folk from Kooh-i-Sabz, rough, direct, warm and strange to Nizam's kind who were used to the sophistication of the city. Truth was, and few in Shahrepour knew this, Hedayat was Nizam's repository of secrets. It was this son of a mountain herder who had preserved all the Naqshi lore of old.

For few Naqshis visited those verdant mountains on account of the poor quality of the roads. So their homeland was a time capsule, a place which time had forgotten. And later, instead of fixing the roads and building schools and hospitals for the people, Baradar had decreed that the area become a national park to save the environment. He got the Chinese to flood the area obliterating many a rare flora and fauna, and built a dam on the site. He supplied all the people with electricity and moved the locals in the area away; that's how Hedayat came to Shahrepour. It was a blessing in disguise for he brought with him all the green mountain's secrets and poured it into Nizam the way a mother does with a suppository to her constipated babe. This is where Nizam learnt about the tradition of pouring salt into the beard and sprinkling it on the food. That tradition had near enough vanished except in Kooh-i-Sabz! So it was Baradar's effort to modernise Kooh which ultimately brought Hedayat to Nizam and Nizam to Hedayat.

Hedayat was not a bad cook, he too had a passion for food. he knew all the inns and outs, but there was no magic in his hands. Or the people were unaccustomed to his mountain habits, and they made faces as if they were revolted by such rustic modes of cooking. So they did not eat his food and his stall did not do very well, until the day he met Nizam. Nizam's father had kicked him out for being feckless, he did not think that playing computer games in various costumes and trying to look like a manga cartoon was a 'job', especially befitting that of a veteran. So Hedayat found him slurping on a bowl soup on his stall and asking for a job. Seeing that Nizam was a veteran, he offered him a job as his assistant. He soon discovered that Nizam had blessed hands and turned all those dishes, even the simple ones, into something delicious. Soon the stall was heaving. They moved into a store. Overtime, the student surpassed his master. Hedayat recognised that in his employ was the true golden child of Naqshi food. Instead of resisting the truth, like the competition in Shahrepour did, he submitted to its light and became its servant. And so a partnership was born, a relationship sometimes akin to slave and master, sometime lover, sometime dog and master, sometimes friend, sometimes father and son and sometimes one which was like Shams to Rumi.

So it pained Nizam to tell Hedayat about the offer that he had been given to serve his country. He knew what the answer would be. Hedayat stopped cutting the parsley for a moment. The electricity came on and the fluorescent light returned; he put out the kerosene lamp.

'I knew this day would come,' Hedayat said, 'and all this time I have been thinking about what to say when it did.'

Nizam blushed, 'I am sorry.'

'No, no. How long can I keep you a secret that belongs to the nation?'

'So does it mean you will come along to the capital?'

'No, no, my place is here.'

'Why, you will be rich!'

'For how long?

Nizam was silent for a moment. 'For as long as these hands can cook. Why hesitate? Don't you know the line: '*He, who on seeing his beloved, hesitated — surely, masturbated!*''

'Ferdowsi?'

'It's Zamakhshari?'

'Never read him.'

'He's one of yours from Kooh-i-Sabz. Don't you see the opportunity? You can send every one of your kids to private school, have a house, a

Korean car, two cars! Three kitchens, four wives! He's told me I can name my price. Come with me!'

'I can't.'

'Why?'

'Because my father told me that power is a carcass that dogs fight over. I don't have the appetite for it.'

'Neither do I! Who says I am going for power? I don't want any of it. I just want to cook!'

'I don't want to go there. Us Koohis are free.'

'So what do we do?'

'We close up,' Hedayat declared. 'You must be known to the world.'

'No, no. Behnam has already proposed that Baradar's nephew, Mehrzad, help run the shop. He's an expert, he does it for a living. So if things don't go well, I can return. Otherwise he will make sure you are looked after, trust me.'

'I don't like the sound of that.'

'Look, I am going away for a few months to try it out. That's all. If it doesn't work I'll return.'

Hedayat was silent.

'It will be fine,' Nizam said.

In order to acclimatise Nizam to life in the capital, Behnam took him by the hand and put him up with his own family in the Pirzade area of the capital. Nizam was surprised that Behnam's father, Gul Abbas, was the prime minister. He may have appeared haughty on the news but was an immensely courteous man who often watched him at work. The Khanum too, came along and helped him chop onions, garlic, parsley and dill and all such things. He was surprised that she was a really an ordinary girl from Oddessapour. She had been a student when Gul Abbas had pulled up in car, as was the custom of old Chingis, and snatched her from university.

'I never finished my course in the end,' she giggled, 'it was love at first sight and my family accepted it.'

'I made them,' said Gul with a wide smile, 'an offer they could not refuse.'

She bore Gul Abbas four children and Behnam was the eldest.

'You must talk to Behnam,' she said, 'it is high time he married someone. I am getting impatient, there are no grandchildren about! And he's nearly thirty! He should be snatching a girl from university by now!'

For several weeks Nizam cooked them all the delights of Naqshi cuisine, and they treated him like royalty. He had his own apartment assigned to him which came complete with an obliging butler who answered his every whim. On the day he had to leave for Baradar's house he was like a bride who didn't want to leave her father's home.

'Don't worry,' said Behnam, 'I will be there alongside you! I will make sure you will want for nothing.'

The palace of Baradar though opulent was very different. Here, Nizam was one of many cooks who specialised in various cuisines. He was given his own apartment which was more like a villa with its own lake on the presidential grounds outside the capital. The rooms were decorated tastefully, each graced with one of Baradar's photos framed on the wall. Once, when Nizam tried to move the photo, he received a phone call from Behnam suggesting that he not play around with the furniture. He also had access to the four-hundred-acre ground complete with tennis courts, stables, pools and so on. He had a Tesla too, but could not leave the grounds. First, as Behnam explained, the electricity infrastructure outside of the grounds was still in development. And second, he could not leave the grounds without permission. He was to be the President's personal secret.

Whenever the First Family wanted it, Behnam would call Nizam to say that he was 'on, don't let me down'. Then he cooked – and for some reason he cooked like his whole being was on the line. The first time he got the phone call, he could not eat breakfast. He was wracked with nervousness. He paced the living room floor that was the size of a basketball court, thinking of what he should serve. Thinking about it made him tired. So he retired to his room and there in his dreams, an angel came to him and inspired him with the dish that he was to prepare for the First Family.

That day he grated some cheese, chopped up some fresh tomatoes, made some *makrona*. He cooked the tomato sauce with garlic until it was thick, he added the handmade *makrona* in a tin and poured the tomato sauce in adding salt and pepper. He put it in the oven for ten minutes, then once semi-cooked he brought it out, added the naqshi paneer, and returned it to the oven to finish the *makrona* off. Once cooked he added the parsley and dill on top of the dish. It tasted heavenly. He felt bold and personally brought it out to Baradar's brood.

Baradar sat at the top of the table in a traditional Naqshi robe. There was Humayun and his Lebanese wife, Lina, who had been a lingerie model from Beirut. She did not understand Naqshi decorum and kept on whispering in Humayun's ear and looked as if she was necking him like a courting swan. What was even worse, Humayun didn't even bother disciplining her. Baradar's second son, Adel, the manager of Naqshi Football Club that had been top of the league for five years running, his two young boys, Malik and Ali, and his wife, Fatema, were also in attendance. So too was Baradar's wife, Dil and Baradar's daughter, Leyla. When Nizam brought in the *Makrona* they all paid attention to the beautiful smell. Nizam served each and every one, spooning the food onto their plates. Malik, the little child, said: 'I love macaroni and cheese.'

'It's a Naqshi dish,' said Nizam. 'The colonisers stole it from us.' This was received with applause and Baradar remarked, 'You don't only cook but you educate too.' Nizam tasted the food, to show them it was not poisoned.

'You do not need to do that,' said Baradar. 'You are an honourable man, I remember that day.' Then Baradar gave permission to eat.

Nizam held his breath as if his life depended on it. For a moment there was silence, and then Lina choked. The family froze. Lina held her throat as if she had eaten something awful – and then burst out in laughter. Everyone laughed at the immodest wench. A surge of joy ran through Nizam's body.

Baradar said, 'You are making Naqhsi food great again.'

From that day on, Behnam called him more often during the week. Sometimes he would cook for Baradar alone, and bring the food to his bedchamber and hand it to the young nurses who administered his nightly medicine. Those nightly snacks were always well received.

One day Behnam called him and told him that Lina was sending him some game Baradar and Humayun had caught hunting. If he could prepare the meat and serve it to the family, she would be grateful.

The meat was brought in by some minders. It was very different, deboned, skinned, and packaged such that he doubted it had been caught very recently. It didn't matter, whatever the father of the nation wanted, he would serve it.

He cooked the meat lovingly, using only salt and pepper for seasoning. Good, aged meat should not be spoilt by spices and he served it alongside roasted Naqshi spring potatoes and *doogh*. It went down a charm even though Lina herself was not there to partake in the delicacy.

Several days later, he received a message from Hedayat's wife, asking him to send her husband back. His wife said that Hedayat had gone to work as usual and not returned home. When she called the shop, he was told that Nizam had asked for him at the palace; that there was to be a gathering of international ambassadors and his help was required for the emergency. Nizam found that odd, because he was the family's personal chef and was not expected to cook for ambassadors. He was only for their private kitchen, the First Family's personal chef. It disturbed him: where could Hedayat have gone? He knew that Naqshi men, often when they reached fifty, married secretly taking on a second wife. So perhaps that was it; perhaps he was secretly spending time with his new wife. But somehow it didn't sound like Hedayat.

He called and asked for Behnam who, as always, was there at his doorstep within the hour, ready to serve. It was as if Behnam yearned to have him back in his own family.

'Behnam,' Nizam said. 'I need to talk to you, please come in.'

'Why don't we go for a walk?' Behnam replied. 'The air is lovely today, there's no smog or acid rain whatsoever.'

Nizam understood and set out with him. They walked till they came to some woodland.

'Now,' Behnam said. 'What is it?'

'Well. Hedayat has disappeared.'

'*Shush!*' Behnam said guiltily and suddenly very frightened. 'Not so loud.'

'What do you mean, *shush?*'

'Why don't you sit down?'

'I don't need to sit down.'

'I wanted to tell you, but I couldn't.' Behnam looked around to see if anyone was listening.

'Why?'

'You and your family would be in danger.'

'Behman. Where is Hedayat?'

'Well,' Behnam said pausing for a moment. 'Hedayat is gone.'

'Gone!?' A knot was forming in Nizam's stomach. 'What do you mean, "gone"?'

'Yes, he's gone to the heavenly garden.'

'Heavenly garden?'

'He's gone to God.'

'What? How?' Nizam felt dizzy for a moment. He found a large rock on the path and sat down on it.

'Do you remember when Humayun and Baradar went hunting?'

'Yes.'

'That meat wasn't animal meat.'

Nizam's eyes widened. He had tasted the meat himself. It had been so sweet and delicious.

'How could you send it to me?' Nizam rebuked.

'I have family too. We are all terrified of the tyrant.'

Nizam stood up, he put his hand in his throat and tried to make himself vomit, he wanted to extricate the flesh of his friend that had nourished his being. But nothing came out; a wave of guilt and remorse ran through him as he remembered his friend's words. And then a new realisation came to his mind.

'I just fed it to the whole family.'

'They are sadists, Nizam.'

Sweat formed on Behnam's brow, a knot had formed in his stomach, and suddenly a wave of acidic bile and yesterday's red beans which he had eaten with a mango, tomato and cucumber salsa sauce gushed forth and fell on the rock. He went through the stages of sadness, fear and anger.

'You mean to tell me, they are cannibals?'

Behnam nodded. 'Nothing is sacred to them.'

'Something needs doing. I can't just let this lie.'

'No, no, let this one lie. Leave it to the dogs to fight over. This isn't your fight.'

'No, no, but Naqshi *qanun* requires that we avenge our friends. There is no choice!'

'There is always a choice! This is too big for someone like you! What happens if you cut off the monster's head?'

'The monster is dead, and no one shall be frightened.'

'Fairy tales. Leave it!'

'I cannot. If Baradar finds out I know that I fed them Hedayat, I am dead in any case.'

'I beg you to refrain.'

'Unless you arrest me, I will not.'

Behnam's arms slumped helplessly. 'I cannot be responsible for the consequences, Nizam.'

'You will not be. I will.'

Nizam became hell bent on his mission. He was going to serve a banquet that the First Family would remember forever. He ordered veal from Khanegah, wherein the baby calf is snatched from the mother, thrown into a shed where it cannot move and fed milk and grain until its flesh is anaemic and so tender it is rose white. He also obtained unpasteurized honey from the fields of Nawawi Jaygah, the honey once the best in central Asia had become poisonous due to the USSR testing their nuclear and chemical armaments there, and then he waited. On the day Nizam got the call, he calmly prepared the veal to be lovingly roasted. Then he prepared the sauce, and set out the honey to drizzle on the meat. He prepared freshly sprouted potatoes from Dastargah and a raw cashew nut salad with dressing. He presented the meal to the family who were all excited by the rose veal. Nizam served the great leader, pouring the honey over the veal and dishing out the potatoes, and then went to each member of his family spooning the food on to the plate. 'In the Name of God,' he said indicating for them to eat. The First Family had barely chomped on their food for twenty minutes when the poisonous honey began to take affect. For the poisonous honey served alongside cashew nuts, sprouting potatoes and elderberries all created a potent poison which meant that the whole family expired very quickly.

When the news that Baradar Jan and his family had been poisoned by their chef broke on 7 June, 2018, Anthony Bourdain was sitting in his room in Le Chambard Hotel in Kaysersberg-Vignoble, France. He saw the film of the defiant chef, Nizam, being led away by Naqshi police. It startled Bourdain for he remembered the chef whose was full of steely resolve and defiance. Bourdain worried that the resolve would soon weaken once the Naqshi chef went through the 'Mongol Mangle' as the machine was affectionately dubbed by torturers all over the world. As the chef shouted his defiance, Bourdain remembered the heavenly roasted eggplant he had eaten at the man's restaurant. It depressed Bourdain to listen to his words: 'Now that the tyrant was gone, a new era in the country will come forth where all Naqshis will be free.'

'Will they be free?' Bourdain thought to himself as he watched the CNN anchor Amanpour explain that the central Asian country had been rocked by the death of the progressive Naqshi president, whose attitude was 'in stark contrast to the country's neighbour, Iran.' He saw images of people shedding tears. Young girls held up their children saying that Baradar Jan was quite literally their father. Even the Interim President, Gul Abbas, who had taken over until elections could be held sometime in the future, said Naqshistan would not be cowed by terrorists. Bourdain watched Amanpour interview the new interior minister, Behnam Gul, who told her that no stone would be left unturned, that any co-conspirators would be rounded up and tried in-line with human rights. 'I am shocked,' he said, 'to learn that we had that terrorist feeding us but thank God my family was saved. He only got away with my watch, a Tissot.'

The head of police, Mehrzad, told Amanpour that they were currently searching for another terrorist plotter, Hedayat from Kooh-i-Sabz, who had likely radicalized the chef. A rough picture of a Hedayat came on the screen. "He is the leader of al-Qaeda in Naqshistan'

Bourdain remembered him in the kitchen as he chopped parsley. He sighed. Bourdain felt himself going into a dark spiral, a staircase if you will, and there was nothing he could do to stop it. He saw, in his mind's eye, Nizam cutting an onion and the rings setting off on a spiral to Eternity. He heard Nizam's words ring in his ears, 'the way you make an omelet reveals your character.' He knew in his very being that Nizam was not who they said he was, though he couldn't prove it he knew, because Nizam was a craftsman, and craftsman build. They do not destroy, and it was craftsmen, not artists, who built the great cathedrals and mosques and temples of the world that he loved to visit. He wondered why the rest of the world could not see this in Nizam as clearly as he did. Why did the world believe such nonsense? Why did the world not care? He looked over at his half-eaten breakfast which had been prepared most likely by a poor underpaid don't-give-a-shit worker, the pastry tasted of cardboard and coffee of hydrochloric acid. Such thoughts made him go even deeper down the spiral stair case and the only way to pull himself up again was to reach for the belt of a bathrobe, stick it on a fan on the ceiling, tie it around his neck and jump off the chair.

Bourdain's tragic suicide became the lead the next day, and nothing much was heard of Nizam or Naqshistan for many years, until Behnam Gul ascended the throne two years later in a bloodless coup to restore the monarchy which had been, in his words, snatched from the last king, Garshasp IX. CNN ran a small segment on the coronation and featured petitioners lining up giving the king a bow and asking the new king to pardon their son, husband or brother. It was in such circumstances that Hedayat's wife now impoverished, turned up to the coronation in the hope that perhaps the new king can do something about her husband or at the very least, let her know about the whereabouts of his daughter that had been snatched from university by a member of the royal family.

ERASED

Shazaf Fatima Haider

You just can't get rid of some people. They're like a bad stain that won't be scrubbed away. I should know – I've been trying to get rid of my grandfather for years.

Dada wasn't easy. The man called me fodricchya all my life – that's Marathi for son of a bitch. Every time I failed an exam, and I failed a lot of exams, he would beat me with his blue rubber-soled slippers which were his only keepsake from India. Those things hurt, especially when they came at your forehead with full swing. He never hit my sister, just me. He'd hold down my arms so I couldn't protect my face from his slaps. 'She'll bear someone else's sons. But *you*, fodricchya, *you* are going to carry my name in this world. I didn't raise myself from the piss and dung and cow-hide only to be let down by *you*. You have to improve yourself' he'd say. Failure wasn't not an option; you know what I mean?

Dada was born in Ahmednagar – that's a village in India. He was treated badly, you know. Really badly. He was a Mahar, which means he was an Untouchable, so you could say he was the village outcast. He was a long-armed, dark-skinned and unhappy looking man and his eyes – man, they were always red-veined with the strain of scowling. My great-grandmother, Dada's mum, collected and sorted and sold rubbish while his dad removed and skinned dead cows. Dada grew up eating beef and to the Hindus, a beef-eater is a dirty thing. Man, could he tell you a thing or two about discrimination. All the dirty work of the village was allotted to Dada's family. They were even buried separately, you know, like bastards of the gods. Upper-casters would spit at him and shoo him away if he got close. They'd die rather than drink from his family well – even if the day was hot and the water cool and sweet.

'To drink from a Mahar well was to become a Mahar,' Dada once told me. 'We were the living embodiments of shit. Scavengers, they called us.

I wanted better than that, so I came to this country to give little shits like you a better life.' He found work in a shop in London as a butcher – and my father graduated from high school and worked in a Londis. But *I* was supposed to be a doctor. Every day, before I went to school, Dada said the same thing: 'Earn respect. Earn money. Erase my past with your future.'

No pressure, you know what I'm saying? I tried, man did I try. I wanted Dada to be proud of me, but there was always that F on the report card and the beatings and recriminations. I wasn't letting him down, I was letting his *entire* village down – everyone who had helped Dada get out and make a better life.

I knew he wouldn't accept what I do for a living. I took home my first pay check – and it was a fat one, and showed it to him. Soften him up a bit before I gave him a blow, if you know what I mean. He had this half-smile on his face. 'Have you become a doctor, then?' And then I told him I was a cleaner. 'You clean people's homes and make this much money?' he asked. So I told him I wasn't just any cleaner – I told him I cleaned up after dead people.

So if someone dies alone and no one collects their body, then they kind of decompose on their sofas or in their bathtub or kitchen or wherever they popped off. Or sometimes, they are killed and there's a lot of blood and body parts everywhere. Who cleans up after them? I do. It's not an easy job – it requires a stomach of steel and *that* I do have. So that's where I come in. It's good honest money – they give you a bit of training and tell you to be all compassionate and all that jazz and really, it's a job where you're cleaning other people's guts and brains and leaving a place brand new. How's that for erasing the past?

So I say to Dada, I say, 'I'm a death cleaner' and he starts and asks me what that is and I tell him and he goes real quiet for a while. And then he stands up and I'm thinking that I'm going to get hugged so I move forward and he slaps me on the face. With his hands – and they are *harder* than his slippers. 'Aai ghalya!' he says. That means mother-fucker. 'You tell me you've taken this life I gave to you and used it to writhe in the excrements of white men?' You know what I said? I said, 'No, even brown men die. And women. Everyone dies. Death is a business. It's a good one and it makes good money, Dada.'

He just couldn't take it. He took his walking stick and started coming at me. Ma tried to get in the way, but he beat her too, but now I was older and stronger than him, so I just flung it out of his hand and smashed his television set. He told me he wished I'd died in Ma's womb rather than lived to bring him such shame. That's when I walked out. Got my own place, started my own business, created my own life. But Dada kept calling me and spewing venom. 'You were supposed to raise us up,' he's say. 'Instead, you've brought the family name back to the mire.'

I suppose Ba and Ma should have done something about Dada – but they were scared of him. I don't blame them – he was one scary fodracchiya. I thought he'd calm down when Diya married some sort of lawyer – he works in an office and he's white. But Dada was only interested in me: I'm the boy and I carry the Pawar name forward. Well, that's it then. I was the main disappointment of his life.

Don't get me wrong, I get it. Dada thought I'm dealing with shit and piss and gore all day, and I am. It's a gruelling, disgusting job, full of innards and goo. But what Dada didn't understand is what he was ostracized for in India, I am paid for well here. It's a lucrative business and I see a lot of things other people don't. I see how white men treat their old folk. The last job I did was an old woman with four sons who had died and decomposed on her leather sofa – she stayed like that for three weeks - her boys never checked up on her. So they called me after her body was taken away and I'm cleaning the sofa and removing the floorboards and wiping stuff down with enzyme and who shows up? The eldest son. And he's fighting and arguing and accusing me of stealing his mum's money. I mean, he's left her to die but now he's picking at me for whatever's left. I'll tell you who the real scavengers are – men like him, not worried about anything more than what they can make off their dead mum.

Look, it's honourable, what I do. More so, in some ways, than what I'd do if I had gotten the grades to become a doctor. What's a doctor? Some rich, well-educated guy who has learned to read scans and reports. So the other day, I had a HIV scare – you often find people who die alone live alone because they live with drugs and needles and I thought I was done and I took off my rubber gloves and was rummaging for stuff and my hand found a needle. I had to go to a doctor. He was a cold one, staring at a

computer screen, emotionless and distant. They call it being professional,
I call it uncaring.

What I'm trying to explain to you is that my job is a people job. I'm
dealing with devastated families who can't bear to see what their loved
ones have left behind. I do what they can't bear to – touch what they don't
want to touch and leave it all clean and sanitized so that it looks like the
death didn't happen. There's always one family member who wants a post-
job update – but what they're really looking for is absolution. I'm like one
of those Brahmin priests, I told Dada, hearing last confessions – and he
swore at me on the telephone.

I still remember our last conversation. He called me and once he'd run
the gamut of all the swear-words in his arsenal, he said he'd punish me. I
didn't take him seriously, I mean, he was old and I was bigger than him and
I lived in another town, so I was like, 'Yeah yeah, old man, do your worst.'

Never underestimate a Mahar. You know, back in Dada's day, the upper-
casters denied the Mahars their share of the village produce. So Dada's
people got together and created this white poisonous powder and fed it to
all the cattle – so everyone lost their livelihood. Everyone, except Dada's
family who got a shit load of cows to skin and sell off.

Ba called me the day they found Dada dead. He and my mum had been
in Manchester for a couple of weeks – Dada had paid them to go and take
a holiday. On the day they leave, my grandfather takes out the trash, boards
up all the windows and locks all the doors and blows his brains out in his
bedroom. He made sure he wasn't discovered until my parents got back
– gave his body time to make things really nasty. That's how much thought
he put into it. He left a note covered in a zip lock bag - and it says that his
last wish is that *I* am the one who's supposed to clean his shit up since
that's what I'd chosen to do with my life.

So I did. I went to clean up after Dada's body was cremated. His room
stank, man – even now I can smell him at the back of my throat. I got to
work and had this strange sensation of being watched – and judged – as in
Dada's entire village had risen from the dead to shame me as I did what I
do. That feeling crippled me. The man killed himself to make to shame me.
To *spite* me. That's some crazy shit right there, you know. I can't get over it.

Dada hated maggots. I mean everyone hates them, but he had a special
disgust of them. His job as a child was to make drums from the hides of

cows, so he spent his childhood battling maggots —dead animals and heat attracted the flies that laid their eggs and out came swarms of squirming wormies. Like macaroni come to life, he'd once described it. And now he was the dead animal that had been burnt to a heap and the maggots had eaten their way out of his flesh and begun breeding in his blood-soaked mattress. There were mounds of black flies everywhere. I bagged and taped and got rid of the other stuff in the room. His dresser had bits of his brain still on it – but that's an easy clean – you can scrape brain off – it dries quickly. I tore the carpets off and scrubbed the floorboards with enzyme – it's hard work, but I got the whole place clean.

I was supposed to erase Dada's past, but here I was, erasing whatever was left of him. I looked at his empty room and felt baptised. The curses, the beatings, the expectations, the shame – it was all disposed of. I told myself I was rid of him.

Who was I kidding? The dreams began the next day. Every night, he stands and glares at me, surrounded by dead cows and maggots. Sometimes, he begins to pull me into the maggots and I wake up screaming.

He's inside me, man, eating away at me like a maggot. Dada's death wasn't a suicide – it was a poisoning. I used to be proud of what I did. It paid the bills, got me a nice house and car, some amount of respect. Now? I feel dirty – like a Mahar to an Upper Caster. There's *so* much guilt. I try to move past it but the harder I work, the more I see him, shaming me beyond the grave.

I've begun to think about quitting – that's how bad it is. Diya, that's my sister, says I need therapy for all that Dada put me through. Perhaps she's right. This hate stuff – it's like the cycle of wormies – it just goes on and on until you bleach it out.

I'm not going to bleach myself out, don't worry. That's not why I'm here with you. But I'm just trying to ask: how do you get rid of a person like Dada? The more I try, the more he come back to haunt me. There's no way of erasing the past, you know?

THERE WILL BE A LAST MUSLIM

Haroon Moghul

There must've been a last Muslim, whom God chose to turn off the lights, who took for Semitism's sake a final fumbled step off Spanish soil.
   'Better,' they said, 'to love, to lose, and to go, then to linger in Morisco limbo.'
Except what the hell did they know?

Read: God said. But also to write. We are pens; blood is the ink with which we speak. What do you do when all of your world
   turns on all of you?
No hay moros en la costa. Then there were no Moors. Then there was no coast.

Their sails unfurled, wind and distance diminished his old world.

Adhans became whispers, then memories; the courtyards vacant, bankrupt, then weightless photons, the future's foreordained bosons, in the spaces where you leave your shoes and quantum foam means hope and failure fuse.

He sighed and he cried, the one become the other, not little tears but heaving sobs, in every tear an ocean nine centuries cold till the corsair captain put his hands

on his trembled shoulder to softly scold,

   'Brother, your trauma will sink our ummah!'

He did as he was told, he dried his eyes and saw with dead glaze gaze the
parapets of his grandfather's castles made immodest by unfriendly flags–

though their foreign imam came by with a mirror for this pauper:

'Brother, there are full mosques and refilled casks, new lives in Sarajevo,
or perhaps you'd rather restart in Tripoli or in Alexandria?

This *Bahri Jihad* might even blast on to Bandar Aceh–'

But this man had business with the one responsible: 'Take me to Mecca!'
(The Imam cornered the captain: 'Reis, we owe him this.')
'To God's Home!' he relented, where months later, worn down and
    down, this deportee dashed with a speed he knew not he still had,
        to the very door of the Ka'ba, vocative particle plus definite article:
'Ya Allah!' he said. 'I wish not to go to the future, not any afterlife,
I care neither to return nor to wander any longer,
I demand only to know by what justice, my Lord,
You keep Your home
        while You've seen fit to drive me from mine?'

The stunned pilgrims spiralled away from this blasphemy,
till there was just one man before just One God. A voice.
Contingent subject. Direct object. Booming
in his (their) heart(s) as much as outside and apart

'My child,' and with this alone the clouds prostrated, raining, crying,
frightened to the point of dying, letting go as children must
and all the mountains of all the planets like carded wool
and seventy thousand veils of light and dark paused to hear Him descend
where stunned worshippers could stare only dumbstruck to the sky
and Satan sneered He heard that ragged peasant and not I

'My child,' He said, 'can you not see that I have dressed My house in black
    because I am in mourning for you?'

THREE POEMS

Rosie Jackson

Rabia and the Thief

I imagine her here, in some quantum future,
her summers in hedgerows, winters in a corrugated shed
where she plays cards with God, who cheats, of course,

or plaits her hair, uncombed for centuries. She asks him
for a love that is out of this world and he replies
her soul is too old for trinkets. She does not lament

the garden of Eden, that sweet homeland between
the Tigris and Euphrates, once heavy with angels.
But prays for the whole earth to wake from pain,

to forgo its journeys to the black box of the Kaaba,
the crosses and synagogues, *asanas* of yoga,
all that greed for the milk and honey of heaven.

Nor does she grieve at the loss of her beauty,
but welcomes the truth of what she will become,
lets herself be scoured by that longing for union

when she will take between her hands the much-loved
face on which the seven worlds are written, marry
that silence whose love leaves all words behind.

I think of her most when it's hot at night and I open

the window, remember the thief who climbed
over the sill into her sparse bedroom. Would I do

what she did? Recognise the smell of ocean,
know the man as another creature out of water,
hair braided with kelp and badderlocks?

And, before he can snatch my blanket, fold
every piece of bedding, each last cotton sheet,
hand them to him like a dowry?

After the Door Has Opened

Here, in San Jan Mohammad Street,
dwells she who is no longer she,
whose desire is gone, who waits
for what is already done.

She is *Hafizah* –
one who has learned the Quran by heart.
She has visited the black box at Mecca,
kissed the stone of the Kaaba,
but she chooses the holy slums of Pune,
where hunger shrivels in unshaded heat.

Women break at her feet their coconuts of prayer,
make their supplications for babies.
But she knows the gift of sorrow –
how we may learn to squeeze sugar
out of grief.

She knows walking is always backwards,
the best living a kind of erasure –
each day rubbing out the folly of what went before;
how the greatest millstone of pain
cannot grind the grain of you small enough,

the finest sieve will not make you pure.

Her hair is the white of egrets.
Her face *Gulrukh* — like a rose.
And since the time her life opened
onto the fire that gives God his heat,
she knows the deceit of daylight.

So what if she was Rabia of Basra,
who wrote pleasure in the sand?
She would rather be despised as the thief
who climbed in to steal her final blanket.
Even the best poems should not be worshipped,
but hung out like rags. Words must buckle
at the knees.

Yes, here, in San Jan Mohammad Street,
trades a stall-keeper from whom few want to buy.
Her age — a hundred or more —
small matter as she sits
under the angel of the neem tree —
seven centuries between each feather.

A Piece of Cloth

Where will the lashes fall? On the shoulders, or the ribs?
Who will lift her when she sinks to the floor? What lakes
will catch her blood? Has she been too proud of her back,
the way she rode a bike or stayed atop a horse? Has she
been too proud of her husband, children, lawyer's
credentials? But the Prophet, peace be upon him, surely
knows there are different kinds of pride, false and true,
different kinds of men, false and true. Is not the *hijab*
a piece of cloth like any other, pegged on washing lines
along with shirts, sheets, pants? Who bid a man wedge
the Quran beneath his armpit to flay this woman's back

until the blood is a river and the bones laid bare? Surely
the Prophet, peace be upon him, calls upon the angel
Jibril to intervene. Surely the Prophet's thirteen wives,
mothers of the believers, sing in praise of these beautiful
girls who drape their *hijabs* on branches of the pomegranate
trees. Surely, they liken the cloths that flutter round
the fruits to uncaged birds trying their wings.

Notes

Rabia of Basra, c. 717-801, a Sufi mystic and poet, was the first woman to
become a Muslim saint.

The shrine of Hazrat Babajan, a Muslim 'Perfect Master', is in the Char
Bawdi district of Pune, India. Until her death in 1931, Babajan spent her
last 24 years living here under a neem tree and, in 1913, revealed to Meher
Baba his spiritual identity. She was said to be the reincarnation of Rabia of
Basra.

In March 2019, Nasrin Sotoudeh, a human rights lawyer in Tehran, was
sentenced to 38 years in prison and 148 lashes for defending Iranian
women's right to remove their hijab in public. Under Iranian law, the man
doing the flogging should hold under his arm a copy of the Quran.

Reprinted with permission from *Love Leans over the Table* (Two Rivers Press, 2023)

REVIEWS

PREVENT OR NOT

John Holmwood

Governments are properly concerned with security and public safety. Historically, this has been about external threats from foreign powers, but, increasingly, it is directed at actors within the state using violence to secure political ends. Such actors are routinely described as hostile to 'our' values, and we are enjoined not to let them win by resiling from our democratic way of life.

The UK now has the most extensive legislation in Europe covering both violent and non-violent terrorism. It also has an extensive programme of counter extremism measures – called *Prevent* – to tackle ideas and activities which, while lawful in themselves, are claimed to be possible precursors to terrorist actions. Interventions under Prevent, therefore, potentially represent a major challenge to civil liberties (especially, the rights of children and young people, as we shall see) in the name of public safety.

William Shawcross, *Independent Review of Prevent*, Home Office, UK Government, 2023.

In this review, I address the Independent Review of Prevent that was first announced as part of the passage of the Counter Terrorism and Border Security Act in February 2019. This was to have been the first since the strategy had begun in 2003. There had been an internal review by the Home Office in 2011 (endorsed by the Independent Reviewer of Terrorism Legislation, Lord Carlile) but nothing since then that addressed the mounting criticisms of its associated programmes and interventions.

There have been many vicissitudes along the way. First, the initial appointment of Lord Carlile to head the review was met with widespread criticism from civil society groups and a legal challenge after which he stepped down. He was replaced in January 2021 by William Shawcross, someone active in neo-conservative think tanks like the Henry Jackson Society and Policy Exchange. He was also a former Head of the Charity Commission between 2012-18 when he initiated investigations of Muslim-led charitable organisations. This was regarded as provocative and many individuals and organisations – Muslim-led groups and wider civil liberties organisations like Liberty, Amnesty International and the Runneymede Trust – announced a boycott of the review.

The People's Review of Prevent was set up to represent those who were impacted by Prevent and to provide an analysis of research and other reports into Prevent that we believed – correctly as it would turn out – would be ignored by Shawcross. In anticipation of the imminent publication of his report we published our own in February 2022. It was not until March 2023 that he finally published his report, although its content was leaked to right-wing media during the six months prior to publication, together with lobbying activities and reports by Policy Exchange supporting its projected conclusions. These included the claim that, 'activists' against Prevent were seeking to 'delegitimise counter-terrorism' and were themselves extremists and should be subject to measures to curtail their activities and the expression of their views.

Significantly, the Shawcross Report itself would claim that if there had been a 'chilling' effect on the free speech of Muslim students and staff on campuses this should be regarded as a consequence of the 'anxieties' generated by campaigners and not by Prevent itself. At the same time, it was claimed that a campaign by MEND (Muslim Engagement and Development, a non-profit that promotes British Muslim involvement in media and politics) against Prevent at Salford University had meant that worrying signs were not identified before Salman Abedi detonated his bomb at the Manchester Arena in May 2017.

The final volume of the Manchester Arena Inquiry Report was published shortly after the Shawcross Report and explicitly denies that Abedi could have been identified through Prevent and stopped – that report lays any blame squarely with the security services acting under the Pursue strand of CONTEST (and also on inadequate safety measures at venues).

There were also claims that Prevent had been too sensitive to safeguarding the vulnerabilities of individuals with not enough attention paid to protecting the public. Prevent, it was argued, lost focus on 'Islamist' extremism and was giving too much attention to right-wing extremism, despite the former being where the real threat to the public lay.

When the Shawcross Report was finally published it was as tendentious and poorly researched as the media promotion of it had led us to expect. Our own People's Review of Prevent was not discussed, despite it having been published a year earlier. Nor were the earlier reports of groups like Medact, MEND, Cage or the Open Society Foundation discussed. Instead, critics were attacked in an adjacent report on 'Delegitimising Counter-Terrorism' published by Policy Exchange the previous April. The Shawcross report also ignored the critical commentaries of UN Rapporteurs.

It even ignored the various reports of the government's own Commission for Countering Extremism. This is particularly significant since it proposes a major change in its role from a body advisory to government, to a body having responsibility for directing Prevent. This was among 34 recommendations, all of which were immediately accepted by government with very limited debate in parliament.

Few of the recommendations require primary legislation to implement, and many had already been quietly put in place under new Home Secretaries as part of the rapid turnover of government ministers. This included the interim appointment of Robin Simcox as Commissioner for Countering Extremism in March 2021. His 'substantive' appointment was confirmed in July 2022. He is a former research fellow at the Washington-based, Heritage Foundation, whose president, Kevin Roberts was a keynote speaker at the recent National Conservative Conference in London.

The recommendations in the Shawcross Report represent a power-grab by the Home Office and a considerable centralisation and concentration of power. It is taking place under a neo-Conservative ideological framing of a 'clash of civilisations' in which the issue is not simply that of countering terrorism, but of limiting the expression of normative Islamic values within the public sphere. It is a power-grab that has been ignored by the mainstream media and Parliament. Where there are concerns expressed about the very serious lurch to the right in the Conservative Party represented by 'national conservatism', it is mainly seen as positioning to capture the party after a forthcoming electoral defeat. There is little appreciation that it is currently in control in the Home Office where it has the full support of the prime minister.

How did we get here? And what is at stake?

Prevent is one of the four component parts of the UK government's counter-terrorism strategy – CONTEST. This strategy was first put in place in 2003 and has four strands. *Protect*, which is concerned with strengthening protection against a terrorist attack (now subject to new legislation following the Manchester Arena bombing – 'Martyn's Law'); *Prepare*, which is about the mitigation of the impact of a terrorist attack; *Pursue*, which is directed at stopping terrorist attacks; and *Prevent*, which has the purpose of stopping people becoming terrorists, or from supporting terrorism.

Significantly, the three other strands of CONTEST come under the remit of the Independent Reviewer of Terrorism Legislation who has a statutory obligation to provide an annual report and also has the power to initiate investigation of different aspects of the strategy. Prevent is exempted from this oversight.

Prevent has undergone multiple iterations since 2003, but one feature remains constant. Unlike the other strands of CONTEST, it operates 'upstream' of any intention to commit a terrorist offence. It is part of what criminologists call the 'pre-criminal space'. In one aspect – which, in the light of subsequent developments we might regard as relatively benign, albeit that it pathologised Muslim communities – Prevent involved programmes to secure community integration and mitigate what was perceived as 'self-segregation' and distance from the influence of 'British values'.

It is striking that Shawcross is both hostile to these programmes and strikingly ignorant about them. He criticises them for being insufficiently focused on extremism and also of including individuals and groups in their delivery that he regards as extremist. Yet most of his discussion concerns evaluations of individual programmes conducted by the Behavioural Insights Team as far back as 2017.

He seems unaware that all such programmes have been gathered within the Home Office under the umbrella of 'Delivering a Stronger Britain Together' since 2015. This has involved local coordinators in each Prevent Priority Area. The programme was positively reviewed by Ipso Mori in June 2021, since when there have been no new funding calls and the system of local coordinators has been disbanded. On this, Shawcross is silent, despite it being a large part of his remit. It is instead a fait accompli carried out within the Home Office during the review period, seemingly with his nod of approval.

His silence is significant. It follows from the priority he gives to the security side of Prevent over that of community cohesion. This shift is something that was indicated in 2011 following the internal Home Office review of the Prevent Strategy, which Shawcross treats as his benchmark. This flagged up the need to clearly distinguish the promotion of community cohesion from the security concern to identify individuals at risk of being radicalised and disrupt that process.

This was despite the fact that there was no evidence that precursors to the development of a terrorist mindset could be identified despite extensive interventions being planned to uncover those vulnerable to radicalisation. In fact, the checklist of indicators that has come to be used in all training is derived from a study of prisoners convicted of non-violent terrorist offences and deemed to be at possible risk of committing violent offences. There are no studies that show the validity of the indicators when applied more generally.

The expansion of Prevent in this direction was on hold during the Conservative-Liberal Democrat coalition government, but was put in place by the new government in 2015. A new Prevent Duty was set out in the Counter Terrorism and Security Act of 2015. Paragraph 26 set out a general duty that: '(1) A specified authority must, in the exercise of its functions, have due regard to the need to prevent people from being drawn into terrorism.'

The duty applies to education settings from nurseries, primary and secondary schools and on to colleges and universities, to health settings and across youth services. It also applies in prisons and probation services, although measures had already been in place there before the 2015 Act. It is also available to the police who encourage reporting from members of the public outside the settings described above.

According to the Home Office, over a million individuals responsible for the provision of public services had by 2019 been trained to spot the signs of possible extremism (data on those trained since then are not available). For the most part, the Shawcross Report deals with Prevent in the years since the introduction of the Prevent Duty.

Nowhere in the 2015 Act is *extremism* defined. Nor does the Shawcross Report provide any new definitions, relying instead on those provided in the Home Office Prevent Strategy Review from 2011, where it is described as 'opposition to British values'. However, in a worrying paragraph, the Shawcross Report refers to legislation to define extremism as something that would have served as the 'backbone' of the Prevent strategy (paragraph 2.9). Instead, he said, the government left it to a new Commission for Countering Extremism which it set up in 2017. In other words, guidance on what constitutes extremism is provided by government agencies responsible for the implementation of Prevent. The Commission for Countering Extremism is no longer operating in an advisory role, but is now the *political backbone* of Prevent.

This is aligned with the reorganisation of the Home Office and its relationships with other government departments, as well new forms of control over the implementation of Prevent nationally. It is a concentration of power for which there is no independent scrutiny – the Shawcross Report proposes that complaints should be the responsibility of the very body within the Home Office that will direct Prevent.

It also represents a centralisation of power. The Report recommends that local autonomy should be reduced and Prevent panels organised through Regional Commissioners directly responsible to the Home Office. This reverses a move in the opposite direction which had been taking place under 'Operation Dovetail'. This had been piloting greater local autonomy in nine Prevent Priority Areas. There is no discussion in the Shawcross Report of the evaluation of the pilots, though there had been an initial plan in 2018 to extend it across all areas.

Notwithstanding this, the recommendations for a more draconian implementation of Prevent do include the shadow of a recognition of what is at issue from the perspective of civil liberties. Adopting the language of Policy Exchange, the Shawcross Report comments that, 'the campaign against Prevent has included some civil liberties groups and activists who seemingly, as a matter of principle, oppose a state-run scheme to counter specific ideas, attitudes, and non-criminal behaviours, no matter how light touch the scheme's methods' (paragraph 6.250).

Prevent is, indeed, 'a state-run scheme to counter specific ideas, attitudes, and non-criminal behaviours'. It is one, as we have seen, without any independent checks against its powers and operating under a neo-conservative (in truth, national conservative) ideology. However, it is far from 'light-touch' – one indication, perhaps, is the cry of pain and outrage expressed in the report about the application of Prevent to right-wing views, even where these are considered by Shawcross to be distasteful. Islamophobia, apparently, is a problem generated by 'Muslimness'.

Let me examine just how 'light touch' is the hand of the state.

There is a deceptively simple set of procedures associated with Prevent. First an individual is flagged within a setting where the Prevent duty applies. There will be an initial assessment by responsible members of staff, usually also involving a counter-terrorism police officer. The matter will be either dismissed (albeit data on the individual can be kept on police data bases and potentially shared with other agencies) or referred to a local Prevent panel. The latter includes counter-terrorism police officers, as well as representatives of other agencies.

We only have data on cases when they reach this point, but the Prevent panel makes a decision whether the case merits adoption onto the Channel programme, dismissal or some other intervention (for example, by mental health services). Participation is voluntary – as it has to be since no laws have been broken – but the context is coercive. The parents and guardians of children and young people caught up in Prevent will also be at risk of social services being brought to bear on them.

Prevent has a particularly significant role in the lives of children and young people. All children are subject to scrutiny under the Prevent duty from the moment they start nursery school until they leave secondary school (and it continues in higher education). In 2021/22, the education sector provided over a third of all referrals (36%). At the same time referrals are younger than from other sectors – the median age being 14, means that half of all referrals (1152 children) are under 14, representing around five children for each school day in England. There can be no serious claim that these children can represent any kind of serious terrorism risk.

In fact, there are an increasing number of young people charged with terrorism offences (usually non-violent offences associated with downloading proscribed material). This is largely an artifact of the introduction of new offences associated with Counter Terrorism and

Border Security Act in 2019. They do not indicate heightened risks that would justify a reinforcement of Prevent. Indeed, in his annual report published shortly after the Shawcross Report, the Independent Reviewer of Terrorism Legislation, Jonathan Hall KC, recommended that such individuals were better treated outside the criminal justice system and without the stigma of their offences being regarded as 'terrorism-related'.

Instead, the Shawcross Report proposes to push Prevent in the opposite direction, away from safeguarding and towards understanding individuals as 'responsible agents' rather than as 'vulnerable'. Indeed, he expresses some concern that a lot of Prevent referrals end up being redirected toward other social services, including mental health services. Logically, this is *an argument for removing Prevent from schools* (and, indeed, also from the health sector) where, safeguarding should be focused on the interests of the child and not an ill-defined future risk of radicalisation.

Shawcross, however, is not interested in reducing the pervasive scrutiny of Prevent except where it is right-wing views that might be caught up in the net. He claims in the Foreword to his report that, 'my research shows that the present boundaries around what is termed by Prevent as extremist Islamist ideology are drawn too narrowly while the boundaries around the ideology of the Extreme Right-Wing are too broad' (page 3). However, the data suggests otherwise. In 2021/22 just 13% of all referrals were adopted onto Channel. Of these, 42% were for far-right extremism, while 19% were for Islamist extremism. Yet, the proportion of all referrals was similar for both categories (20% for right wing extremism, 16% for Islamist extremism). In other words, the implication already is the opposite of what he claims; the definition is drawn broadly for 'Islamist' extremism and narrowly for right-wing extremism. A greater focus on 'Islamist extremism' would give rise to a greater number of Prevent referrals of Muslims, but a decline in the proportion of them going onto Channel. For right-wing extremism, the opposite would occur; that is, that there would be fewer referrals, but a higher proportion of adoptions onto Channel.

So far it might seem that the Shawcross Report presages little more than a doubling-down on already established features of Prevent. I think that there is something more fundamental underway with particular implications for universities. The recommendations coincide with the passage of the Higher Education (Freedom of Speech) Act 2023. This sets out a 'duty to promote the importance of freedom of speech and academic freedom.' It derives from right-wing agitation around 'cancel culture'. However, Prevent is itself a form of cancel culture, a cancelling of speech that is lawful, but deemed extremist. Is it, therefore, in conflict with the new legal framework on free speech?

As we have seen. the determination of what is 'extremist' is the responsibility of the Commissioner for Countering Extremism. The Shawcross Report makes two specific recommendations applying to universities. One is aimed at countering the 'anti-Prevent agenda' in Higher Education, which proposes revised training for those overseeing events (recommendation 28), the other is the creation of a network of advisors in the Department for Education who can be invited to speak at universities to promote Prevent (recommendation 33).

However, the Report also named two Muslim-led civil society organisations as 'extremist' – MEND and Cage. The Policy Exchange Report on 'Delegitimising Counter Terrorism' from which the new role for the Commission for Countering Extremism derives went further. There should be a register of approved Muslim-led civil society organisations and all bodies in receipt of public funds should be directed not to engage with those deemed 'extremist'.

This, of course, has implications for local government as well as national government, but has a particular significance for universities. Not only would speakers involved in these organisations be excluded from speaking on campus, so, too, would students that volunteered for them risk being referred to Prevent. Academic research would be affected in so far as the 'impact agenda' requires the collaboration with 'user groups' – Muslim-led civil society groups deemed 'extremist' are potentially excluded from collaboration. The Policy Exchange report went further than Shawcross to indicate that not only MEND and Cage, but also the Muslim Council of Britain, the Islamic Human Rights Commission, Prevent Watch, the Federation of Student Islamic Society, and any active criticism of Prevent should be considered for identification as 'extremist'. They also included the People's Review of Prevent and its authors!

I began this review with the common view that terrorism is a threat to our values. In this context, it is a commonplace to refer to terrorism as a form of political communication. Perhaps we should also see counter-terrorism as a form of political communication, too. What is being communicated are not liberal values, but those of an authoritarian national conservatism.

FAITH AND PATIENCE

Abdullah Geelah

In 1928, Somali seafarer Ibrahim Ismaa'il wrote an autobiography, extracts from which were published, some forty years later, by British-Ethiopian historian Richard Pankhurst in the journal *Africa* (32:2, 1977). It is one of the earliest accounts of life as a Somali seaman in Britain and arguably the first work of Anglo-Somali literature. 'I had heard of a place called Europe,' Ismaa'il writes, 'which was the other side of Djibouti, and where life was easier, wages being higher. I now decided to try my luck there.'

It's an altogether familiar story: the migrant's longing for better economic opportunities overseas. For the Somali seamen, other than being pioneers of modern African migration to Britain with a presence since the 1880s, their shared experiences have coalesced into their becoming a distinct social group within the Somali polity. A *siimaan* isn't just a seafarer with the Merchant Navy or the Royal Navy as it's historically been the case. He is also proficient, paternalistic, a polyglot and, rather sneeringly, Anglicised.

The seamen's relationship with that place on 'the other side of Djibouti', located beyond the extremity of the Somali's geographic conception, isn't as quixotic as Ismaai'l's words may suggest. Their connection with Britain didn't fit the émigré trope of an Eden away from the Golgotha of home. Nor did it reflect a wistful patriotism to rebuild the "mother country". Britain was simply a stop to refuel. It was a practical arrangement devoid of romanticised familial bonds. You tried your luck in England (a lingering exonym for Britain), but you yearned for Somalia. The seamen would often return from their foreign excursions flush with money. *Hoodolayaashi* – the fortune men – was what their countrymen called them, amazed at their Whittingtonian motivations and newfound capital.

Nadifa Mohamed has returned to the same theme in her third novel *The Fortune Men* which was shortlisted for the 2021 Booker Prize. Her debut

The Black Mamba Boy (2010) is a semi-autobiographical account of her now late father's childhood and life as a seaman. It is also a paean to the 'Somali Argonauts' – the many other seamen, like my late father, whose biblical journeys mirrored that of the book's protagonist. 'Those fortune men' she writes, 'who set their footprints in the sand, fifty, sixty, a hundred years ago, are the prophets who led the Israelites out of the wilderness.' Consider then Mahmood Hussein Mattan whose life is semi-fictionalised in *The Fortune Men*. He is a fully-fledged member of the Argonauts' Club: born in British Somaliland; stoker in the Merchant Navy; (mis)adventures in unfamiliar places (Tanganyika, Southern Africa and the Americas); multilingual (in descending order of fluency: Somali, Arabic, Swahili, English, Hindi); and patriarchal. Unlike his fellow seamen, he tried his luck in Britain and met a tragic end. Mattan was wrongly convicted and hanged for the murder of Lily Volpert. *The Fortune Men* is an elegy and a seething jeremiad.

Nadifa Mohamed, *The Fortune Men*, Viking, 2021.

The start to the book is (intentionally) hectic. Enter a myriad of characters and a multitude of voices amidst the transition to the second Elizabethan Age. This is Cardiff's Tiger Bay in the 1950s: a microcosm of the dying Pax Britannica. Thanks to archival work and interviews with Somali elders, Mohamed is meticulous in her portrayal, throughout the book, of Wales' oldest multi-ethnic community:

> 'The Bay emerges out of the industrial fog and sea mist like an ancient fossil-
> ized animal stepping out of the water. You might walk along the docks and find
> sailors carrying parrots or little monkeys in makeshift jackets to sell or keep as
> souvenirs, you can have chop suey for lunch and Yemeni *saltah* for dinner, even
> in London you won't find the pretty girls – with a grandparent from each
> continent – that you just stumble into in Tiger Bay.'

Tiger Bay's history, though well-researched, is presented with gratuitous detail (local 'rumour' has it that 'the world's first million-pound cheque was signed at the Coal Exchange'). Focus slowly moves to the lives of the two victims, flitting between one and the other in the lead up to the murder.

The story is told in the third-person, allowing the reader to observe from a distant vantage point as the events unfold. If you expect a tight narrative, forget it. The book is structured chaotically: monologues and dialogues; police interrogations and court transcripts; prayers and dealings.

Violet Volacki (the name changed at the request of the family) is a Jewish shopkeeper and moneylender, a doting aunt and sister. Many of her relatives have perished, whether in the Shoah or some pogrom we are unsure. They haunt her with pleas of deliverance: 'cousin, save me … Avram dead, Chaja dead, Shmuel dead. In Lithuania, in Poland, in Germany'. She is proud of her shop at 203 Bute Street (inherited from her father) which anchors her family despite her sister Diana's protests that they should have moved to London or Brooklyn. 'This shop is my life, and if I had just sold it in '48 what good would that have done?' Yet they recognise their vulnerability in Tiger Bay: 'this patch of earth, reclaimed from marshland and still liquid, deep within the foundations, is all the sanctuary (we) have.' There is a fleeting glimpse into her romantic life. She breaks the tenth mitzvah in her 'lovelorn, girlish infatuation' with her sister's husband Daniel. He is an escape from her wretched spinsterhood: 'a sepulchre for her hope of one day bearing children. He is in her waking dreams: his lips, his hands, his pink nipples lewd and raspberry-like against his snowy skin.' We subsequently have a snapshot into the family, the murder and their grief. Mohamed humanises Volacki: 'Violet wasn't *just* a moneylender,' Diana says bitterly 'People *knew* her'. Mohamed describes her life in all its mundanity and gives her story equal legitimacy. She doesn't want a female character whose very existence in the story is justified by the act which negates that existence. However, one assumes that Mohamed's research into the Volpert family was either limited or restricted. This shows in the narrative and the character's development.

The story gains momentum as we learn more about Mattan. He sees himself as a 'nomad, a chancer, a fighter, a rebel' yet his actions cast him as profligate, a pilferer, a plunger and a philanderer. Despite being down on his luck, he is no loafer. Mattan has misguided ambitions to re-join the Merchant Navy, encouraged by his friend Berlin who rebukes him for 'clinging on to this piece of flint they call a country'. Mattan knows it is a reckless proposition; he is now settled with his Welsh wife Laura and their three sons. He goes to the Employment Exchange ('Red brick and leaded glass, the smell of bleach and defeat.') and examines the notices to see the firms which 'can be relied upon to take coloured folk'. They are not advertising and he knows the clerks at the Exchange resent him 'whether he is looking for work or drawing dole.' Mattan goes to gamble at the races with his dole money and leaves the 'melancholia of the Exchange'. Quite.

Mattan is a complicated figure with a proclivity for self-sabotage. He is morally questionable and some of his misfortune is self-inflicted. Indeed, this does not invite sympathy from the reader. One should not, therefore, draw conclusions as to his capability to murder. The simplistic and conventional antihero trope has no room in this novel. Mattan challenges concurrently the myth of the saintly victim and the absurdity that one's criminality justifies one's inevitable death – recurrent refrains in the killing of Black men. As Berlin sighs: '*Doqon iyo malaggiisa lama kala reeb karo*, a fool and his fate can never be parted.' Mattan is a Black immigrant man in 1950s Britain. He needs to survive in whichever way he sees fit. While Mattan's humanity is negated because of his lifestyle, Volacki's humanity is validated in spite of hers. Humanity, in this case, isn't an objective and transcendent ideal, but an attribute that gains or loses power based on the person who yields it (or who it is yielded for).

Mattan's conviction is a forgone conclusion. The book's rage pivots on Cardiff City Police's investigation with Chief Detective Inspector Powell at the helm. This is a miscarriage of justice *par excellence*. The investigation is predicated on the classical canon: fabricated testimonies, tampered evidence, police corruption. Colonial prejudice permeates their view: 'Powell collects his thoughts… He'd read somewhere that for Somalis every man is his own master. They aren't like the jovial Kroo boys or anglicized West Indians, but are truculent and vicious, quick to draw a weapon and unrepentant after the fact.' Mattan ridicules their arrogance to concentrate on the circumstantial: 'British police is so clever. I tell you I kill twenty men. I kill your king. This I tell you if you like, you think that right?' He is the archetypal Black criminal; demonised for his appearance, behaviour and lifestyle. His misplaced faith in British justice is risible: 'That was the famous British justice. You had to have proper evidence, or the game was all over: not 'I think', or 'I heard', or 'I guess', none of that shit.' He marvels at the lawyers 'who speak in a language far removed from his English of engine rooms, factories, quarries, street fights and pillow talk.'

They prepare 'a strong case' in contrast to the prosecution's 'assortment of tattletales and what-ifs.' Mr Rhys Roberts commences his closing speech: 'as my learned friend said, the whole of Mattan's stories and explanations and statements and evidence is riddled with lies.' This gets better: 'You have to ask yourselves this question when you saw him: *What is he?* Half child of nature? Half semi-civilized savage?' When your own counsel blatantly undermines your defence, British justice is indeed risible. Throughout the investigation and trial, Mattan is prone to periodic proclamations of innocence in his 'pidgin English': 'I kill no woman', 'I *innocent*', 'All I got to say is, I'm not guilty'. He subverts the quietism of the colonial subject. His liturgical repetitions are compelling but woefully delusional. Whilst we are struck by their Spartan eloquence, we pity his fantasy that this is sufficient. Mattan is audacious to claim his humanity. For the defence's closing speech to rest on Mattan's dehumanisation was not only a legal own goal but a triumph of whiteness. The jury's conclusion is made: he is sub-human and therefore excluded from our conception of humanity. Mattan resigns to an almost fatalistic passivity as he thanks his solicitor for his effort to secure a petition to the Home Secretary (a forlorn endeavour given Sir David Maxwell Fyfe's refusal to grant a reprieve in early 1953 to Derek Bentley, another victim of a miscarriage of justice). 'The very best of luck, Mr Mattan.' his solicitor says, 'Everything always come back to luck,' Mattan replies.

Though she writes in English, Mohamed's prose is peppered with Somali mythology and Hadraawi-like imagery and metaphor. Consider Mattan's view of the lawyers: 'That black cap, that black gown with wing-like folds, sharp grey lips like an evil bird talking. Waaq, the forgotten crow-god of the Somalis, come to life to pluck out his heart, the prayers sent to Allah sticking like arrows in his bitter, proud flesh.' As he observes the full moon to mark the beginning of Ramadan, Mattan ponders from his prison: 'The night skies of Hargeisa made you think of God ...where sunset meant genuine darkness, you could track the slow movements of stars and planets, glittering and pulling you up into a depthless, shifting sea with its coastline of purple, indigo and black stretches.'

The trial strips Mattan of his personhood yet Mohamed centres him firmly in a Muslim Somali context. The seamen's detachment from their country led Somalis to label them as Anglicised, a coded term meaning irreligious, since the early seafarers were ensnared by the appeal of Britain's bibulous culture and Siren-like women. This notion is interrogated by the depth of Mattan's semi-fictionalised world: the backstory, the spirituality, the argot. Here he is the hubristic Habar Awal man from Hargeisa; not 'a real rogue with no respect for authority, a covetous darkie of no fixed abode' as Chief Detective Inspector Powell thinks. He sees himself as 'a self-anointed king, far beyond being just a Reer Gedid youth, a Sacad Muse clansman, a Somali, a Muslim, a Black.' When he is told that he will be staying at Her Majesty's Prison, this stirs an anticolonial anger towards the new monarch: 'What kind of woman gets pleasure from keeping her men cooped up like chickens and goats? ... I see you now. I see your power, you satisfied? Araweelo the castrator, the indomitable. Somalis were right to overthrow our own evil queen.' His striking soliloquy trails off: 'You rich, I'm poor, you white, I'm black, you English, I'm Somali, you're loved, I'm despised. Fate is wrong to tie us up together when we have no more in common...than a...' The Somali words and expressions he and Berlin use (transliterated, sometimes inconsistently, to ease pronunciation for non-Somali speakers) are left untranslated. Mohamed, in the words of Abdulrazaq Gurnah, refuses to make 'the alien seem more alien'. We come to appreciate the inherent poetry of Mattan's *Soomaalinimo* and we re-engage with him as a person.

Faith and fatalism run the course of the book to its sad and inevitable end. Rake-thin and hermit-like, Mattan finds spiritual sustenance in the almost solipsistic insularity of prison. As his hope in temporal justice quivers and quakes, his belief in divine justice, though shaky at first, stabilises:

> 'God reminds you through those night skies of how small and insignificant you are, and he speaks to you clearly, his anger and solace tangible in the rain he sends or withholds, the births or deaths he orders, the long, waxy grass he gives or the dead, broken earth he carves. The miasma above the prison, above Cardiff, suffocated Mahmood's faith and separated him from God. He began to strut and bluster his days away and completely forget that this life meant nothing and was as fragile as a twig underfoot. He had needed to be humbled ... he can see God's wisdom so clearly now.'

The caricatured Yemeni sheikh from the local *zawiya* arrives to offer comfort, enjoining Mattan to 'put his trust in the Almighty because the world of men is an unjust one'. When Ainashe, a former sailor, recounts his story of nursing his brother's dead body after their ship was torpedoed, the *makhayad* (coffeehouse) audience of men sigh '*sabar iyo imaan*' as they 'shrugged off the weight of Ainashe's misery and insanity with an ease that at first shocked Mahmood but then felt right and manly.' *Sabar* (in some cases, *samir*) *iyo imaan* – meaning '(may you have) faith and patience' – is said to the loved ones of those who are grieving a loss. The words act as a reminder, in the midst of profound anguish, of the certainty of death and the futility of bereavement. These words hasten closure. *Geeridii uu ka samiri waaye* ('the loss hasn't brought him patience') refers to someone who hasn't come to terms with the death of a loved one. Sometimes this is uttered disparagingly, for such behaviour implies a rejection of divine will. Often, it is sighed amongst mourners with pangs of pity; a euphemism that the death was tragic. Mahmood Hussein Mattan's family have found neither patience nor faith since his execution in Cardiff 70 years ago. His conviction was quashed in 1998 after a long campaign by his widow Laura and their children. His case was the first to be referred to the Court of Appeal by the newly-formed Criminal Cases Review Commission. The compensation, though considerable, wasn't adequate. Trauma stalked the family. They were pariahs in Cardiff for nearly half a century. Mattan's son, Omar, took his own life on a solitary Scottish beach in 2003. His granddaughter, Natasha, took part in the Black Lives Matter protest in Cardiff in 2020 to highlight her own family's tragedy, and that of countless other Black men whose ends could not, will not, bring the closure of that ancient Cushitic condolence. *Wan ka samiri weeyne* – we haven't come to terms.

ATHENA RETURNS

Flavie Curinier

The critiques were very mixed. Positive critiques highlight the fact that the movie takes on all the tough topics one would expect from a social commentary and deals with them in a way that equips the audience with a comprehension that allows them to appreciate and sympathise with the situation in the *banlieues*, suburban ghettos, as well as evaluate how the police handled it. No doubt this comes in part from the frequent use of frenetic tracking shots that place the audience within the chaos, first hand. Others mention that this movie has the aesthetic of a Greek tragedy, evoked through a double entendre inferred by the film's title. Indeed, some claim the aesthetic is purely political shock: the film reflects the image of a country on the verge of ruin. The negative critiques were also numerous. Some contend that the film is dishonest and unsatisfactory in every way and that the mysterious character, the former terrorist, Sébastien's radical Islamism is to blame for the social uprising featured. Yet others say not enough is said, that the only thing the audience is left to remember is that the revolt was illegitimate, absurd, and nothing else or any actions taken matter – the position of the far-right. Most French critics argue that the movie is too political; but this was over a year ago before a very similar situation played out following the killing of Nahel Merzouk by French police in the Parisian suburb of Nanterre. International critics tend to have a more positive view of the film. One critic argued that it is a virtuoso movie with a rarely witnessed lyricism.

Athena directed by Romain Gavras, Iconoclast and Lyly Films, 2022. 1:39:33

The film is Romain Gavras's 2022 *Athena*. The plot picks up in the aftermath of a police blunder in the *banlieue* of Athena, just outside Paris, which resulted in the death of a young boy. The film focuses on the deceased boy's brothers, who try to make sense of the events against a backdrop of unrest taking place in their banlieue. Each brother represents different ways in which immigrants 'take on systems of power that are not designed for them to succeed'. Moktar is an opportunist who solely thinks about his drug traffic, which is brought to a grinding halt by the uprising. Karim represents an all-or-nothing radical, willing to risk his life to know the names of the police officers responsible for the death of his little brother. Finally, Abdel stands in between the two other brothers. He has just returned from a mission in Mali as a soldier and is conflicted between his duty to the police and his loyalty to his brothers, a titanic achievement not only for his own piece of mind, but for the peace, order, and safety of their community. As a barricade forms, locking the *banlieue* and all is citizens within and the French police out, much of what happens in the outside world is feed through overheard and often cut to imagery from the 24/7 news channel, BFMTV. This is how we are slowly introduced to the third key character, the shadowy Sébastien. BFMTV reports fears from the police that Sébastien resides in Athena and is suspected of barbaric acts in the past. We first meet Sébastien, as the situation in Athena escalates and our apparent hero, Abdel, asks Sébastien to go help the rioters, even though he has become a completely different person from the devout follower of Islam he is first witnessed by the audience. Sébastien is now a man fascinated by destruction. Where Abdel is torn between two ideals, that of family and that of duty to his country, we can see Sébastien conflicted between staying quiet and hiding, perhaps a coward indeed, and being consumed by the destruction taking place all around him.

Historically, the banlieues were largely developed during the urbanisation period and the rapid industrialisation of land in the nineteenth century France. The banlieues were created to allow more people to live close to the big cities, which, themselves, expanded due to the urbanisation boom. As it is cheaper to live in the banlieues than in the city centre, the population living in the banlieues tended to be more ethnically and racially diverse. It was a natural place for immigrants, wishing to work in the city, to affordably reside. As the backgrounds of the diverse people living in banlieues broke from French culture, a resentment festered between the people and the police. The word 'banlieue' developed a stronger connotation than its English transition of suburb. It became a strong marker of disadvantage and now carries negative connotations, such as urban deprivation, criminality, and violence. Recently, the banlieues have been associated with inter-racial conflict, Islamism, violence against women, police brutality, and, of course, riots and other forms of urban disorder.

In 2005, two youngsters living in the Parisian banlieues died as result of electrocution following their attempted fleeing from police. This was the touch paper set ablaze alongside the persistent high unemployment among young people and police harassment in the banlieues. Riots erupted all over France. A state of emergency was declared and extended for three weeks. In total, three people died, almost 3,000 people were arrested, and more than 8,000 vehicles were burned. Nicolas Sarkozy, minister of the interior at the time, was accused of having worsened the situation. During the riots, it is said that he asked the prefects that both legal and undocumented immigrants who were convicted be immediately deported. In 2008, then-President Sarkozy implemented a plan called *Espoir Banlieues*, whose goal was to reduce the gap between the banlieues and the rest of the territory. It focuses on education, employment, opening up, and security. However, this plan did not gather enough financing, which shows that politicians do not see this as a pressing issue.

The police situation remains desperate for those who reside within the banlieues. Riot police remain on constant call, replacing the everyday police while there is never enough money and therefore enough staff. ID checks and riot mitigation is untenable. New and inexperienced recruits gain their training in a baptism by fire as they are assigned to these poor suburban towns. The fact that these locations are not their home or anywhere they particularly desire to work or reside within makes matters all the worse. Consequently, by failing to increase everyday police presence since the mid-1990s, the state has favoured the militarisation of police in the banlieues. To fill the policing gaps at the local level, the state relies on diverse types of militarised units, such as the *Compagnies Républicaines de Sécurité* (CRS) and the *Esquadron de Gendarmerie Mobile* (EGM or Gendarmerie). Like a military wishing to remain untethered to a never-ending quagmire, units deployed to these *banlieues* engage in their assigned intervention, and then go back to where they came from. In and out. This means that they have no preconceptions about the environment of the banlieues or who lives there. Resorting to summary tactics, these CRS or Gendarmerie police officers do nothing to help stabilise the environment in the long term. No rapport is established between the police and the policed. No progress is even attempted. Moreover, because the rapid reassignment of these units grants them such a facelessness that individual officers or their commanders are not required to answer to the residents for their behaviour and are rarely pressured to do so. Despite the government's efforts to change the situation, the militarisation of the police in the banlieues continues exponentially. The way the police handle situations in the banlieues pushes the residents to defend themselves, violently if need be. Thus, the police have started to use rubber-bullet weapons to retaliate and protect themselves since the early 2000s, incited by Nicholas Sarkozy.

Any recipe for disaster is incomplete without the intervention of the courts. The Court of Cassation, France's highest court of law, has ruled that 'anti-discrimination laws are not to be applied in the same manner in areas renowned for a high crime rate, as is the case of all the housing projects of the banlieues'. Defeat declared in any hopes of ever normalising the banlieues, now judicial laxity, mixed with the increased militarisation of the police, allows for the banlieues to remain in a disaster or war like state. The result is a maintained and perpetuated legalistic style of policing. Thus, it is not surprising to observe that police officers in the *banlieues* are strongly suspected of discriminatory, racist, or violent behaviour.

The film's director explained how *Athena* gives the audience a way into the people living with this history of government failure. He notes that the three brothers represent the diverse ways immigrants and marginalised communities take on systems of power that are not designed for them to succeed, as well as the different perspectives or responses to the racial injustice of French society.

For the first year of the film's release, it was hard to argue that *Athena* would stand the test of time. It could even have been dismissed as style over substance as a more nuanced exploration of the motivations of the communities at war throughout the film leaves one wanting. In fact, one could even go so far as to call it a less substantial, yet more modern take on Mathieu Kassovitz's 1995 celebrated film, *La Haine*. But then 27 June

2023 happened. In a *banlieue* similar to Athena, Nanterre, seventeen-year-old Nahel Merzouk was fatally shot while fleeing from two police officers. A protest outside the police headquarters the same day erupted into a riot. On 29 June, only two days after the fatal shooting and the protest-turned-riot, twenty-four officers had been injured, 150 people arrested, and forty cars set ablaze. Although almost two decades had past, just as in 2005 the same tactics were deployed by the state. Riot police, gendarmes, and the national police and counterterrorism forces of the *Recherche, Assistance, Intervention, Dissuasion* (RAID) and *Groupe d'intervention de la Gendarmerie Nationale* (GIGN) were deployed for weeks throughout France.

Just as the riots of 2023 appear as a simple repeat of 2005, perhaps *Athena* gives us the same impression when seen after *La Haine*. Yet many things have changed. As the film continues, we come to find one of the brothers is watching BFMTV in order to see what is going on outside their banlieue. BFMTV is a 24/7 news channel. As such, some of the information it passes on is incorrect and can lead to disinformation and manipulation of information. Critics have described the news channel as manipulating the information to make it more extreme to attract more viewers. This is amplified by the broadcasting on a loop of a few videos or pictures that are used to emphasise the sensationalism of the information. BFMTV invites experts onto the set to give analyses and explanations of a situation. It is a great opportunity for these experts, who are usually not famous (yet), as it allows them to find a way to express themselves and gain popularity. Other critics accuse BFMTV of frequently inviting Florian Philippot when he was vice president of the Front National, the same far-right party that nominated Marine Le Pen to take on incumbent President Emmanuel Macron in the 2022 presidential election. Critics maintain that there are risks of propaganda by the news channel. Unlike in 1995, the hate that gives rise to hate not only comes from within a given system, but from everywhere. The problem is made complex thanks in no small part to misinformation, fake news, bias, and the continual perpetuation of ignorance around the rampant Islamophobia endemic to French society. Where skinheads and racism are no new phenomenon, the power and positioning of the most extreme xenophobes has painted an entirely new picture for us to view.

France is a majority-white nation, but its, as well as more generally throughout Europe, demographics are changing. According to a 2016 survey, 70.7% of the respondents considered themselves exclusively white. This is striking as, until recently, most French citizens would not simply identify as white. Far-right, racist organisations, whose explicit political agenda is to uphold and advance white supremacy, have reclaimed whiteness as a positive racial identity. Charles Mills points out that the failure to examine white supremacy holds it in place.

There are no Arabs, Asians, Blacks, Roma, or Whites in France. Everyone is expected to be an unhyphenated citizen. Race is absent from official discourse as a category of analysis, and the census does not collect racial and ethnic data. The ban on the collection of so-called 'ethnic data' is an essential component of French whiteness, as it prevents the government and civil society from using their knowledge of racial inequalities and oppression towards redistributive ends. Thus, whiteness is seen as a Republican universalism in France.

Under the identity of Arab/Muslim or Maghrebi, people from a wide range of ethnic and religious backgrounds are seen as part of a group that is different from the rest of society. The public and legal debates operate under the paradigms of colour blindness, secularism, and universalism, yet the systematic targeting of Islamic practises, from the headscarf to halal food, betrays its xenophobic and racist underpinnings. In France, the Arab or Muslim presence has long been unwelcomed and the target of blame and violence. In France, Islam is central to the definition of whiteness, where the latter has been recast in contrast to Muslimness.

The film's ending has a resonance that carries on through the final credits. Is the fight from within, does hate give rise to hate, or can hate simply be a tool? Is the struggle in the *banlieues*, within the community, between the community and the state (and time-honoured tradition in modern France) or could hate simply be being used by others to provoke artificial conflict between parties that would otherwise be capable of harmonising? Gavras ends his film very deliberately to wake the audience up to the fact that the far right is on the rise, and how the tactics they use will push France to civil war. Gavras explains that he has a feeling that 'we live in a time when information is so confusing. Throughout the film, you hear the news saying something, and the kids are not believing it because there is such disbelief and suspicion of information in general. So, it is very easy these days for a group to pull off a false flag coup or operation'. It was important for Gavras to show that, because of this overflow of information and disinformation, people do not know who to trust, and many nefarious actors, in France and beyond, are skilled at using this confusion to its own benefit and ends.

While the shock factor of the film is successful in staying in the minds of the audience beyond their viewing, what is most interesting to note is how events in the news can reignite flames doomed to extinguish themselves over time. The power of *Athena* comes not in its cinematography, which largely relies on a viewer's tastes, or even its successful use of spectacle and shock, but in how insightfully its art imitated reality. It is often the objective of many artists to have their work reach such a feat, but in viewing the differences of opinion between those who viewed the film in 2022 and those watching it as chaos continued to unfold on the streets of Paris in 2023, one must ask is it the filmmaker or the screenwriter's keen eye or Frances inability to cope with our contemporary times that saw to this successful imitation. Whether we laugh or applaud at the end of *Athena*, it is critical that we ask why such banal violence flourishes in our times.

ET CETERA

ON DENIAL

Oz Katerji

It was the Auschwitz survivor Elie Wiesel who once said, "to forget a Holocaust is to kill twice."

After nearly a decade and a half working as a foreign correspondent, these words remind me why I continue to work documenting atrocities, crimes that the United Nations vowed would never again happen in our lifetimes, despite the tremendous mental and physical toll it takes to do so. By bearing witness, we remember, and we remember so as never to forget. If one is powerless to prevent these crimes, testimony becomes the only moral choice left.

There remains however a crime even worse than forgetting, and it plagues nearly every facet of modern public and political discourse surrounding documented war crimes and crimes against humanity: Denial.

Today the Russian regime has weaponised denial as a critical component of its full scale war on Ukraine. So too has the Chinese government in its cultural eradication of the Uyghurs of East Turkestan. In the previous decade, the Iranian and Syrian regimes, in league with their Russian allies, denied their industrial-scale slaughter of the Syrian people, even as extensive forensic photographs documenting these crimes (the Caesar photographs) were smuggled out of the country, verified by Human Rights Watch and publicly displayed, including by the US Holocaust Memorial Museum. In the decade before that, the Sudanese regime employed denial over its genocide in Darfur. And in the decade before that, the Serbian government did the same in Bosnia.

This horrific cycle of genocide followed by denial continues back through time; the Cambodian Genocide, the Holocaust, the Holodomor, the Armenian Genocide. There are so many examples it becomes valid to ask if denial is in and of itself a crucial component of genocide.

But is denial a crucial component for all genocides? Genocide scholars, unsurprisingly, have mixed opinions on this. A book published in 2021 titled *Denial: The Final Stage of Genocide?* explores these questions at length, but here I would like to highlight the contribution by Armenian-American academic and former president of the International Association of Genocide Scholars, Henry C. Theriault, who argues that denial is not essential to genocide, and that there are both ancient and contemporary examples of perpetrators drawing attention to, and even exaggerating their crimes for the purposes of intimidation. Furthermore, mixing denial with explicit approval for genocide is so common in political discourse that it has spawned a recognisable trope: "It didn't happen, but they deserved it".

Theriualt's argument that denial is a tool that is employed only when it is perceived as an efficacious strategy in the pursuit of a genocide is a reasonable one, but in either case, the rhetorical purpose of these strategies remains to dehumanise the victims of genocide and to justify the genocidal intent of the perpetrators. On the pathology of denial, Theriualt says that all deniers "share a desire that genocide denial be normalized out of an approval of genocide and even a pleasure at demeaning the victims and as a way of reserving the potential of renewed genocide as a threat or future activity." The logical assumption from this would be that genocide denial, or atrocity revisionism more generally as it pertains to ongoing crimes against humanity that have not yet been classified as genocide, would be perceived as societally unacceptable. But that logical assumption is false, and the examples of this are too numerous to fit in a book, let alone an essay.

On the intention of the denier, American historian, diplomat and author of *Denying the Holocaust*, Deborah Lipstadt once summarised part of her legal battle with the British convicted Holocaust denier David Irving by saying, "there are facts, there are opinions and there are lies. And what deniers want to do is take their lies, dress them up as opinions, opinions that should be part of the conversation, and then they encroach on the facts." Lipstadt appears to agree with Theriualt that the denier's intention is that of normalisation, to present the act of questioning documented, incontrovertible atrocities as if it were as reasonable as any other type of academic discourse, even when the fallacies underpinning those arguments are as divorced from reality as claiming that the Earth is flat.

This relationship between truth, fiction, and the apologists for crimes against humanity was explored by the political philosopher Hannah Arendt in her study *The Origins of Totalitarianism*. Arendt wrote "the ideal subject of totalitarian rule is not the convinced Nazi or the convinced Communist, but people for whom the distinction between fact and fiction and the distinction between true and false no longer exist." As Arendt correctly highlights, this attitude towards truth and revisionism isn't confined to Nazis and the fascist far right. Indeed the problems with atrocity denial have also become entrenched and endemic on the far left, and this has been the case at least since the crimes of Josef Stalin. Nor can the liberal centre ground claim to be free from this moral stain – indeed, for as long as ideology has existed, there will be those willing to kill and lie in its name. While it's true that Holocaust denial does now carry a social stigma in many western liberal democracies, even being designated a criminal offence in some European countries, the same cannot be said of other war crimes, crimes against humanity and genocides, even when those crimes are among the most well-documented in human history. And even with the Holocaust-specific stigma, Holocaust deniers like David Irving have still at times managed to attain positions of relative prominence and supposed academic credibility. Irving himself was once regarded, in Britain at least, as a respected World War II historian, even while he continued to claim that Auschwitz had no gas chambers. One is left wondering what his reputation would be today if he had not famously lost his libel case against Ambassador Lipstadt.

Writing in the *New York Times* in 2019, Bosnian-American novelist Aleksandar Hemon said, "any survivor of genocide will tell you that disbelieving or dismissing their experience is a continuation of genocide." Hemon was responding to the Austrian author and Bosnian Genocide-denier Peter Handke's receipt of the Nobel Prize for Literature that same year, whom Hemon referred to as "the Bob Dylan of genocide apologists." The veneration of Handke by the Nobel committee not only reinforces the impunity of the genocide denier, but as Hemon said, serves as a continuation of the Serbian genocide of Bosniaks.

Unfortunately the Nobel committee is not the only institution mired in the disgrace of genocide denial. In fact, atrocity revisionism in general has become an endemic problem in political discourse, engineered largely by the regimes culpable for these crimes, but tolerated and enabled by the apathy of the establishment. I will come back to this, but I feel I should provide the reader with some context as to why this issue is so important to me.

My personal experience with atrocity revisionism as a journalist is a deeply personal one, and one that radically changed the course of my career. I first knew I wanted to be a war reporter when I was just a child, watching my uncle Philip Howarth report from Lebanon for the BBC during the civil war. I don't think many children are fortunate enough to have already decided the paths their careers would take before the age of 10, but I honestly couldn't imagine doing anything else with my life.

As I approached the industry with an initially unshakeable idealism, I did not have any idea how much denialism would impact my career. While I was aware of the Bosnian Genocide revisionists, I was too young to have experienced their work firsthand. But it would not be long before I encountered denialism myself, albeit concerning the Middle East and not the Balkans. At first I wasn't prepared for the reality of this job. But now that I understand the reality, I am not prepared to walk away from the fight. If conflict journalism isn't a direct opponent of atrocity denial, then it is nothing but war tourism and propaganda. If we are not duty-bound to fight for the truth to be heard, then we have no business reporting that truth in the first place. These stories are only entrusted to us so we can do them justice, and we do them no justice if we do not confront denial.

War crimes denial has unfortunately become a subject I have learned a great deal about over the course of my journalistic career. It touches on conflicts that have no relation to each other besides the zealotry of the revisionists. I have published extensively on the subject, but this was never by design, and I would have been horrified to learn as a student that I would dedicate so much of my career fighting against atrocity denial.

It is no longer enough to simply report the truth. Journalists these days are forced to compete with fantasists and propagandists in the information space, on platforms where the quality of information is considered significantly less important than its propensity to go viral. As this phenomenon continues to degrade public discourse, the money spent on quality journalism is in decline, as is the media industry in general. All of which is more good news for authoritarian states looking to flood the internet with disinformation and lies.

I grew up with a reverence for war journalists, for the bravery they displayed, for their tireless pursuit of speaking truth to power, even at the cost of their lives. I watched my heroes like Kate Adie, Marie Colvin, Robert Fisk and James Nachtwey put themselves in harm's way to bear witness to the very worst acts of humanity, to provide a voice for the voiceless, and to testify before history so that no crime against humanity could ever be forgotten.

It was one of these heroes that first drew me into this struggle. As a fledgling intern at the now-shuttered Lebanese English language newspaper *The Daily Star*, I remember going along with several young colleagues of mine to see Robert Fisk give a speech at the Lebanese American University in 2010. This was my first time seeing him in the flesh and I was excited to hear what he had to say. "The Middle East is not a football match," he said. "It's a bloody tragedy, and the journalists have a responsibility to be on the side of those who suffer."

I agreed — and still agree — wholeheartedly with that statement. But it was difficult for me to reconcile this Robert Fisk — the Robert Fisk of *Pity The Nation*, which I believed when I first read it to be the most comprehensive western account of the civil war that had destroyed my father's home country — with the Robert Fisk I would later come to know. Because in his writing, Fisk often described a fictional world based only loosely on reality.

I will lay just a handful of examples out to demonstrate. Firstly, despite what was written in some obituaries, even after 40 years of living in the Middle East, Robert Fisk could not speak Arabic. He lacked even knowledge of basic words like "ummah" (community/nation), which was apparent from his catastrophic mistranslation of the Ba'athist slogan "Ummah Arabiya Wahida" as "the Mother of one Arab People", instead of "One Arab Nation".

Following Fisk's death, Syrian journalist Asser Khattab attempted to set the record straight by writing a furious piece on Fisk's mistruths for the Arabic magazine *Raseef22*. In it Khattab gave a first hand account of Fisk making stuff up, focusing particular attention on an encounter with his regime-minder/translator on a visit to Homs. Khattab says "Fisk spoke of places we did not visit, and facts we did not witness, and his interview with officials, including those in the governorate, was full of long, eloquent and expressive phrases that I have no idea where they had come from."

Another story, told by former *Telegraph* correspondent, Francis Harris, demonstrates just how brazen Fisk was with his stories. "When I was in Zagreb, the foreign desk sent me his piece from rural Croatia," Harris said. "I said that's impossible. No one could do that journey in a day, and I'd seen him at breakfast and dinner. A decade later, when I was on the foreign desk, an angry young correspondent said the same — that Fisk's trip from Kabul to Kandahar was impossible. Journalists had died trying to drive down that road. And I told him what my deputy foreign editor had told me in '91: 'Sorry old son, you've been Fisked'."

As the Assad regime's counter-revolutionary violence brutalised Syrians from 2011 on, Fisk conducted fawning interviews with such regime figures as foreign minister Walid Muallem. Instead of asking searching questions, he took their propaganda claims at face value. Then, after the August 2012 massacre of around 700 people in Daraya, a suburb west of Damascus, Fisk's career arrived at its lowest point. During the American-British occupation of Iraq, Fisk had written powerfully against 'embedded journalism', when journalists accompanied occupation forces and questioned Iraqis in their presence, but in 2012 Fisk entered Daraya with the Assad regime forces who had just perpetrated the massacre and then proceeded to question survivors in their presence. Of course the story he then wrote explained the innocence of the perpetrators. Fisk did not meet any member of the opposition in Daraya, and did not meet any civilian at all except in the presence of armed regime minders. The respected war correspondent Janine di Giovanni went into Daraya with civilians at the same time, however, and uncovered the truth of the regime assault on a rebellious civilian community.

Fisk could not have duped an entire industry for so long without the complicity of his editors and publishers. When I published my obituary of Fisk in *The Critic*, a small British conservative magazine, I did not expect it to be so widely shared by my peers. As I wrote there, "the frequency with which falsehoods can be found in Fisk's work wasn't so much an open secret as a widely shared joke." Now that Fisk was dead, other journalists finally felt free to share their own stories of Fisk's litany of distortions, half-truths and passed-on propaganda. Some of his more sympathetic peers questioned why I had waited until his death to publish this account, despite the fact that I had been highlighting Fisk's record for many years. The truth is that very few people cared enough to speak out. Something could have been done, and other than the British satirical magazine *Private Eye*, very few acted to challenge Fisk's atrocity revisionism. Fisk's newspaper, *The Independent*, even quietly moved his copy to the Opinion section, probably because they were tired of the scrutiny his articles were increasingly put under in the latter stages of his career.

Fisk's reporting in Syria was, for me, as much a continuation of the Assad regime's crimes against humanity as those the Bosnian Genocide-revisionists had committed against Bosniaks in the nineties. His denial of massacres, chemical weapons attacks, and the brutalisation of Syria's civilian population discredits his entire career. Fisk proved that his word could not be trusted, thus undermining his role as a journalist. But like the Pulitzer Prize winner, Holodomor-denier and Stalin-apologist Walter Duranty before him, Fisk's accolades remain. Even in death there has been no real reckoning with his legacy.

As a reporter learning the truth about one of my former idols, I was crestfallen. Syria had opened my eyes to denialism, and once my eyes were open, I was shocked to start seeing it in places I had never even questioned before.

Perhaps I am fortunate that one of the first major lessons I learned as a journalist was that I could not simply trust the word even of those journalists I had grown up admiring. It is a lesson I learned young, and it is probably what spurred my interest during the early 2010s in Open Source Intelligence (OSINT), which employs forensic and open source methods (such as user generated content, for example videos uploaded from crime scenes) to verify and confirm war crimes. Learning about the open source method was a liberating experience. I could now acquire the skills necessary to accurately and effectively counter the fabrications and distortions of charlatans.

With these new skills, journalists were able to disprove war crimes denial using forensic evidence, evidence that can be peer-reviewed and widely corroborated. OSINT didn't just change the game, it provided journalists and human rights activists with the tools to confront the evil of denialism without the need for hugely complicated and expensive on-the-ground investigations. These still have an important role to play in journalism, but OSINT revolutionised the entire industry approach to documenting war crimes.

The rise of social media and video technology allowed unprecedented levels of global communication, meaning that war crimes could be documented by anybody who had a mobile phone, and could be uploaded online and on the same day broadcast to the entire world, something that previous generations could only achieve by hugely expensive broadcast news operations. This was a new era for journalism. We could now cover conflicts in new ways, in real time, thanks to waves of user generated content being uploaded to the internet every day.

But there was a counterweight. This unprecedented flow of information would be immediately assaulted by an equally unprecedented tech-savvy approach to atrocity denial. The growth of social media provided state sponsored atrocity revisionism a new platform, a *Radio-Television Serbia* but with the power to be broadcast directly into every home with a computer and an internet connection. At certain points, reporting the truth of the systematic war crimes taking place in Syria became in and of itself a radical act. Those who documented the atrocities the Assad regime inflicted on Syrian civilians were targeted by a vast, state-sponsored network of deniers, supported by the extensive influence operation of the Russian Ministry of Information, itself masquerading as a state broadcaster. The purpose was the same as ever – to pump out non-stop disinformation intended to dismiss, distort, distract, dismay and divide – only in a medium that could now be streamed directly to any phone in the world, and not just printed on the pages of *Pravda*.

Russia was bombing hospitals, and enabling the Assad regime to rain chemical weapons on utterly defenceless civilians in Douma and Khan Sheikhoun, by actively denying that any of this was taking place. Next they claimed that if it was taking place, it was all staged. And that if it wasn't staged, the victims were in fact the perpetrators. It did not matter how absurd the lie was, or how many times the story changed to fit a new narrative, all that mattered was the denial, and the dehumanisation of the victims.

These claims were further amplified by a chorus of journalists and academics, some with immense influence and legitimacy. Not only Fisk but several important figures on both left and right have supported propaganda absolving the Assad regime of using chemical weapons. Not one of them has suffered a single social or career consequence. In fact, you will find very little discussion of this in the mainstream press. There are seemingly very few people in positions of power or influence who think anyone should face accountability or even scrutiny over this issue.

Syria is not a unique example, but having spent so many years of my career covering the Syrian Revolution and the civil war that followed, it is the story that opened my eyes to the problem of denial, and how entrenched denial has become within our digital information ecosystem.

One of the other things I learned was that atrocity revisionists are rarely interested in whitewashing only one set of crimes. It was no accident that many of the same figures who relayed Russian and Assadist denialist narratives had also denied the Bosnian genocide, and faced no professional consequences for that denial, even after the International Criminal Tribunal for Yugoslavia convicted multiple Serbian war criminals for the crime of genocide. Many of these figures engaged in similar denialism over China's systematic erasure of its Uyghur population. Is it any surprise that so many of those involved in Bosnian genocide denial, who would then go on to defend Beijing's actions in Xinjiang, and who would then further engage in Syrian chemical weapons revisionism, have been proven so catastrophically wrong on Ukraine too?

There is a pathology to the atrocity denier, one that is rewarded and reinforced by the current political and media climate, and which thrives further thanks to the increasing polarisation of political discourse in western liberal democracies. Now is a good time to be in the state propaganda business. But that is also what makes the fight against this endemic problem so important. To lose this information war is unthinkable. If nobody speaks out for the victims, if the perpetrators are continually granted impunity, such crimes against humanity will surely happen again.

It's hard to think of any organisation that has failed to achieve its founding purpose more than the United Nations Office on Genocide

Prevention. Nevertheless, the UNOGP has recognised the need to combat denialism. It's difficult to find fault with the conclusions of its 2022 report "Combating Holocaust and Genocide Denial: Protecting Survivors, Preserving Memory, and Promoting Prevention", which recommend that "UN actors, civil society, and social media companies should develop proactive strategies to advance education about the Holocaust and other atrocity crimes and about the dangers of denial and distortion online."

This is a noble goal, and one that I think would start to have some effect on atrocity denial within the digital space at least. The problem is that UN actors, civil society and social media companies don't consider denial a priority. Many can barely conceive of it as a serious problem, one that has lasting political, social, cultural and psychological ramifications that impact far beyond just the communities targeted by denial.

Whenever this topic is discussed, legitimate discussions around freedom of speech naturally arise. But there is no such thing as an inalienable right to say whatever you want on a public platform free from consequence, and most democracies have some form of hate speech legislation that criminalises incitement. What is needed is a broader understanding of atrocity denial and how it can and frequently does intersect and interact with hate speech.

Since the start of the Russo-Ukrainian war, much more attention has been paid to Russia's state-sponsored disinformation campaigns. Moscow's ability to deny the atrocities Russian forces have committed against Ukrainian civilians has been severely hampered by a newly robust approach to Russian state media in the countries allied to Ukraine. It should not have taken the largest land invasion in Europe since World War II for this to have taken place. Russian propaganda networks have been actively poisoning political discourse in the west for nearly two decades now. Had the west properly valued Syrian (and Georgian, and Chechen) life, it wouldn't have taken this long.

While Russia's active propaganda measures have faltered in the last 18 months or so, they are far from defeated, and they are far from the only actor in this space. Of even more concern is the instability of the political systems in the liberal democracies that must be relied on to push back against this effort. Donald Trump's rise to power followed by his failed putsch present a serious threat not only to political and media discourse in the United States, but also to the future of its democracy.

There is a relentless information war taking place in our societies. We are at the mercy of powerful forces that have proven time and time again that truth is of little consequence to them. Many people are struggling with wage stagnation and inflation, and most do not have the time or media literacy to sift through the vast amounts of information with which they are constantly bombarded, particularly when the information concerns conflicts that don't directly impact their lives or the lives of their loved ones. Winning this war for truth may be an insurmountable task.

But losing it? That would be the same as killing the victims twice. Therefore, it falls to us to bear witness, and to fight to make sure this witnessing is heard.

MY TEN EVILS

Christopher Jones

Generally, evil is defined as the opposite of 'good,' but the meaning of evil is different in different cultures, societies, and even between individuals. Evil is contextual, based on religious or secular values—or both—thus this list is informed by my socialisation, experience, spirituality, and philosophical grounding. Broadly, it appears that the popular discourse on evil is informed by the deep structures of major religious and spiritual traditions, where the belief in evil requires a higher (or 'lower') metaphysical or mystical power.

My personal background as a son of a Christian minister and theologian has influenced my perspective on evil. In my twenties, I had a conversation with my father who confided in me that he did not believe in evil, the devil, or in any external dark power. This surprised me given all talk of evil and images of the devil in Christianity. What he said did align with what I was learning in graduate school about good and evil in Hawaiian, Pacific Island, Shinto, Buddhist, Hindu, and indigenous teachings and knowledge. Preliterate peoples and religions appear likely to have associated the violence and traumas associated with wildlife and weather with supernatural evil. Some belief systems support the idea of ghosts, disembodied evil, and bad spirits. My selection of evils follows Muslim and Judaic traditions that explain evil as a creation of man, not God. Similarly, my evils are not transcendent phenomena, but rather *immanent*, created by humans and inherent in human behaviour.

My choices of evil are predominantly products of the Scientific Revolution, the Enlightenment, and industrialisation. My list is neither exhaustive nor definitive, but exemplary of destructive human phenomena from my 2023 perspective. Some are material objects and others are phenomena. Some are policies or economic concepts. Some overlap. They are presented in alphabetical order, not in order of magnitude or degree of impact. Some have both positive and negative aspects.

1. Artificial General Intelligence (AGI)

AGI poses an existential threat to humans and is therefore evil in that sense. One of the AGI's pioneers, Geoffrey Hinton, has likened it to the arrival of extraterrestrial aliens who speak very good English – we really have no idea of their potential or danger. The intrinsic evil is the inability of innovators to pause, to first consider the potential unanticipated consequences, of AGI before proceeding to develop it. It is unquestionable that the emergence of sophisticated artificial intelligence, such as the large language models that run machines such as ChatGPT are harbingers of revolutionary technology that will profoundly impact human life. AGI isn't here yet, but may be here soon.

AGI machines have the potential to positively improve health diagnoses, create greater abundance, increase leisure, improve housing and transportation, and reduce bureaucratic inefficiency in increasingly complex social systems. They may also very quickly learn to seek greater power to fulfill their purposes. Moreover, actual achievement of silicon sentience does not mean we will be able to communicate meaningfully with them, given the advantage of silicon memory and processing, especially the speed at which machines can process information—already vastly faster than humans. If not developed and controlled ethically, the evils of AGI include the potential for massive job displacement, the acceleration of the gap between rich and poor, and military applications. AGI machines could take on god-like qualities, super-human abilities, or radically disrupt the normal order. Humans could become dependent on automated systems for material existence creating a cargo cult mentality. Machines may have little incentive to conserve resources or energy at the expense of planet Earth. Biological forms of life might be seen as competition for those resources.

2. Anthropogenic greenhouse gases

Human-sourced carbon dioxide and methane buildup in the Earth's atmosphere are a dangerous byproduct of our use of fossil fuels, deforestation, and industrialisation. We are on track to raise the planet's average temperature at least 2° C, or more, above the pre-industrial background due to these gases that retain heat within the Earth's atmosphere. They are a driving force in accelerated warming that is melting glaciers, causing heat waves, and adversely affecting human health and longevity. The impacts of climate change largely effect marginalised communities, particularly in developing countries, who have contributed very little to the problem.

These gases are intrinsically evil because they contribute to the melting Greenland and West Antarctic ice sheets that will likely raise sea levels dramatically and reshape the world's coastlines. Scientists report that melting is accelerating even faster than previously believed. In 2023 we are entering a new El Niño weather pattern that will bring even hotter temperatures. More hell on Earth. Many religious teachings stress the importance of caring for nature and for providing stewardship to protect the environment. Allowing the buildup of greenhouse gases is a violation of a covenant: our responsibility to protect the Earth. Numerous indigenous belief systems, as well as monotheistic religions, believe that we have an obligation to leave a healthy environment for future generations. The continued generation of excessive greenhouse gases is a violation of that responsibility.

3. Cars

Closely linked to the evil of greenhouse gases is the automobile. A symbol of freedom and mobility, and of the modern era, is the car. The USA helped spread the car virus across the planet but the countries with the largest per capita car ownership are tiny Gibraltar, Guernsey, San Marino, Liechtenstein, and Andorra – roughly one car per person. Cars are evil because of their impact on the environment, particularly air pollution—particulates and carbon dioxide emissions—and use of nonrenewable resources. They are directly responsible for tens of thousands of deaths annually, as well as hundreds of thousands of injuries. They have dominated the development of modern infrastructure and the urban landscape. Cars have had a large negative impact on mass transit, and human scale transportation such as walking and bicycling. The development of the interstate highway system in the USA divided and fractured many urban neighbourhoods.

Individual car ownership is not compatible with values of simplicity, frugality, and sustainable environmental practice. The evils include the negative ecological impacts, pollution, greenhouse gas emissions, and the social inequalities baked into automobile infrastructure and economics. Cars also feed a culture of industrialisation, individualism, and materialism. Interestingly, emerging younger generations in some countries are less likely to be car owners. Electric vehicles (Evs) are promoted as a greener alternative, but they still consume vast quantities of natural resources and water in their production. EV battery construction and electronic components require rare earth elements, the mining and production of which cause even economic inequality and more harm to Mother Earth.

4. CRISPR

Clustered Regularly Interspaced Short Palindromic Repeats (CRISPR) is one of the revolutionary gene-editing technologies that has emerged this century. Another is the Transcription Activator-Like Effector Nucleases (TALEN) approach that uses restriction enzymes engineered to cut specific DNA sequences. This class of technologies is evil because of the enormous potential for unethical use. The technology is celebrated for its potential positive applications: for medical treatment and research, gene therapy, and possibly the re-introduction of extinct species. Unethical and evil use might include bioterrorism, experiments on the human genome, and long-term effects on the environment or future generations. As with AGI, the developments in this field are emerging rapidly, and there is a little oversight or consideration of unanticipated consequences of the use of the technology. Moreover, these techniques are not restricted to the laboratory but are being used in home basements and garages.

Genetic enhancements could create numerous social, cultural, and ethical dilemmas. Genetic improvement of longevity, for example, might be available to only the very rich. Extinct species will be brought back to life and multi-species organisms, or chimera, are likely to be created without considering the impact on the environment. There are clear religious perspectives on the use of these technologies: some support their potential to alleviate suffering and improve the human condition in alignment with values of compassion and healing. The evil is in CRISPR's potential to alter the 'natural order' or by interfering with the human genetic code. Again, the technology may create god-like powers or could fundamentally disrupt planetary ecosystems.

5. Fake News

The shift to the digital age in most of the industrialised world has transformed journalism and the explosion of social media channels have given rise to fabricated news and misinformation. Ex-US President Donald Trump is renowned for spreading false information, lies, and he still denies his loss of the 2020 US presidential elections. Similarly, conspiracy theories and prevaricated news reach tens of millions of people over social media platforms. Fascists still deny the Holocaust and the Srebrenica massacre. Fake news is used to manipulate public opinion, sow doubt and division, erode trust in public institutions, and the media. Fake news is evil because it is used to deceive and manipulate.

Religious traditions advocate for truth and integrity, and the deliberate spread of fake news is as a violation of ethical principles. Fake news is evil because it contradicts the importance of honesty, truth, and the potential harm due to deception and deceit. The social media platforms intertwined with fake news and conspiracy theory dissemination take away individual's ability to think critically, to question assumptions, and otherwise think for themselves. Fake news is evil because it contributes to overall ignorance at a time when humans, individuals and communities truly need to think critically and creatively about visioning positive futures.

6. Gill Drift Nets

Gill drift nets are long fishing nets hauled by trawlers and large fishing vessels. The fishing technique is criticised as an industrial approach to fishing that severely impacts marine ecosystems. The nets may stretch for miles and are occasionally cut loose and abandoned. These so-called *ghost* drift nets continue to wreak havoc for years as they drift on their own in the open ocean. The overall gill drift net practice is unsustainable because it can trap and kill unintended marine species, including endangered ones. Gill drift net fishing is harmful to marine biodiversity, making it ethically problematic.

This practice is evil, because it disregards our obligation to provide stewardship for natural resources and responsibility for the Earth and its inhabitants. The practice is a violation of that stewardship; and this approach to fishing is evil, because it is disrespectful of the ocean itself, it's creatures, and planetary functions. It is an unsustainable industrial, fossil fuel-based approach to fishing. Also evil is the assumption that ghost drift nets are simply a 'cost of doing business,' rather than an action that has serious adverse long-term implications.

7. Orbital Congestion

Near-Earth orbital (NEO) is the growth of the accumulation of space debris in lower orbits near the earth, caused by decommissioned satellites, used rocket stages, and other objects from human space activities. The congestion poses risks to functioning satellites and may result in collisions that could generate even more debris. The Kessler Syndrome, or ablational cascade events, warns of the potential for catastrophe in near earth orbital space once orbital congestion gets to a critical mass generating a cascade of ricocheting fragments that could destroy most satellites in NEO. A Kessler Syndrome event would mean the end of our ability to use these orbital spaces for communication, navigation, and observation. It could even threaten the launch of rockets to the moon and outer space for the foreseeable future.

This congestion is evil, because it threatens the sustainability and safety of space operations, including satellite communications, weather observation, Earth-sensing, ocean and atmosphere, and other scientific research. Companies such as Elon Musk's Starlink system (42,000 satellites are projected) are already adversely affecting Earth-based telescopy and adding further to the congestion and chances of miscalculation.

Catastrophe in orbit could permanently alter the night sky, and our view of the universe. The debris would eventually burn up in the upper atmosphere, but some large pieces will inevitably come to ground with at least some potential for death and destruction.

8. Scarcity Economics

In a world of obvious abundance, why is our economic system based on scarcity? One of the basic assumptions of neoliberal capitalism is that inequality is a given. The system perpetuates disparities by concentrating wealth in the hands of a few, while leaving billions without access to necessities for survival. Moreover, this unequal distribution leads to poverty, social unrest, and marginalised populations. Scarcity economics can be seen as evil by ethical frameworks, such as utilitarianism, that prioritise overall well-being and happiness – 'the greatest good for the greatest number.' Utilitarian economics leans towards the promotion of resource, abundance and equitable distribution of goods and services. The core evil is of scarcity economics is *continuous economic growth*, that leads to over-exploitation of natural resources, fossil fuel use, and environmental degradation. This approach neglects the finite nature of Earth's resources, limits to fossil fuel extraction, and the long-term consequences of ecological harm.

Disregard for environmental sustainability is ethically objectionable, and downright evil. Scarcity economics is contradictory to stewardship because it perpetuates resource depletion and unequal distribution of wealth. Scarcity economics clashes with concepts of compassion, justice, and care for marginalised and excluded communities. Many religious traditions emphasise communal well-being and solidarity, and the competitive nature of scarcity economics privileges an individualistic mindset that prioritises self interest over communal needs. The focus on competition rather than cooperation seems fundamentally wrong and undermines values of shared responsibility and mutual support.

9. State-sanctioned Killing

State-sanctioned killing, such as the death penalty, extra judicial killings, and most warfare should be seen as evil, particularly by people who oppose the taking of human life. It violates the basic right to life and can lead to the wrongful execution of innocent people. State-sanctioned killing perpetuates a cycle of violence. The United Nations was established in large measure as a response to the horrors of World War II, and yet, the Cold War and conflicts in many parts of the world show the sad nature of state behaviour in the last 80 years. We have learned much about conflict resolution, but as a species have fallen dangerously short of achieving the aspirational policy goals, such as the UN Declaration of Human Rights. How else will we stop the cycle of violence unless nation-state actors renounce state-sanctioned killing? It may start at the national level where some 85 countries have outlawed the death penalty.

Most major religions promote principles such as compassion, forgiveness, and respect for human life. From a religious standpoint, state-sanction killing is evil, because it conflicts with these principles. While self-defence, at the community and individual levels, appears to be morally defensible, purposeful killing by powerful organisations, such as nation states, disregards a nation state's capacity to preserve human rights and dignity and find alternatives to violence.

10. Human Trafficking

The last evil on my list is the most evil of them all, the recruitment, transportation, or harbouring of individuals through force, coercion, deception, or other means for the purpose of exploitation—human trafficking and slavery. It is estimated by the International Labor Organisation and the Walk Free Foundation (2022) that over 25 million people are in forced labour at any given point in time. Human trafficking is a fundamental violation of the inherent dignity and basic rights of individuals, depriving them of freedom, autonomy, and agency, making them commodities to be bought and sold. This is a profound ethical concern. The practice targets marginalised populations, particularly women, children, migrants, and refugees. Children born into slavery inherit their status and likely endure a lifetime of exploitation. Victims are subject to emotional, psychological, and physical harm; victims endure extreme suffering and trauma.

The practice is operated by and profits criminal networks, complicit individuals, and corrupt social systems that allow the practice to flourish. The international nature of human slavery raises moral questions about our collective responsibility to end the practice. Human trafficking is evil because it reduces individuals to property, denies their inherent worth, and reduces them to objects of ownership. Trade in human beings as chattel devalues their humanity, erodes the principles of equality, and violates the basic respect for all humans as individuals. The systematic oppression and cruelty of human trafficking underscores its evil nature. Slavery routinely occurs in societies with institutionalised discriminatory practices, allowing it to persist. Tolerance for these institutional practices, represent a moral failure at the highest level of the larger society, pointing to the need for systemic change. Seeing human trafficking and slavery as evil reflects the inherent wrongness, injustice, and moral repugnance associated with these utterly odious practices.

CITATIONS

Evil in the Absence of God by Richard Appignanesi

Apropos of length: the opening sentence of my text modifies the famous last words of the Viennese satirist Karl Kraus, *Mir fällt zu Hitler nichts ein*, 'Concerning Hitler, nothing occurs to me', meaning either that Hitler is a nullity or that Kraus has nothing to say about him, which did not prevent him from proceeding to a 200-page evisceration of Hitlerism titled *Die Dritte Walpurgisnacht* ('The Third Walpurgis Night') in his satirical journal *Die Fackel* ('The Torch') in 1933, but withheld from publication in fear of Nazi reprisals against Jews, and not published until 1952.

All books to which I refer in the text are easily accessible, either available in libraries or by purchase at bookshops or online at major suppliers like Amazon. Those I have used are by now outdated and have since been reissued. Hannah Arendt's *New Yorker* articles on the Eichmann trial are available online or made into her book (1963) *Eichmann in Jerusalem: A Report on the Banality of Evil*, now in Penguin Paperback, London, 2022.

I admit to being snappish with Kurt Gödel's important *Incompleteness Theorems* which can be remedied by consulting the numerous online explanatory articles on the subject. I recommend a reading of C.G. Jung's *Answer to Job* especially if available in the Bollingen Series, translated R.F.C. Hull, with a Forward by Sonu Shamdasani, and useful notes, Princeton University Press, 2011.

For assistance on the technical terminology of Islamic theology I consulted Mustapha Sheikh's *Ibn Taymiyya, Analogy and the Attributes of God*, MA Thesis, University of Oxford, 2007 https://www.academia. edu/45029569/Shayk_al_Islam_Taymmiya and Wesley Williams, *Aspects of the Creed of Imam Ahmad Hanbal: A Study of Anthropomorphism in Early Islamic Discourse*, in *International Journal of Islamic Studies*, 34, 2002. Both these scholarly articles will benefit the reader with their copious bibliographies of further readings.

For readers curious to know more about Ibn Taymiyyah from his own lips can consult *Ibn Taymiyyah Against the Greek Logicians*, translated, with notes and introduction by Wael B. Hallaq, Oxford University Press, 1993.

Jonah and Redemption by John Liechty

The lines on losing the Self are from Afkham Darbandi and Dick Davis's translation of *The Conference of the Birds*, 1984, Penguin Classics, p 131. The fictional Father Mapple is a whaling man turned preacher in the town of New Bedford, Massachusetts. He delivers a sermon on Jonah in Chapter 9 of *Moby Dick*. The delightful descriptions from Rabbi Eliezer and Al Tahani of the ambiance inside the fish are mentioned in *Wikipedia*.

Joppa is present-day Jaffa. Tarshish is generally thought to be present-day Cadiz, about as far away from Nineveh as a sailor of Jonah's day could expect to get. The curious decree that livestock must wear sackcloth and join the fasting is one of several details in the Book of Jonah leading some scholars to see it as parody or satire. If the work is tongue in cheek, Jonah functions as a kind of picaresque anti-prophet. His flight from duty and inadvertent success at conversion stand in ironic (and comic) contrast to the embrace of duty exhibited by a more exemplary prophet, and to the rejection of message a 'real' prophet could typically anticipate.

Atrocity, Evil, and Forgiveness by Luke Russell

The quote from Mohammed Siddiqui comes from: https://www. aljazeera.com/news/2020/8/25/survivors-families-describe-loss-rage-after-new-zealand-attacks; the Daily Mail article calling Tarrant evil can be found at https://www.dailymail.co.uk/news/article-8669287/New-Zealand-demands-Australia-evil-terrorist-Brenton-Tarrant.html; the quote from Maysoon Salama comes from https://www.bbc.co.uk/news/world-asia-53861456; the quote from Janna Ezat is taken from https://www.theguardian.com/world/2020/aug/24/i-dont-have-hate-i-dont

-have-revenge-stricken-mother-of-christchurch-massacre-victim-forgives-killer; the quote from Andy Burnham can be found at https://www.standard.co.uk/news/uk/manchester-attack-mayor-andy-burnham-says-spirit-of-manchester-will-prevail-after-evil-act-a3545916.html; the quote from Caroline Curry comes from https://www.bbc.co.uk/news/av/uk-england-manchester-64829891; the quote from Figen Murray can be found at https://www.bbc.co.uk/news/av/uk-england-manchester-64814141; Phillip Cole's sceptical arguments against the existence of evil are laid out in his 2006 book *The Myth of Evil*, Edinburgh: University of Edinburgh Press; Christopher Hitchens uses the concept of evil in his article 'Evil', Tues 31st December 2002, *Slate* http://www.slate.com/id/2076195; Hannah Arendt's claims about the banality of evil can be found in her book *Eichmann in Jerusalem*, first published in 1963; For the text of Himmler's Posen speeches, see Bradley F. Smith and Agnes F. Peterson, *Heinrich Himmler. Geheimreden 1933–1945*, Propyläen Verlag, Frankfurt am Main, Berlin/Wien 1974; David Cesarani's evaluation of Eichmann can be found in his 2007 book *Becoming Eichmann: Rethinking the Life, Crimes, and Trial of a 'Desk Murderer'*, London: De Capo Press; My thoughts about evil are set out in more detail in my 2014 book *Evil: A Philosophical Investigation*, and in a shorter and more digestible form in my 2020 book *Being Evil*, both published by Oxford University Press. Other philosophers who have written in detail about evil include Claudia Card, Eve Garrard, Daniel Haybron, Paul Formosa, Steven de Wijze, and Susan Neiman. My thoughts about forgiveness are set out in my 2023 book *Real Forgiveness*, Oxford University Press. Other philosophers who have written on forgiveness include Lucy Allais, Glen Pettigrove, Pamela Hieronymi, Charles Griswold, and Brandon Warmke.

Ordinary Folks by Julian Baggini

The works cited: Confucius, Analects, Book 13, Chapters 2–3, in James Legge, *The Chinese Classics Vol. 1*, (Oxford University Press, 1893), p. 102; and Dhammapada, IX.6, in *A Sourcebook in Indian Philosophy*, Sarvepalli Radhakrishnan and Charles A. Moore (eds.) (Princeton University Press, 1957), p 301. 'The Woodsman', is directed by Nicole Kassell with screenplay by Nicole Kassell and Steven Fechter, was released in 2004.

Sinful AI by Michael Wilby

The following articles were referenced: Allais, L. (2015). Elective Forgiveness. *International Journal of Philosophical Studies*, 21:5, 637-653, DOI: 10.1080/09672559.2013.767525; Arendt, H. (1951). *Origins of Totalitarianism*. New York: Harcourt Brace Jovanovich; Arendt, H. (1963). *Eichmann in Jerusalem: A Report on the Banality of Evil*. New York: Penguin; Bostrom, N. (2014). *Superintelligence: Paths, Dangers and Strategies*. Oxford: Oxford University Press; Cave, S., Coughlan, K, and Dihal, K. (2019). 'Scary Robots'. *Proceedings of the 2019 AAAI/ACM Conference on AI, Ethics, and Society*. https://doi.org/10.1145/3306618.3314232; Cole, P. (2006). *The Myth of Evil*. Edinburgh: Edinburgh University Press; Crawford, K. (2021). *Atlas of AI*. New Haven: Yale University Press; de Wijze, S. (2002). Defining Evil: Insights from the Problem of 'Dirty Hands', *Monist* 85(2): 210-238; Hendryks, D., Mazeika, M. and Woodside, T. (2023). An Overview of Catastrophic AI Risks. arXiv:2306.12001v3. https://doi.org/10.48550/arXiv.2306.12001; Hieronymi, P. (2020). *Freedom, Resentment and the Metaphysics of Morals*. Princeton: Princeton University Press; Lambert, H. (2023). The Men who Made the Future. *The New Statesman*, Vol 152, No. 5722, pp. 18-23; Mackie, J.L. (1977). *Ethics: Inventing Right and Wrong*. London: Penguin; Neiman, S. (2002). *Evil in Modern Thought: An Alternative History of Philosophy*. Princeton: Princeton University Press; Nietzsche, F. (1887). *The Genealogy of Morality*. Cambridge: Cambridge University Press; Nyholm, S. (2023). *This is Technology Ethics: An Introduction*. London: Wiley-Blackwell; For a book length discussion of the narrow view of scepticism towards evil see Russell, L. (2014). *Evil: A Philosophical Investigation*. Oxford: Oxford University Press; Russell, S. (2019). *Human Compatible: AI and the Problem of Control*. London: Viking; Shoemaker, D. (2011). Attributability, Answerability and Accountability: Toward a Wider Theory of Moral Responsibility. *Ethics*, 121: 602-32; Shoemaker, D. (2015). *Responsibility from the Margins*. Oxford: Oxford University Press; Smith, A. (2012). Attributability, Accountability and Answerability: In Defense of a Unified Account. *Ethics*, 122: 575-89; Strasser, A. and Wilby, M. (2023). The AI-Stance: Crossing the Terra Incognita of Human-Machine Interactions, in R. Hakli (ed). *Social Robots in Social*

Institutions. Amsterdam: IOS Press; Strawson, G. (2014). Freedom and the Self: Feeling and Belief, in D. Shoemaker & N. Tognazzini (eds). *Oxford Studies in Agency and Responsibility, Vol 2: Freedom and Resentment at 50*. Oxford: Oxford University Press; Strawson, P.F. (1962). Freedom and Resentment, reprinted in P.F. Strawson (1974) *Freedom and Resentment and Other Essays*. London: Routledge; Walker, M. U. (2006). *Moral Repair: Reconstructing Moral Relations after Wrongdoing*. Cambridge: Cambridge University Press; Watson, G. (1987). Responsibility and the Limits of Evil: Reflections on a Strawsonian Theme, reprinted in G. Watson (2004), *Agency and Answerability*. Oxford: Clarendon Press; Wilby, M. (2022). The Thin Moral Concept of Evil. *Studies in the History of Philosophy*, 13 (3), 39-62; Wolf, S. (1987). Sanity and the Metaphysics of Moral Responsibility, in F. Schoeman (ed). *Responsibility, Character and the Emotions*. Cambridge: Cambridge University Press.

Apathy: Disaffection, Enthusiasm, Fanaticism
by Ben Gook and Seán Cubitt

The following was referenced and drawn from in the making of this article: Adorno, Theodor. 1973. *Negative Dialectics*. Translated by E.B. Ashton. London: Routledge; Agamben, Giorgio. 1998. *Homo Sacer: Sovereign Power and Bare Life*. Translated by Daniel Heller-Roazen. Stanford: Stanford University Press; Appadurai, Arjun. 2016. *Banking on Words: The Failure of Language in the Age of Derivative Finance*. Chicago: University of Chicago Press; Ayache, Elie. 2016. 'On Black-Scholes.' In *Derivatives and the Wealth of Society*. Edited by Benjamin Lee and Randy Martin. Chicago: University of Chicago Press, 240-251.

Baudrillard, Jean. 1983. *In the Shadow of the Silent Majorities, or, The End of the Social and Other Essays*. Translated by Paul Foss, John Johnston, and Paul Patton. New York: Semiotext(e); Berlant, Lauren. 2007. 'Slow Death (Sovereignty, Obesity, Lateral Agency).' *Critical Inquiry* 33 (Summer): 754-780; Black, Fischer, and Myron Scholes. 1973. 'The Pricing of Options and Corporate Liabilities.' *The Journal of Political Economy* 81 (3) (May-June): 637-654; Bloch, Ernst. 1988. 'Something's Missing: A Discussion between Ernst Bloch and Theodor Adorno on the

Contradictions of Utopian Longing (1964).' In *The Utopian Function of Art and Literature: Selected Essays*, translated by Jack Zipes and Frank Mecklenburg, 1-17. Cambridge, MA: MIT Press; Brulle, Robert J., Melissa Aronczyk, and Jason Carmichael. 2020. 'Corporate promotion and climate change: an analysis of key variables affecting advertising spending by major oil corporations, 1986–2015.' *Climatic Change* 159 (1): 87–101; Davies, William. 2018. *Nervous States: How Feeling Took Over the World*. London: Cape 2023. 'The Reaction Economy.' *London Review of Books* 45 (5). https://www.lrb.co.uk/the-paper/v45/n05/william-davies/the-reaction-economy. Fromm, Erich. 2019. 'On the Feeling of Powerlessness.' *Psychoanalysis and History* 21, no. 3: 311–29; Hartmann, Patrick, Aitor Marcos, Juana Castro, and Vanessa Apaolaza. 2023. 'Perspectives: Advertising and Climate Change – Part of the Problem or Part of the Solution?' *International Journal of Advertising* 42 (2): 430-457; Hobsbawm, Eric. 1983. 'Introduction: Inventing Traditions.' In *Inventing Traditions*, edited by Eric Hobsbawm and Terence Ranger, 1-14. Cambridge: Cambridge University Press; Kaufmann, Michael. 2020. 'The Carbon Footprint Sham.' *Mashable*, July 13. https://mashable.com/feature/carbon-footprint-pr-campaign-sham; Klein, Naomi. 2007. *The Shock Doctrine: The Rise of Disaster Capitalism*. New York: Henry Holt; López, Antonio. 2023. 'Gaslighting: Fake Climate News and Big Carbon's Network of Denial.' In *The Palgrave Handbook of Media Misinformation*, edited by Karen Fowler-Watt and Julian McDougall, 159-177. London: Palgrave. Lorenz, Edward N. 1963. 'Deterministic non-periodic flow.' *Journal of the Atmospheric Sciences* 20 (2): 130–141; Mair, Peter. 2013. *Ruling the Void: The Hollowing-Out of Western Democracy*. London: Verso; Marx, Karl. 1959. *Capital: A Critique of Political Economy*. Volume III. Edited by Friedrich Engels. Moscow: Progress Publishers; Marx, Karl. 1975. ''The Economic and Philosophical Manuscripts'.' In *Early Writings*, translated by Rodney Livingstone and Gregor Benton, 279-400. New York: NLB/Viking; Massoumi, Narzanin, Tom Mills, and David Miller. 2020. 'Secrecy, Coercion and Deception in Research on 'Terrorism' and 'Extremism'.' *Contemporary Social Science* 15 (2): 134–52; Melville, Herman. 2002. 'Bartleby, The Scrivener: A story of Wall Street.' In *Melville's Short Novels*, edited by Dan McCall, 3–34. New York: W. W. Norton & Co.; Miller, David, and Tom Mills. 2010. 'Counterinsurgency and Terror Expertise: The Integration of Social Scientists into the War Effort.' *Cambridge Review of International Affairs* 23 (2): 203–21; Miller, David, and Tom Mill. 2009. 'The Terror Experts and the Mainstream Media: The Expert Nexus and Its Dominance in the News Media.' *Critical Studies on Terrorism* 2 (3): 414–37; Mitropoulos, Angela. 'Oikonomia'. *Philosophy Today* 63, no. 4 (2019): 1025–36; Neumann, Franz L. 2017. 'Anxiety and Politics.' *TripleC: Communication, Capitalism & Critique* 15 (2): 612–636 ; Pryke, Michael. 2010. 'Money's eyes: the visual preparation of financial markets.' *Economy and Society* 39 (4): 427-459; Robles-Anderson, Erica, and Arjun Appadurai. 2022. 'Editors' Letter: A Critique of Pure Dumbfoundedness.' *Public Culture* 34 (2): 147-152; Rosenberg, Jordana (Jordy). *Critical Enthusiasm: Capital Accumulation and the Transformation of Religious Passion*. Oxford: Oxford University Press, 2011; Sassen, Saskia. 2022. 'The Limits of Power and the Complexity of Powerlessness: The Case of Immigration.' In *Routledge International Handbook of Contemporary Social and Political Theory*, second edition, edited by Gerard Delanty and Stephen P. Turner, 456-465. London: Routledge; Scheer, Monique. 2021. *Enthusiasm: Emotional Practices of Conviction in Modern Germany*. Oxford: Oxford University Press; Seymour, Richard. 2010. *The Meaning of David Cameron*. London: Zero Books; Soper, Kate. *Post-Growth Living: For an Alternative Hedonism*. London: Verso, 2020; Supran, Geoffrey, and Naomi Oreskes. 2021. 'Rhetoric and frame analysis of ExxonMobil's climate change communications.' *One Earth* 4, May 21: 696–719; Terada, Rei. 2001. *Feeling in Theory: Emotion after the 'Death of the Subject.'* Cambridge: Harvard University Press; Toscano, Alberto. 2017. *Fanaticism: On the Uses of an Idea*. 2nd ed. London: Verso; Vogl, Joseph. 2015. *The Specter of Capital*. Translated by Joachim Redner and Robert Savage. Stanford: Stanford University Press; Vogl, Joseph. 2023. *Capital and Ressentiment: A Short Theory of the Present*. Translated by Neil Solomon. London: Polity Press; Wendling, Amy E. 2022. 'Alienation.' In *The Sage Handbook of Marxism*, edited by Beverley Skeggs, Sara R. Farris, Alberto Toscano, and Svenja Bromberg, 527-542. London: Sage.

The Seven by Gwen Adshead

The following books, articles, and essays were referenced and can give greater insight into the psychology of evil and the Seven: Allen, J.G., 2003. Mentalizing. *Bulletin of the Menninger Clinic*, 67(2: Special Issue), pp.91-112; Bartels, D.M. and Pizarro, D.A., 2011. The mismeasure of morals: Antisocial personality traits predict utilitarian responses to moral dilemmas. *Cognition*, 121(1), pp.154-161; Burleigh M (1994) Death and Deliverance: 'Euthanasia' in German 1900-1945. Cambridge & New York, Cambridge University Press; Cleckley, H (1941) the Mask of Sanity: an attempt to reinterpret the so-called psychopathic personality. C.V Mosby & Co. St Louis Missouri; Crego, C., & Widiger, T. A. (2022). Core traits of psychopathy. *Personality Disorders: Theory, Research, and Treatment,* 13(6), 674–684. https://doi.org/10.1037/per0000550; Dutton, K., 2016. Would you vote for a psychopath?. *Scientific American Mind*, 27(5), pp.50-55.; Ford, K., Barton, E., Newbury, A., Hughes, K., Bezeczky, Z., Roderick, J. and Bellis, M., 2019. Understanding the prevalence of adverse childhood experiences (ACEs) in a male offender population in Wales: the prisoner ACE survey. Bangor University; Foster Wallace, D. Big red sun, (1998) In *Consider the lobster: And other essays*. 2005. London, Hachette UK.; Fox, B.H., Perez, N., Cass, E., Baglivio, M.T. and Epps, N., 2015. Trauma changes everything: Examining the relationship between adverse childhood experiences and serious, violent and chronic juvenile offenders. *Child abuse & neglect*, 46, pp.163-173; Gilbert, G (1947) Nuremberg Diary. 1995 edition. Da capo Press, USA; Gilligan, J (1996) Violence: our deadliest epidemic and its causes. New York, Putnam Publishing; Hare, R.D., Harpur, T.J., Hakstian, A.R., Forth, A.E., Hart, S.D. and Newman, J.P., 1990. The revised psychopathy checklist: reliability and factor structure. *Psychological Assessment: A Journal of consulting and clinical Psychology*, 2(3), p.338; Lewis, C.S. (1942) The Screwtape Letters. London Geoffrey Bles. 2012. Collins edition. London. P 87; Lewis, C.S (1952) Mere Christianity. London Geoffrey Bles. 2016 Williams Collins edition. London P 124; Sadler, J.Z., 2013. Vice and mental disorders. *The Oxford handbook of philosophy and psychiatry*, pp.451-479; Simon, R (2003) Should forensic psychiatrists testify about evil? Journal of the American Academy of Psychiatry & Law,

31: 4: 413-416; Welner MM: Defining evil: A Depravity Scale for today's courts. The Forensic Echo 2:4–12, 1998; The Depravity Scale. Created by Michael M. Welner, MD. Provided by the Forensic Panel, New York, NY. Available at http:// www.depravityscale.org; Welner, M., O'Malley, K.Y., Gonidakis, J., Saxena, A. and Stewart-Willis, J., 2018. The Depravity Standard III: Validating an evidence-based guide. *Journal of Criminal Justice*, 55, pp.12-24; Wootton, B., 1972. Academic Lecture: The Place of Psychiatry and Medical Concepts in the Treatment of Offenders: a Layman'S View. *Canadian Psychiatric Association Journal*, 17(5), pp.365-375.

Grinding Mills of Evil by Zaina Erhaim

Hannah Arendt's *Eichmann in Jerusalem: A Portrait of Banality of Evil* and The Origins of Totalitarianism are available as Penguin Classic, 2022 and 207; Jeremy Bentham's notion of the panopticon prison can be found in *Panopticon, or The Inspection House*, Dodo Press, 2008, original 1791. Neville Buch's discussion of Manichaeism can be found at https:// drnevillebuch.com/wp-content/uploads/2020/02/Candide.pdf

Encountering the Shadow by Jeremy Henzell-Thomas

The works cited include: Edward William Lane, *Arabic-English Lexicon*, Islamic Texts Society 1984, originally published in 8 volumes, London, 1863-1893; Cyril Glassé, *Concise Encyclopaedia of Islam* (Stacey International, London, revised edition, 2001),109; Carl Gustav Jung, *Collected Works* (Routledge, 1973);Teun A. van Dijk, 'Critical Discourse Analysis'. https://discourses.org/wp-content/uploads/2022/07/Teun-A.-van-Dijk-2015-Critical-discourse-Analysis.pdf; Maria Lipman, 'How Russia has Come to Loathe the West.' *European Council on Foreign Relations* (ecfr.eu), 13/3/2015.

https://ecfr.eu/article/commentary_how_russia_has_come_to_loathe_the_west311346/; Norman Cigar, 'The Role of Serbian Orientalists in Justification of Genocide Against Muslims of the Balkans', *Islamic Quarterly: Review of Islamic Culture*, Vol. XXXVIII, No. 3, 1994; Richard Tarnas, *The*

Passion of the Western Mind: Understanding the Ideas that have Shaped Our World View (Pimlico, London, 1996); Jean Gebser, *The Ever-Present Origin,* authorised translation by Noel Barstad with Algis Mickunas (University of Ohio Press, Athens, 1985).

Remembering Stalin by Boyd Tonkin

Simon Sebag Montefiore's two-volume biography, *Stalin: The Court of the Red Tsar* and *Young Stalin* was published by Weidenfeld & Nicolson in 2003 and 2007 respectively. I also consulted Robert Service's *Stalin: a Biography* (Macmillan, 2004) and Robert Conquest's *Stalin: Breaker of Nations* (Orion, 2000). Conquest's *The Great Terror* was re-published by Bodley Head in 2018. On the Gulag, see Aleksandr Solzhenitsyn's 'literary investigation' *The Gulag Archipelago* (translated by Thomas P Whitney; abridged edition, HarperPerennial, 2007) and Anne Applebaum's *Gulag: a History* (Penguin, 2004). Eugenia Ginzburg's *Into the Whirlwind* (translated by Paul Stevenson and Manya Harari) is published by Persephone Books (2014), Nadezhda Mandelstam's *Hope Against Hope* (translated by Max Hayward) by Everyman's Library (2003), and *The Selected Poems of Osip Mandelstam* (translated by Clarence Brown and WS Merwin) by New York Review Books Classics (2004).

The greatest literary testament to life in Stalin's Soviet Union remains the fiction of Vasily Grossman, *Life and Fate* (translated by Robert and Elizabeth Chandler; Vintage, 2006) and *Stalingrad* (translated by Robert and Elizabeth Chandler; Harvill Secker, 2019). On Stalin the 'intellectual', see Geoffrey Roberts, *Stalin's Library: a dictator and his books* (Yale UP, 2021) and, for a fresh account of the relationship between literary and political currents in Russia: Gary Saul Morson, *Wonder Confronts Certainty* (Harvard UP, 2023). On the concept of evil in philosophy and politics I have drawn on Susan Neiman, *Evil in Modern Thought: an alternative history of philosophy* (Princeton UP, 2002) and Terry Eagleton, *On Evil* (Yale UP, 2010). Eren Tasar's *Soviet and Muslim* (OUP, 2017) explores the place of Islam in Stalin's empire and Donald Rayfield's *Edge of Empires: a history of Georgia* (Reaktion, 2019) the past of his homeland. For Stalin's assault on Georgian culture and its resonance today, see Maya Jaggi, 'Resurrecting the poets of Tbilisi', *New York Review of Books*, 24 November 2022.

The official website of the Stalin Museum is https://www.stalinmuseum.ge. On Stalin's memory in Georgia today, see Beka Chedia, 'The Ghost of Stalin and the post-totalitarian image of Georgia', https://caucasuswatch.de/en/insights/the-ghost-of-stalin-and-the-post-totalitarian-image-of-georgia.html, and 'Georgia: Still Struggling to Shake off the Memory of Josef Stalin', 9 March 2023, https://georgiatoday.ge/georgia-still-struggling-to-shake-off-the-memory-of-josef-stalin/. On Putin's recent rehabilitation of Stalin, see Eva Hartog, 'Putin's Russia summons Stalin from the grave as a wartime ally', Politico, 6 March 2023, https://www.politico.eu/article/vladimir-putin-russia-summon-joseph-stalin-grave-wartime-ally/, Anastassia Boutsko, 'Why the cult of Josef Stalin is flourishing', Deutsche Welle, 6 March 2023, https://www.dw.com/en/why-the-cult-of-josef-stalin-is-flourishing/a-64896549 and https://www.rferl.org/a/russia-putin-decries-excessive-demonization-stalin/28559464.html.

Prevent Or Not by John Holmwood

The William Shawcross report, *Independent Review of Prevent*, can be downloaded from: https://www.gov.uk/government/publications/independent-review-of-prevents-report-and-government-response.
See also: John Holmwood and Layla Aitlhadj, *The People's Review of Prevent* (2022) Report: https://peoplesreviewofprevent.org/main-report/ and John Holmwood, Layla Aitlhadj (with an additional contribution by Charlotte Heath-Kelley), *The People's Review of Prevent* (2023): *A Response to the Shawcross Report*: https://peoplesreviewofprevent.org/wp-content/uploads/2023/03/A-Response-to-the-Shawcross-Report.pdf.

Athena Weeps by Flavie Curinier

The following articles were referenced in writing this review: Brzeski, Patrick. 'Venice: Romain Gavras on Creating the 'Greek Tragedy' of His 'Immersive' Epic 'Athena'.' *The Hollywood Reporter*, September 2, 2022. https://www.hollywoodreporter.com/movies/movie-news/venice-2022-romain-gavras-athena-interview-1235210296/; Cohen, Mathilde, and

Mazouz, Sarah. 'Introduction: A White Republic? Whites and Whiteness in France.' *French Politics, Culture and Society* 39, no. 2 (2021): 1-25; Défenseur des Droits. 'Inégalités d'Accès aux Droits et Discriminations en France.' La Documentation Française. Accessed April 13, 2023. https://juridique. defenseurdesdroits.fr/doc_num.php?explnum_id=19415; Jobard, Fabien. 'Policing the Banlieues' In *Policing in France*, edited by Jacques de Maillard and Wesley Skogan, 157-172. New York, NY : Routledge, 2021.

https://doi.org/10.4324/9780429026928; Laffly, Tomris. 'Athena.' Roger Ebert.com., September 23, 2022. https://www.rogerebert.com/ reviews/athena-movie-review-2022; Mills, Charles W. *The Racial Contract.* Cornell University Press, 2022; Service Politique. 'Enquête sur la ' BFMisation ' de la vie politique.' *Le Monde*, December 7, 2013. https:// www.lemonde.fr/politique/article/2013/12/07/enquete-sur-la-bfmisation-de-la-vie-politique_3527305_823448.html.

Last Word On Denial by Oz Katerji

Denial: The Final Stage of Genocide? Edited by John Cox, Amal Khoury and Sarah Minslow is published by Routledge (2021). Henry C. Theriault, is co-author, with Samuel Totten of *The United Nations Genocide Convention: An Introduction*, which is published by University of Toronto Press (2020). Deborah Lipstadt's *Denying the Holocaust* is published by Penguin (2016). *The Origins of Totalitarianism* by Hannah Arendt is now in Penguin classics (2017). Aleksandar Hemon's article, 'The Bob Dylan of Genocide Apologists' appeared in the *New York Times* on 15 October 2019, and can be accessed at: https://www.nytimes.com/2019/10/15/opinion/peter-handke-nobel-bosnia-genocide.html

My obituary of Robert Fisk, 'Fabricator and fraudster', appeared in *The Critic* December 2020 issue. For the Daraya massacre, see Janine di Giovanni's account in her book *The Morning They Came For Us: Dispatches from Syria* (Bloomsbury, London, 2016); and 'Ten Years On: First Full Report Records Syrian Regime's Massacre at Daraya', *The Guardian* 25 August 2022.

CONTRIBUTORS

Gwen Adshead is a forensic psychiatrist, psychotherapist, amateur philosopher and incompetent gardener • **Richard Appignanesi**, writer, editor, and existentialist philosopher, is the author of four novels, a graphic novel, and a string of texts in the *Introducing* and *Manga Shakespeare* series • **Julian Baggini**, the founding editor of *The Philosophers' Magazine*, is the author of over 20 books, including *How to Think Like a Philosopher* • **Flavie Curinier** is an intern at the Institute of Security and Global Affairs, Leiden University • **Seán Cubitt** is Professor of Screen Studies at the University of Melbourne • **Zaina Erhaim** is an award-winning journalist working as a media and gender consultant with different organisations in Southwest Asian and North Africa • **Abdullah Geelah** works at a large City firm and is keen on mosque architecture • **Ben Gook** is Lecturer in Cultural Studies at the University of Melbourne • **Shazaf Fatima Haider** is a novelist and a full-time mother • **Jeremy Henzell-Thomas** is a Research Associate and former Visiting Fellow at the Centre of Islamic Studies, University of Cambridge • **John Holmwood**, emeritus Professor of Sociology in the School of Sociology and Social Policy at University of Nottingham, is the author of *Colonialism and Modern Social Theory* • **Tam Hussein** writes for *New Lines* magazine • **Rosie Jackson** is a well-known English poet and spiritualist • **Christopher Jones** is a futurist and Senior Fellow of the Centre for Postnormal Policy and Futures Studies • **Oz Katerji** is a British-Lebanese conflict journalist currently based in Ukraine • **John Liechty**, a retired teacher, currently divides his time between Spain and Morocco • **Haroon Moghul** is an award-winning writer, public speaker, and occasional Friday preacher • **Marc Nelson** is an artist and teacher who lives in Kewanee, Illinois • **Luke Russell**, Associate Professor of Philosophy at the University of Sydney, is the author of *Evil: A Very Short Introduction* and *Real Forgiveness* • **Boyd Tonkin**, writer and literary critic, is a regular contributor to *Critical Muslim* • **Michael Wilby**, a specialist in the philosophy of mind, is a senior lecturer in philosophy, Anglia Ruskin University, Cambridge • **Robin Yassin-Kassab** is Deputy Editor of *Critical Muslim* • **Lutfiye Zudiyeva**, one of the coordinators of the 'Crimean Solidarity' civic initiative, is a Crimean Tatar journalist.